THE
FORGOTTEN
CHRIST

THE
FORGOTTEN
CHRIST

Exploring the majesty and mystery
of God incarnate

Edited by Stephen Clark

APOLLOS

APOLLOS (an imprint of Inter-Varsity Press)
Norton Street, Nottingham NG7 3HR, England
Email: ivp@ivpbooks.com
Website: www.ivpbooks.com

First published 2007
Reprinted 2008

British Library Cataloguing-in-Publication Data
A catalogue record for this book is available from the British Library.

ISBN: 978–1–84474–210–3

Set in Monotype Garamond 11/13pt
Typeset in Great Britain by Servis Filmsetting Ltd, Manchester
Printed and bound in Great Britain by Ashford Colour Press Ltd, Gosport,
Hampshire

*Inter-Varsity Press publishes Christian books that are true to the Bible and that communicate
the gospel, develop discipleship and strengthen the church for its mission in the world.*

*Inter-Varsity Press is closely linked with the Universities and Colleges Christian Fellowship,
a student movement connecting Christian Unions in universities and colleges throughout Great
Britain, and a member movement of the International Fellowship of Evangelical Students.
Website: www.uccf.org.uk.*

CONTENTS

CONTRIBUTORS

Greg Beale is Professor of Biblical Studies, Wheaton College, Illinois, USA.

Stephen Clark is minister of Freeschool Court Evangelical Church, Bridgend, UK.

Philip H. Eveson is Principal, London Theological Seminary, UK.

Richard B. Gaffin, Jr., is Charles Krahe Professor of Biblical and Systematic Theology, Westminster Theological Seminary, Pennsylvania, USA.

A. T. B. McGowan is Principal, Highland Theological College, Dingwall, UK.

Matthew Sleeman is Lecturer in New Testament Studies and New Testament Greek, Oak Hill Theological College, London, UK.

Paul Wells is Professor of Systematic Theology, Faculté Libre de Théologie Réformée, Aix en Provence, France.

PREFACE

These chapters were first prepared as papers for the 2007 Affinity Theological Study Conference. Launched in 2004, Affinity describes itself as a 'Church-centred Partnership for Bible-centred Christianity'. It is a growing network of approximately 1,300 churches located throughout Great Britain and Ireland.

We live at a time when majority 'evangelicalism' is no longer defined by what the Bible says and when, in particular, it seems to know little, and care even less, about the nature and role of Christ's church. Perhaps, as a result, there has proved to be a strong desire among those who see the necessity of maintaining and proclaiming the objective truths of the gospel for the kind of encouragement Affinity provides.

Our aim is to act as a catalyst, promoting the exchange of resources between essentially like-minded churches, while seeking to dismantle the 'glass walls' that can so easily isolate Bible-centred church groupings from one another. Affinity facilitates the formation and development of regional and local church partnerships. It is eager to support the planting and recommissioning of congregations that wish to find ways of engaging their culture without compromising doctrinal purity.

On behalf of the churches, Affinity is also involved in researching and analysing current thinking and social trends in the light of Scripture. Part of that brief means keeping its constituency informed of the moral and ethical implications of impending parliamentary legislation. This function is mainly performed by *The Bulletin* – a unique resource freely downloadable in booklet form from the website (www.affinity.org.uk). When deemed necessary, we issue statements and make appropriate representation to Government departments and the media.

Affinity is committed to advancing and deepening an understanding and acceptance of biblical Christianity. Inevitably, we find ourselves monitoring the ever-increasing number of challenges to orthodox doctrine that appear to be sheltering under the umbrella of evangelicalism. The effect of the postmodernist mindset with which many contemporary theologians approach the biblical data is revealed in the sense of insecurity and uncertainty it eventually produces within the churches. As we cannot be satisfied with the false peace that comes from denying the existence of the Bible's propositional truth claims, we must therefore work all the harder to clarify, defend and proclaim them. Apart from arranging conferences, Affinity produces a theological journal, *Foundations*, and also *Table Talk*, an occasional theological briefing for church leaders.

The Forgotten Christ will certainly not be forgotten by those fortunate enough to have been present over the three days of the event. As always at an Affinity Theological Study Conference, the papers had been distributed several weeks beforehand to those attending, and were not read but rather were commented on by their authors. Then followed small group and plenary sessions filled with stimulating debate of the highest calibre. Feedback was unanimously and strongly positive. I am extremely grateful to all our speakers – each of whom was on top form.

Unfortunately, Stephen Clark, our conference convener, was unable to be with us, but I want to thank him for all his hard work – and for his introduction to the present volume. Gladly, I must also mention Ian Herring and Barbara Homrighausen, on whose administrative skills we again depended. One final word – the 2009 Affinity Theological Study Conference will, God willing, be considering the subject of Covenant and Law.

Jonathan Stephen
Director, Affinity
Principal, Wales Evangelical School of Theology

INTRODUCTION

Stephen Clark

'The Word became flesh and made his dwelling among us' (John 1:14 NIV). With these sublime words John identifies both the majesty and the mystery of the person of Jesus Christ: majesty, because he is the Word, and John has already told us that the Word not only was with God but was God (v. 1); mystery, because flesh, in this context, denotes human nature, and so John has told us that God became man. The remainder of his Gospel sets before the reader the glory of this person who is both God and man. While the New Testament displays rich diversity in its portrayal of Jesus, underlying this diversity and expressed through it is a uniform conviction that Jesus Christ is God and man. This is the Jesus the church is to proclaim to a needy and dying world and to keep before God's people in order that each one may be presented mature in Christ (Col. 1:28). This is the real Jesus; there is no other.

The church has sometimes struggled to maintain this balanced emphasis upon the majesty and mystery of the person of Christ. Sometimes emphasis upon his deity has been at the expense of taking seriously his humanity: this is what is known as *Docetism*. At

other times the church's concentration upon the humanity of
Christ has eclipsed his deity. There has also been the heresy known
as *Nestorianism*, which separated off the humanity from the deity of
Jesus in such a way that one was effectively left with two personal
agents. When these errors have been avoided, it has not been
unknown for something of the mystery of the person of Christ to
be lost: if our approach to Christology is basically no different
from that of the mathematician who engages in a merely mental
exercise to ensure that his equations balance, then we have gone
profoundly astray in our *approach*, even though our doctrinal formulation is correct. A proper Christology is inextricably linked to
doxology. This shines through on just about every page of the
New Testament.

In this connection some have sought to drive a wedge between
a *functional* approach to the person of Christ and an *ontological*
approach. This distinction is sometimes employed in the following
way: the functional approach emphasizes what Jesus means to me
and to others. Many great hymns of the church have this emphasis. It is an essentially *religious and devotional* approach to the person
of Jesus. By contrast, it may be claimed, the ontological approach
is philosophical, sterile and arid, and is not true to the New
Testament emphases. The New Testament is replete with people
whose lives were transformed by Jesus. When the New Testament
writers spoke of Jesus, they were seeking to give expression to the
greatness of what he meant to them. It is sometimes said that to
take this language in an ontological sense is to be guilty of a theological category error.[1] When a young woman who is head over
heels in love describes her fiancé, she uses exalted language to
express what he *means to her*. What she does not do is give an
account of his dimensions, size of his feet and so on, for that kind
of description would not serve her purpose. In the same way, it
may be claimed, a *theological* approach to the person of Christ, such
as characterized the Councils of the church in the first four to five
centuries, is fundamentally misconceived.

---

1. See e.g. W. David Stacey, *Groundwork of Biblical Studies* (London: Epworth,
   1979), pp. 436–437.

The problem with arguing in this way lies not in the distinction between a functional and an ontological approach but, rather, in regarding these categories as mutually exclusive. A moment's reflection should soon demonstrate that driving a wedge between them creates all kinds of problems. *Why* is it Jesus who is so special, rather than, say, John the Baptist, or Paul? If all one can do is to testify to what Jesus means to me, my neighbour may well ask what this has to do with him. Indeed, contrary to a somewhat revisionist reading of early church history, it appears to be quite clear that the Church Fathers' emphasis upon the deity of Christ was the result of their conviction that Jesus could not be the Saviour we need, if he were not truly God.[2] In other words, the ontological question (Who is Jesus?) underpins the functional questions that concern his significance for us.

It was the great achievement of the Council of Chalcedon to preserve both the majesty and the mystery of the person of Christ, by giving expression to each aspect of the biblical teaching without trying to solve the mystery of how there could be one personal agent who was fully divine and fully human. Andrew McGowan paints the background to that Council and points to the biblical basis of the creed to which it gave rise. This is an important chapter. Too frequently theologians have tried to drive a wedge between the biblical Christ and the Christ of Chalcedon. While it is readily admitted that ecclesiastical politics were involved in the early church councils (once you adopt Constantine's position, this will be inevitable), and while one may lament the

---

2. For example, the following words from the great Athanasius' work *On the Incarnation* (*De incarnatione verbi Dei*) establish this point: 'or what was required for such and such recall, but the Word of God, which had also at the beginning made everything out of nought. For His it was once more both to bring the corruptible to incorruption . . . For being Word of the Father, and above all, He alone of natural fitness was both able to recreate everything, and worthy to suffer on behalf of all and to be ambassador of all with the Father.' The translation is that found in Philip Schaff and Henry Wace (eds.), *The Nicene and Post-Nicene Fathers of the Christian Church*, 2nd series, vol. 4 (Edinburgh: T. & T. Clark, 1891 [repr. 1987]), p. 40.

carnality frequently displayed by some of those who were involved, one cannot but be thankful that Chalcedon fixed the parameters of a truly biblical account of the person of Christ and, in Augustine's memorable words, 'put a fence around the mystery' and 'denied denials of the truth'.

In view of the commitment of each of the contributors to this volume to a high view of Scripture, none addresses the question as to whether the New Testament writers drove a wedge between the true Jesus and the Jesus whom they worshipped and portrayed in their writings. This being the case, I shall make a few brief comments upon this matter. Although the roots of this kind of thinking (that the New Testament does not present a faithful account of the historical Jesus) really go back to the Enlightenment, with the German scholar H. S. Reimarus starting the ball rolling, we need to be alert to the fact that there is a public perception that the Christ of the church and of the Bible cannot be identified with a real, historical person: he is, rather, the creation of his disciples. This approach has endless varieties. What they have in common is a conviction that the Gospels are not historically reliable. In a global village and a multicultural society we cannot expect the world to listen to our message of the uniqueness of Jesus Christ or to take us seriously unless we can deal with this issue.

The research since the 1970s or so that has come to be denoted by the term 'Third Quest' has emphasized the *Jewishness* of Jesus and of his context. This should never have been lost sight of in the first place. What this emphasis has done, however, is to show that a title such as 'Son of Man' was precisely the sort of self-designation Jesus might employ because of its ambiguity.[3] He could, at one and the same time, be understood as using it as no more than a circumlocution for 'I' while also making a profound

---

3. See the following three penetrating essays in Harold H. Rowdon, *Christ the Lord: Studies in Christology Presented to Donald Guthrie* (Leicester: IVP, 1982). The essays are F. F. Bruce, 'The Background to the Son of Man Sayings', pp. 50–70; Robert D. Rowe, 'Is Daniel's "Son of Man" Messianic?', pp. 71–96; D. A. Carson, 'Christological Ambiguities in the Gospel of Matthew', pp. 97–114.

Christological claim for himself by it (see Matt. 16:13, 15; Mark 8:27; cf. Matt. 26:64). *After* the resurrection and Jesus' teaching of his disciples during the forty-day period before his ascension, all this fell into place for the disciples, a fact clearly borne out by dying Stephen's reference to the Son of Man being at God's right hand (Acts 7:56). The important point to observe, however, is that although the Gospel writers represent Jesus frequently applying this term to himself, it is hardly ever used of him by Luke in Acts or by Peter, Paul, James or John in their letters. If the early church were simply projecting back on to Jesus the elevated status they came to confer upon him, how is it that 'Son of Man' appears so frequently in the Gospels but hardly elsewhere? The answer, surely, is that the Gospel writers were not guilty of anachronism. Furthermore, *after* the crucifixion and resurrection of Jesus there was no longer any need to apply an ambiguous title to him.

We must also understand the phrase 'Son of God' against its Old Testament background. It is used of Israel at the time of the exodus, as well as of the kings of the Davidic dynasty (see Exod. 4:22–23; Hos. 11:1; 2 Sam. 7:11–16; Ps. 2:7). This being so, it was natural that it would apply to the Davidic king par excellence. What this means is that for Jesus' contemporaries the phrase was synonymous with 'Messiah'.[4] But the Old Testament promise of the Messiah was of one who would not only be descended from David but, also, would be 'the mighty God' (Isa. 9:6). This, it seems, was lost on Jesus' contemporaries but it is clear that he was aware that the Messiah was far more than merely a descendant of David (Matt. 22:41–46 and parallels). John's Gospel particularly highlights the divine status that being Son of God entailed for him.

What this brief survey demonstrates is that the disciples' understanding of Jesus was a developing one, with his resurrection and post-resurrection teaching crystallizing for the disciples the precise identity of Jesus. That divine status should have been predicated of him by fiercely monotheistic Jews underlines the impact upon them of his person, his deeds, his resurrection and his teaching. While

---

4. This seems fairly clear from Peter's words in Matt. 16:16, where the phrase 'Son of God' stands in apposition to 'the Christ' and is epexegetic of it.

they set forth in their writings what Andrew McGowan calls a Christology 'from above', it was also a Christology 'from behind' and 'from within'; that is to say, it derived from what the Old Testament said of the Messiah. But they were able to grasp this only after the redemptive events of crucifixion and resurrection had taken place and after Jesus had explained to them how everything fitted together. This approach to Christology maintains a high view of Scripture, and is able to give due weight to the developing nature of the disciples' understanding of who Jesus was,[5] while also locating Jesus firmly in his historical and geographical context.

The mystery of Christ's person resides not only in the fact that he is God and man. We need to reckon with the fact that there is mystery in the Being of God as well as mystery in human nature. In the case of the God-Man, therefore, we have three mysteries in one person! A human being, for example, begins as a zygote and develops, via the various stages of gestation, through babyhood, childhood, adolescence and on into adulthood. There is profound mystery in the whole area of personal identity and of continuity through time. This mystery applies as much to Jesus Christ as to any other human being. Philip Eveson explores some of the relevance of this with respect to the inner and psychological life of Christ. His thoughtful chapter will repay careful study.

The mystery of God's Being, of course, is infinitely greater than that of a human being. One perennial problem reflective Christians have to grapple with is the question 'Can God suffer?' Put into theological language, is God *passible*? It may well be that some of the differences between those who believe God to be passible and those

---

5. Thomas's confession in John 20:28 illustrates this point. Only a week earlier he could not accept that Jesus had risen from the dead. Such scepticism was hardly possible if he believed that Jesus was God-Man. But after the appearance of Jesus to him, he makes his great confession. Admittedly, he expresses himself *functionally*: '*My* Lord and *my* God'. But for a Jew to make such a confession would have been blasphemous unless he believed that Jesus was, *ontologically*, Lord and God. Furthermore, this confession can be seen as the climax of John's Gospel, expressing in personal terms what John had stated ontologically in the Prologue, especially in v. 1.

who hold that he is impassible are more imagined than real. Where there are real differences, there is the danger of exaggerating them. 'Passibilists' will rightly emphasize those passages of Scripture which assert that God is angry with human sin, that he is grieved by it, that he is moved with pity and mercy, and so forth. Of course, they are aware that the Bible uses anthropomorphisms, and that 'impassibilists' will regard such passages as being anthropomorphic. The point of an anthropomorphism, however, is just this: there is a reality to which it relates. Therefore, the 'passibilist' will contend that one cannot simply dismiss the matter with the word 'anthropomorphism'. 'Impassibilists' will rightly emphasize the fact that God is sovereign and that nothing happens in the universe outside, and apart from, his sovereign decree. What this means, of course, is that while God's anger, pity, mercy, grief and so on are never empty charades, these qualities must be somewhat different in him from what they are in us precisely because he is sovereign, whereas we are not.[6]

This discussion of the passible–impassible debate is important for a proper appreciation of the profundities connected with our Lord's cry of dereliction. Put simply, the question is this: 'Did the incarnation confer upon Jesus a capacity to suffer that he did not possess as the eternal Word?' The answer of the letter to the Hebrews is surely in the affirmative (see e.g. Heb. 2:5–18; 4:14 – 5:10; 9:26–27). It is one aspect of the glory of Christ that he can sympathize with his suffering and tempted people. While it is true that different Persons of the Trinity perform different works, the unity of the divine nature that they share is such that an act of one person is an act of the whole Godhead; this point notwithstanding, in the work of atonement suffering is never predicated of the Father or of the Spirit but only of the Son. To be true, the

---

6. Helpful discussion of the issues involved in a consideration of divine impassibility and divine passibility will be found in the following: D. A. Carson, *Divine Sovereignty and Human Responsibility: Biblical Perspectives in Tension* (London: HarperCollins, 1981); *The Difficult Doctrine of the Love of God* (Leicester: IVP, 2000); B. B. Warfield, 'Imitating the Incarnation,' in *The Person and Work of Christ* (Philadelphia: Presbyterian & Reformed, 1950), pp. 570–571; Thomas G. Weinandy, *Does God Suffer?* (Edinburgh: T. & T. Clark, 2000).

greatness of God's love that prompted the giving of his Son means there was cost to the Father. This must never be minimized. At the same time, it is the sufferings of the Son that are emphasized. These sufferings were borne in the human nature of Christ. As Paul Wells makes clear, Jesus bore them as the Mediator; there was no 'rupture' in the Godhead. At the same time, the *communio idiomatum* means that, though these sufferings were in the human nature, they are ascribed to the person.[7] Professor Wells's chapter is both theologically lucid and profoundly moving.

It is important in this connection not to lose sight of the fact that each human being is made in God's image and, therefore, human nature was an appropriate and fitting 'vehicle' for the incarnation. C. S. Lewis once said that if we wish to know what incarnation means, we should try to imagine what it would be like for a human being to become a slug.[8] This, however, is a misleading – and a dangerously misleading – analogy. Human beings are made in God's image and likeness; slugs are not made in our likeness. In other words, there is a certain congruence between God and human beings that does not exist between God and any other creature, or between human beings and slugs. To put it baldly, God could not have been incarnated as a dog or a donkey. To say that he could do so is not to magnify his omnipotence; rather, it is to be guilty of blasphemy.

One strand of biblical teaching concerning the incarnation emphasizes the condescension involved in God taking human nature to himself. Paul's great treatment of this theme in Philippians 2 emphasizes that it was in accord with God's character to do this. Another strand of biblical teaching emphasizes that the vindication and triumph of Christ in his resurrection, ascension

---

7. There is an important distinction between the *communio idiomatum* and the *communicatico idiomatum*: the former denotes the ascription of attributes and activities of one of the two natures of Christ's person; the latter denotes the transfer of attributes or activities of one of Christ's two natures to the other nature. The former is the biblical position. See John Murray, *Collected writings of John Murray*. Vol. 2: *Select Lectures in Systematic Theology* (Edinburgh: Banner of Truth Trust, 1977), p. 140.

8. *Mere Christianity* (New York: Macmillan, 1977), p. 155.

and coming again is something done on behalf of his people as their representative. As 'Rabbi' John Duncan quaintly expressed it, Jesus has raised the dust of the earth to the throne of heaven.[9] While evangelicals give due emphasis to the incarnation (the Christmas period ensures this), one cannot say the same with respect to the ascension. Yet the New Testament lays great emphasis upon the fact and the theological significance of the ascension, as well as upon the heavenly ministry of Christ. The ascension is not only tied, theologically, very tightly to the gift of the Holy Spirit and to the church's mission in the world but also to elucidating the true destiny of the people of God. Matthew Sleeman and Richard Gaffin explore these themes in their respective chapters and throw much needed light on this aspect of biblical teaching.

The great mystery of how the eternal Word, who was God, could join himself to human nature, with all the developmental characteristics of human beings that this would entail, and remain one personal agent is so profound that many adopt a reductionist approach to the person of Christ.[10] Some feel that to say of the same person at the same time that he knows everything and that he does not know everything, and that he is almighty but also weak and frail is to talk incoherent and illogical nonsense rather than profound mystery. But an analogy from the physical world may help to elucidate this point. To classical physics light could either be a wave motion through a medium ('the ether') or consist of a stream of particles. By the early twentieth century enough data had been gathered to demonstrate that while there was no such medium as the ether, through which light waves could be propagated, light consisted of 'packets of energy', photons, which had the characteristics of both particles and waves. One could describe light as a wave motion or as particles; what was not to be done, however, was to adopt a 'reductionist' approach

---

9. 'In the exaltation of Jesus the dust of the earth has been exalted to the throne of the universe.' Quotes in J. Douglas Macmillan, *Jesus – Power without Measure: The Work of the Spirit in the Life of our Lord* (Bridgend: Evangelical Press of Wales, 1990), pp. 152–153.

10. A. N. S. Lane appears to do this in his chapter 'Christology beyond Chalcedon', in Rowdon, *Christ the Lord*, pp. 257–281, esp. p. 272.

whereby one description would rule out the other. In the world of quantum mechanics one can specify a particle's momentum or its position at any one time, but not both at the same time. Is this so very far removed from the mystery of the person of Christ?[11] One may say that he was almighty, and this is true. One may say that he was frail and weak, and this also is true. It would be false, however, to say that *only* one of them could be true. Underlying these two aspects is the unity of his Person. As the late John Murray wonderfully expressed it, in the person of Christ there are two centres of consciousness but only one of self-consciousness.[12]

Christology, we have seen, is not only a theological concern but is also doxological. This being so, it is fitting that the final chapter of the book addresses the subject of the person of Christ in the book of Revelation. Too frequently this book is read through a 'not yet' eschatological lens. But the book is profoundly Christological and, for that reason, its eschatological perspectives are those of the 'already' as well as of the 'not yet'. Greg Beale's exegetically and linguistically penetrating treatment of self-designations of Christ in Revelation demonstrates that language from the Old Testament that describes Yahweh is applied in the last book of the Bible to Jesus. We are reminded that the worship of Jesus is no mere academic affair: we live in a world where idolatry can be presented in such an attractive light that we need the focus of Revelation upon the fact that such idolatries are really grotesque beasts, monstrous parodies of the true God. The Lamb is worthy of glory in 'Immanuel's Land' and is therefore to be glorified in and by his saints on earth. It is the prayer of the contributors and of the editor that this volume will serve to promote the glory of Christ among his people, to strengthen their devotion and enhance their worship of, and witness to, him in our needy generation.

© Stephen Clark, 2007

---

11. For discussion of 'complementarity' in quantum theory and Christology, see e.g. Alister McGrath, *Science and Religion: An Introduction* (Oxford: Blackwell, 1999), pp. 165–174.

12. Murray, *Collected Writings*, vol. 2, p. 138.

1. AFFIRMING CHALCEDON

A. T. B. McGowan

Introduction

The intention of this chapter is to set out the core Christological teaching of the Council of Chalcedon, to demonstrate that this was soundly based on the teaching of Scripture and to argue that it should remain the teaching of the church. It is important to do this because many modern theologians have rejected the teaching of Chalcedon. The chapter is divided into four sections: (1) a study of the Chalcedonian Definition, demonstrating its historical and theological roots; (2) a survey of the biblical evidence concerning the person of Christ, which is generally used to demonstrate Chalcedon's coherence with Scripture; (3) an analysis of the current Christological confusion and its roots in the Enlightenment; and (4) an affirmation of the profound theological significance of Chalcedon.

The Christology of Chalcedon

About 450 delegates attended the Council of Chalcedon in 451.[1]
The Council covered many topics but the central issue concerned
the person of Christ. After much debate, a formula was arrived
at called the Definition of Faith, now commonly known as
the Chalcedonian Definition. In addition to this, the Council
reaffirmed the decisions of previous councils, not least the ones
at Nicaea (325) and Constantinople (381). In other words, the
Definition of Faith was not viewed as a replacement for the
Niceno-Constantinopolitan Creed but a spelling out of its central
tenets, an expansion of its key themes, answering some new questions. The Chalcedonian Definition remains today the classic
statement on Christological matters and has been accepted historically by virtually all churches, whether Orthodox, Roman Catholic
or Protestant. Here is the statement on the person of Christ:

> Following the holy Fathers we teach with one voice that the Son [of
> God] and our Lord Jesus Christ is to be confessed as one and the same
> [person], that he is perfect in Godhead and perfect in manhood, very
> God and very man, of a reasonable soul and [human] body consisting,
> consubstantial with the Father as touching his Godhead, and
> consubstantial with us as touching his manhood; made in all things like
> unto us, sin only excepted; begotten of his Father before the worlds
> according to his Godhead; but in these last days for us men and for our
> salvation born [into the world] of the Virgin Mary, the Mother of God
> according to his manhood. This one and the same Jesus Christ, the only-
> begotten Son [of God] must be confessed to be in two natures,
> unconfusedly, immutably, indivisibly, inseparably [united], and that
> without the distinction of natures being taken away by such union, but
> rather the peculiar property of each nature being preserved and being

---

1. For a study of Chalcedon, see H. R. Mackintosh, *The Doctrine of the Person
   of Jesus Christ* (Edinburgh: T. & T. Clark, 1937), pp. 196–222; R. V. Sellers,
   The Council of Chalcedon: A Historical and Doctrinal Survey (London: SPCK,
   1961); Gerald Bray, *Creeds, Councils and Christ* (Fearn: Mentor, 1997),
   pp. 144–171.

united in one Person and subsistence, not separated or divided into two persons, but one and the same Son and only-begotten, God the Word, our Lord Jesus Christ, as the Prophets of old time have spoken concerning him, and as the Lord Jesus Christ hath taught us, and as the Creed of the Fathers hath delivered to us.[2]

The problem with this statement is that it cannot be fully understood without a knowledge of some of the Christological debates that took place during the period leading up to Chalcedon. This is because many of the statements in the Definition are taken from earlier conciliar decisions, or are written in response to views the Council of Chalcedon itself regarded as heretical. To unfold the teaching of Chalcedon, then, we need some background.

Early Christology

It was not until the fourth century that the church gave sustained attention to the doctrine of the person of Christ.[3] There had, of course, been earlier Christological discussions, mostly in response to heresies. On the one hand, there were those who overemphasized Jesus' humanity, such as the Ebionites, Jewish Christians who believed that Jesus was the son of Mary and Joseph but became Son of God at his baptism; or the Adoptionists like Paul of Samosata. On the other hand there were those who overemphasized his deity, such as the Docetists and the Sabellians.[4]

---

2. Henry R. Percival, 'The Seven Ecumenical Councils', in Philip Schaff and Henry Wace (eds.), A *Select Library of Nicene and Post-Nicene Fathers of the Christian Church*, 2nd series, vol. 14 (Grand Rapids: Eerdmans, n.d.), pp. 264–265.
3. For a study of the earliest Christological reflections, see I. H. Marshall, 'The Development of Christology in the Early Church', *Tyndale Bulletin* 18 (1967), pp. 77–93; and J. D. G. Dunn, *Christology in the Making: A New Testament Inquiry into the Origins of the Doctrine of the Incarnation* (London: SCM, 1980).
4. For a detailed study of these and other early Christological debates, see J. N. D. Kelly, *Early Christian Doctrines* (London: A. & C. Black, 1989), pp. 138–162.

It was not until the Arian controversy in the fourth century, however, that the church began to define its Christology with care. Arius, who was a presbyter of Alexandria, held to a strong monotheistic position and did not believe that Jesus was God. Rather, he believed Jesus to be the first and greatest of all created beings. Alexander, Bishop of Alexandria, opposed Arius, insisting that Jesus was truly God. He did not deny that Jesus was generated by the Father but, following the teaching of Origen, insisted that this was an eternal generation.[5]

The Council of Nicaea

The emperor Constantine came to rule over the whole Roman Empire in 324, with a strong desire for a united Christianity in a united empire, and called the Council of Nicaea in 325 to settle this matter of the relation between the Son and the Father.[6] At this Council, Alexander and his party insisted on the word *homoousios*, 'of the same essence', as being the best way to describe the relationship the Son of God has with the Father. This was opposed by the Arians.[7] The battle, however, was not just between Arius and his supporters as over against Alexander and his supporters. There was another group in between, a moderate party, which wanted a compromise. This group (often called the 'semi-Arians') was led by the great church historian Eusebius, who was a much better historian than he was a theologian! This middle group wanted to substitute the word *homoiousios* for the word *homoousios*. This compromise word *homoiousios* meant 'of similar essence'.

---

5. Mackintosh, *Doctrine of the Person*, pp. 164–170.

6. For a study of this Council and the controversy from which it originated, see Kelly, *Early Christian Doctrines*, pp. 223–251. Rowan Williams, *Arius: Heresy and Tradition* (London: Darton Longman & Todd, 1987); Maurice Wiles, *Archetypal Heresy: Arianism through the Centuries* (Oxford: Clarendon, 1996); and Lewis Ayres, *Nicaea and its Legacy: An Approach to Fourth-Century Trinitarian Theology* (Oxford: Oxford University Press, 2004).

7. This title should not necessarily be taken to mean a unified perspective. As Williams points out, 'there was no such thing in the fourth century as a single, coherent "Arian" party' (*Arius*, p. 233).

This underlines the complexity of the matter. Here was the major battle over the doctrine of the Trinity and it rested on one Greek letter and the difference made by this one Greek letter was colossal. These three groups, then, met at Nicaea to settle the matter once and for all. The Council (after the emperor intervened) concluded that what Alexander said was orthodox and rejected the Arian and the Semi-Arian positions. The word *homoousios* was affirmed. This meant that the church was stating unambiguously that Jesus Christ was a divine person and was of one essence with the Father.

The aftermath

The matter didn't end there, however, and the arguments raged on. Because it was the emperor who settled the matter, many within the church were dissatisfied. Hence, for a long time there were Arians and semi-Arians in the church despite the decision. Eventually, Arius and his followers were excommunicated. By this time, however, Arius had sought and found help and support from outside Egypt and the matter became more than a local case of church discipline. In particular, he enlisted the help of a number of bishops who shared his views.

It was Alexander's successor, the bishop and theologian Athanasius, who provided the main theological opposition to the views of Arius. Although he was only a young man when the controversy broke out, he had accompanied the bishop to the Council of Nicaea. Although he went to Nicaea only in support of his bishop, even then his theological brilliance was recognized and for the next forty years his was the major theological voice of orthodoxy and he was the principal opponent of Arian and semi-Arian views.

As Athanasius battled against the Arians,[8] he was very often left in a small minority among the bishops and was even

---

8. Even to speak of the 'Arians' in this sense, however, is also challenged by Williams. He writes, 'The textbook picture of an Arian system, defended by self-conscious doctrinal dissidents inspired by the teachings of the Alexandrian presbyter is the invention of Athanasius' polemic; most non-Nicenes would probably have been as little likely to call themselves Arians as Nicenes were to call themselves Athanasians' (ibid., p. 234).

occasionally entirely alone. The various emperors tended to side with the majority and so five times Athanasius was removed from his position and forced into exile. For a considerable period, the church in the west took the side of Athanasius, whereas the church in the east became more or less completely semi-Arian. Various councils were held to settle the matter, but without success. At one point, the emperor Constantius by various means brought the western bishops into line with the east and so almost the whole of Christendom was opposed to Athanasius and the Nicene party.

Eventually, however, this was turned round. This happened partly because the Arian party became more and more divided and because a more extreme group within it came to the fore. Several Church Fathers were involved in the return to orthodoxy, including Basil, Gregory of Nyssa and Gregory of Nazianzus (called the 'Cappadocian Fathers'). The Arians had imperial support from 353 to 378, but thereafter declined. The Council of Constantinople met in 381 and affirmed Nicene orthodoxy. It was the version of the Nicene Creed adopted by this Council (including an affirmation of the divinity of the Holy Spirit) that is the version still used today;[9] hence it is more properly called the 'Niceno-Constantinopolitan Creed'.[10]

Between Nicaea and Chalcedon

Now one might have expected that, following upon the Council of Nicaea, the key theological issues had been settled, but it was

---

9. Although in the western church it has the added *filioque* (and from the Son) clause, to assert that the Holy Spirit proceeds not only from the Father but also from the Son. This was first added to the western version of the Creed in 589 by the Council of Toledo and was one of the reasons for the great schism in 1054 between the eastern and the western Church.

10. For theological reflections on this Creed, see T. F. Torrance (ed.), *The Incarnation: Ecumenical Studies in the Nicene-Constantinopolitan Creed A.D. 381* (Edinburgh: Handsel, 1981).

not so.[11] Part of the problem that contributed to the Christological battles that followed was the fact that there were two rival theological schools at work and they had different emphases. The Alexandrians were concerned to emphasize the unity of Christ, whereas the Antiochenes wanted to stress the distinctness of the two natures of Christ. The fact that Jesus was both God and man had been agreed, but beyond that there was no agreement. There was now a new question to be answered: Given that Jesus is God and man at the same time, how is this possible? To that question there was a variety of answers, three of which were ultimately rejected as heretical.

Apollinaris

Apollinaris argued that the divine Logos took the place of Christ's mind or spirit. This meant that Christ had no human spirit or human mind. The problem with this solution was that it essentially denied the incarnation. If the Logos simply took the place of the human mind or spirit, then you cannot say that the Logos became flesh. The church rejected the solution offered by Apollinaris but did not offer an alternative. The question still remained: Precisely how are the divine and the human related in the person of Jesus Christ?

Nestorius

Nestorius was another to offer a solution. He was reputed to have argued that Christ was two persons, a divine person and a human person. Nestorius was attacked by Cyril, Bishop of Alexandria, who believed and taught that Christ was one person with two natures, one human and one divine. At the request of Cyril, the emperor called a council of the church in 431, the Council of Ephesus. At this Council Nestorius was condemned. Many scholars now believe that this judgment was unfair and that the heresy was really created by the followers of

---

11. For a more detailed study of the period between Nicaea and Chalcedon, see Kelly, *Early Christian Doctrines*, pp. 280–343; and Frances M. Young, *From Nicaea to Chalcedon* (London: SCM, 1983).

Nestorius and not by Nestorius himself. As Alan Richardson says:

> [Nestorius] used a word for 'nature' which the Alexandrians now used only for 'person' in the sense of the person of Christ. When, therefore, he intended to speak of the two natures or aspects of Christ (divine and human), he was understood to mean that Christ was two persons.[12]

Richardson supports his argument by saying that certain writings of Nestorius were discovered earlier this century that clarify his position.[13] Whether or not he himself was to blame, however, the heresy of Nestorianism did exist and required a response. Cyril provided this, although his motives have been questioned.[14]

Eutyches

A third person to come forward with a proposed solution to the problem was Eutyches. He argued that Christ was two natures prior to the incarnation but at the incarnation the divine nature swallowed up the human nature and so Christ had only a divine nature. His body, argued Eutyches, was a divine body and not like ours at all.

Once again the situation was complicated by a dispute between Alexandria and Constantinople for control of the eastern church. Dioscorus was Bishop of Alexandria and Flavian, Bishop of Constantinople. Dioscorus supported Eutyches. Flavian held a synod in 448 that condemned this heresy. The emperor called a synod in 449, at which the other party were in control and Eutyches was affirmed. Indeed, violence broke out and Flavian died later of injuries received! The whole church was appalled at these events. The Bishop of Rome

---

12. Alan Richardson, *Creeds in the Making* (London: SCM, 1967), p. 78.

13. Ibid, p. 77.

14. As the bishop of Alexandria, it has been suggested that he was principally concerned to establish himself as the sole leader of the church. The see of Constantinople, held by Nestorius, provided the only credible challenge to Alexandria in the east.

excommunicated Dioscorus and when a new emperor, Marcian, came to the throne in 450 he called a council of the church. This met at Chalcedon in 451.

The Council of Chalcedon

Having come full circle, we are now in a better position to understand the Christological statement issued at the Council of Chalcedon. The Council of Nicaea had said that Jesus was both God and man. The Council of Chalcedon now had to take this further and decide how this was possible, especially in response to the various suggestions that had been offered and rejected. The two great influences upon the Council of Chalcedon were Cyril of Alexandria and Pope Leo the Great. There are regular references in the Acts of the Council of Chalcedon to 'the Blessed Cyril' or 'Cyril of Blessed Memory'. The two letters of Cyril (to Nestorius and to John of Antioch) and the *Tome* of Leo[15] were all read at Session II of the Council. Leo's *Tome*, in particular, summed up the key issues and received the support of the Council. The Council duly declared that Jesus Christ was 'one person with two natures'.

This decision, however, required further clarification. If we accept that Jesus Christ has a divine nature and a human nature and that these two natures are united in the one person of Jesus Christ, we must ask about the union between these natures. The answer given by the Council of Chalcedon was that the natures were 'unconfusedly, immutably, indivisibly, inseparably [united], and that without the distinction of natures being taken away by such union, but rather the peculiar property of each nature being preserved'.[16]

In this statement, the Council was guarding against the three errors outlined above. It is important to affirm, as Chalcedon did, that the two natures of Christ remain as two natures. This is to guard against the view that somehow the two natures were fused together into something different, something neither

---

15. Percival, 'Seven Ecumenical Councils', pp. 254–258.
16. Ibid, pp. 264–265.

God nor man, but an amalgam. This was a direct response to Eutyches who, as we saw above, argued that Christ had two natures before the union but only one afterwards. Louis Berkhof says this,

> The one divine person, who possessed a divine nature from eternity, assumed a human nature, and now has both. This must be maintained over against those who, while admitting that the divine person assumed a human nature, jeopardize the integrity of the two natures by conceiving of them as having been fused or mixed into a *tertium quid*, a sort of divine-human nature.[17]

On the other hand, the Council had to be equally determined in affirming that the two natures were truly united. This was to guard against those like Nestorius (or his followers) who would separate the natures. It is instructive to go through the Chalcedonian Definition and to note the sections that sum up previous councils (especially Nicaea and Constantinople) and those sections that specifically respond to Arius, Nestorius, Apollinarus and Eutyches.

The church, through this great council, taught that, at the incarnation, the second person of the Trinity, God the Son (or Logos), took to himself a human nature and was born as Jesus of Nazareth. The Son of God thus had two natures, one divine and one human, both of which were subsumed under the one acting subject. What we must now ask is whether or not this is true to Scripture. Do the Scriptures identify the man Jesus with God in this way? Can both his deity and humanity be found in Scripture? In other words, can the decisions of the Council be supported by the teaching of Scripture?[18] The following is an analysis of the Scriptures used by the Fathers and their successors to justify their position.

---

17. Louis Berkhof, *Systematic Theology* (Edinburgh: Banner of Truth, 1971), p. 322.

18. For a short but powerful defence of Chalcedon, see Gerald Bray, 'Can we Dispense with Chalcedon?', *Themelios* 3.2 (1978), pp. 2–9.

Biblical teaching on the person of Christ

In the Synoptic Gospels of Matthew and Luke we have the
infancy narratives, which affirm that Jesus was born miracu-
lously, that his mother was a virgin when she gave birth and that
the conception of Jesus came about by the action of God the
Holy Spirit. In other words, there was an incarnation (God
becoming human) such that the one to whom Mary gave birth
was God himself. This is why the Chalcedonian Definition calls
Mary the 'Mother of God' (or 'God-Bearer'). It is also Matthew
who records that one of the names given to Jesus was
Emmanuel, meaning 'God with us' (Matt. 1:23). Neither Mark's
nor John's Gospel contains an infancy narrative, but the prologue to John's Gospel has perhaps the strongest statement of
the deity of Jesus: 'In the beginning was the Word, and the Word
was with God, and the Word was God. He was in the beginning
with God. All things were made through him, and without him
was not any thing made that was made' (John 1:1–3). It is clear
from the later verses in the Prologue (14–18) that the Logos
referred to in these verses is Jesus of Nazareth. John is thus
claiming that Jesus is God and that he was the agent of creation
itself.

From the beginning of the public ministry of Jesus, there is
controversy over his identity, just as there is over the identity of
John the Baptist, a figure with whom he is closely related in
the Gospels, even in the infancy narratives (Luke 1:36–45). The
Baptist had been challenged as to whether he was one of the
figures expected by the Jews, based on prophetic statements in
parts of the Old Testament, namely, the Messiah, the Prophet or
Elijah (John 1:19–28). He denied all three designations, although
Jesus later identified him as the fulfilment of the prophecy regarding the Elijah who was to come before the Messiah (Matt. 11:7–15;
cf. Mal. 4:5). Jesus too was constantly challenged as to his identity.
Sometimes it was couched in terms of authority: 'And when he
entered the temple, the chief priests and the elders of the people
came up to him as he was teaching, and said, "By what authority
are you doing these things, and who gave you this authority?"'
(Matt. 21:23). At other times it was more direct: 'Are you the Son

of God, then?' (Luke 22:70). As a general rule, Jesus did not answer these questions directly.

At the beginning of his ministry, most people treated him as if he were no more than a wandering rabbi from Nazareth. Many people, including his own family, thought that he was mad when he acted and spoke in a way that seemed to make claims to a special status. Nor was it the case that the doubters gradually became convinced of his claims. Indeed, many of those who followed him initially, later deserted him and the crowds who cheered him when he entered Jerusalem were quick to cry 'Crucify him!' a week later. Even his disciples seemed to be uncertain as to his identity, despite having seen so much dramatic evidence of astonishing power, not least people being healed and raised from the dead. There were, however, points when clarity and faith seemed to shine through. For example, at Caesarea Philippi, when Jesus asked the disciples, 'Who do people say that the Son of Man is?', he received a range of answers; but, when he then asked them for their own opinions, Peter declared, 'You are the Christ, the Son of the living God' (Matt. 16:13–16). These points of insight rarely lasted, however, and the same Peter ran away terrified when Jesus was arrested. It was only after the resurrection that the followers of Jesus truly understood and thereafter consistently maintained his identity as the Son of God.

The humanity of Jesus is rarely doubted today, although it was by some in the early days of the church. Under the influence of Greek philosophy they believed that spirit and flesh were incompatible and the idea of a God (who is spirit) taking flesh was incomprehensible; hence the Docetic claim that Jesus only 'appeared' to be a man but was in reality pure spirit. Today the problem usually concerns the affirmation of his deity. Nevertheless, it is worth pointing out that Jesus had a real humanity. He could eat and drink (even in his resurrection body); he could be tired and sleep; he could be angry; he could weep. Above all he could bleed and die.

It is clear, however, that the writers of the New Testament also affirmed his deity. This is particularly clear in John's Gospel, both in the recorded words of Jesus himself and in the reflections of John. We have already noted the claim to deity contained in the prologue to the Gospel (1:1–3). One striking passage is John 8:56–59, when some Jews challenged Jesus as to whether or not he was greater than Abraham. Jesus answered, 'Your father Abraham rejoiced that he would see my day. He saw it and was glad.' The Jews replied, 'You are not yet fifty years old, and have you seen Abraham?' Jesus responded, 'Truly, truly, I say to you, before Abraham was, I am.' Given that 'I am' was a recognized name for God among the Jews, ever since God had told Moses that was his name (Exod. 3:14), there can be little doubt that Jesus, in using these words, was claiming to be God.[19] That was certainly what those present understood him to mean because, we are told, 'they picked up stones to throw at him'. It does not say so specifically in the text but clearly they were going to stone him for blasphemy. On another occasion the Jews again tried to stone him for blasphemy because he had said 'I and the Father are one' (John 10:30). On this occasion, however, the Jews were very specific about the reasons for the stoning. Jesus had taunted them by asking for which of his many good works he was to be stoned. They replied, 'It is not for a good work that we are going to stone you but for blasphemy, because you, being a man, make yourself God' (John 10:33).

For orthodox Christological and trinitarian thinking, it is imperative to insist that there is no God lying behind Jesus to whom he points but rather that he is himself the revelation of the living God; thus, God reveals himself in and through himself. An incident recorded by John highlights this truth. We are told (John 14:8–9) that Philip, one of the disciples, said that if Jesus would simply show them the Father, then they would be satisfied. Jesus replied, 'Have I been with you so long, and you still do not know me, Philip? Whoever has seen me has seen the Father. How can

---

19. The majority of interpreters today find the proper background to *egō eimi* in John 8:24, 28, 58 in Isa. 40 – 55 (cf. esp. 41:4; 43:10, 13, 25; 46:4; 48:12). In the Hebrew, God discloses himself in the declaration *'ănî hû'*, 'I am he'; this expression is consistently rendered in the Septuagint as *egō eimi*. Isa. 43:10 is especially close to Johannine language; 43:11–13 alludes directly to Exod. 3:14.

you say, "Show us the Father"?' This identification with the Father is further emphasized in John 17:5 where, in his high priestly prayer, Jesus says, 'And now, Father, glorify me in your own presence with the glory that I had with you before the world existed.' This surely underlines the consistency of John's Christology.

It is in the Epistles, however, that the clearest statements about Jesus' deity are to be found. This is surely what we would expect. After the momentous events of the resurrection and ascension and after a time of prayer and theological reflection, the earliest Christians were able to express very clearly what the Holy Spirit had given them to understand. Paul expresses a very high Christology in such passages as Ephesians 1:20–23 when he says that God raised Christ from the dead,

> and seated him at his right hand in the heavenly places, far above all rule and authority and power and dominion, and above every name that is named, not only in this age but also in the one to come. And he put all things under his feet and gave him as head over all things to the church, which is his body, the fullness of him who fills all in all.

This is clearly not the description of a mere man! Even more striking is Colossians 1:15–20, where Paul affirms that Jesus 'is the image of the invisible God', that he was the agent of creation, that he holds everything in being and that he is in all things pre-eminent. Paul concludes this great peroration by saying, 'For in him all the fullness of God was pleased to dwell'. There can surely be no doubt that Paul was affirming Christ's deity? If there was, the words that follow shortly thereafter add confirmation, 'in him the whole fullness of deity dwells bodily' (2:9).

The most important passage in Paul's writings concerning the true identity of Jesus is found in Philippians 2:5–11. Using Christ as the example of supreme humility, Paul writes:

> Have this mind among yourselves, which is yours in Christ Jesus, who, though he was in the form of God, did not count equality with God a thing to be grasped, but made himself nothing, taking the form of a servant, being born in the likeness of men.

Here is God the Son, accepting the Father's will and submitting to an incarnation. The end result, of course, is a restoration to his previous glory:

> Therefore God has highly exalted him and bestowed on him the name that is above every name, so that at the name of Jesus every knee should bow, in heaven and on earth and under the earth, and every tongue confess that Jesus Christ is Lord, to the glory of God the Father.

We could, of course look to many other passages in Paul's writings, but shall confine ourselves to two further passages, where Paul leaves us in no doubt as to his belief in the deity of Christ. In Titus 2:13 he describes Jesus as 'our great God and Saviour Jesus Christ' and in Romans 9:5 he speaks of 'the Christ who is God over all'. We should note in passing that the apostle Peter also describes Jesus in this way (2 Pet. 1:1).

The writer to the Hebrews also affirms a high Christology.[20] Were we to go through the whole epistle we could see the comparisons he makes between Jesus and the angels, between Jesus and Moses, between Jesus and the high priest and so on, all to the same effect, namely, the superiority of Jesus because of his deity. We need go no further, however, than the opening verses of the epistle, where we read this:

> Long ago, at many times and in many ways, God spoke to our fathers by the prophets, but in these last days he has spoken to us by his Son, whom he appointed the heir of all things, through whom also he created the world. He is the radiance of the glory of God and the exact imprint of his nature, and he upholds the universe by the word of his power.

Notice, Jesus Christ is the precise imprint of the nature of God and he upholds the universe.

If further evidence were needed, we could consider the Old

---

20. Mackintosh, *Doctrine of the Person*, pp. 78–87.

Testament witness to Christ.[21] Or, we could refer to the many studies that have been undertaken of the names used by and about Jesus, such as 'Lord', 'Son of Man', 'Son of God', 'Messiah' and so on. The use of these terms can be demonstrated to be making significant theological claims.[22]

The Scriptures are quite clear, then, that Jesus is man but is also God and that he claimed this for himself. The deity of Christ is thus an essential (perhaps *the* essential) element of Christian theology. From this brief summary of the evidence we can affirm that nothing in the Chalcedonian Definition is contrary to Scripture. Certainly, the Definition goes well beyond Scripture in its use of language and terminology and makes distinctions the church had yet to make when the New Testament was completed. Nevertheless, the New Testament is clearly set on a trajectory perfectly in keeping with Chalcedon.

Scripture and tradition

It is important to remember, however, that the Chalcedonian Definition, although important, does not have the authority we accord to the voice of God speaking by his Holy Spirit in Scripture. The church has almost universally accepted the decisions of the Ecumenical Councils and we do well to think carefully before rejecting such time honoured and respected formulations, but they do not have final authority. When Robert Reymond rejected aspects of conciliar teaching on the Trinity in his volume of systematic theology,[23] there were wide and sustained protests and condemnations. Those who objected to his theological

---

21. For a summary of the evidence, see Robert L. Reymond, *Jesus Divine Messiah: The New and Old Testament Witness* (Fearn: Mentor, 2003), pp. 63–165.

22. See Donald Guthrie, *New Testament Theology* (Leicester: IVP, 1981), pp. 235–321; G. E. Ladd, *A Theology of the New Testament* (Grand Rapids: Eerdmans, 1974), pp. 135–172; D. Macleod, *Jesus Is Lord: Christology Yesterday and Today* (Fearn: Mentor, 2000), pp. 78–87.

23. Robert L. Reymond, *A New Systematic Theology of the Christian Faith* (Nashville: Thomas Nelson, 1998).

conclusions had, of course, every right to argue with him on the detail. What was inappropriate for Protestant theologians was the argument that he had no right to challenge or disagree with such august bodies as the Councils of Nicaea or Chalcedon.

This points out the need for an evangelical theology of tradition. Tradition must not be regarded as an authority to be put alongside Scripture, as in Roman Catholicism, or as a body of church teaching that includes Scripture, as in Eastern Orthodoxy but it must be recognized as a vital strand of our theology. We are not the first Christians to reflect on Scripture and we do value the work of those who have gone before us. In the Reformed tradition of Protestantism we value certain confessional statements to the point where we use them as an entry test for ordinands and as a theological canon for purposes of discipline. This is effectively to have a theology of tradition because we are elevating a human statement to the point where we require affirmation of it as well as of Scripture. This has always been the case. As Herman Bavinck has shown us, the Reformers did not reject tradition per se but only bad tradition![24]

Post-Enlightenment Christology

Despite the teaching of Scripture on this matter as summarized by the church in the Chalcedonian Definition and despite the virtually unanimous testimony of the Christian church throughout its history, many theologians now reject the doctrine of the deity of Christ. Cardinal Basil Hume summarized the position well when, in his last book, he wrote:

> Is it not the case that in our day people do not easily admit, and accept, the limitations to their understanding of the great truths of our religion? There is a pride of the mind which rejects what it cannot understand and denies what it cannot prove. How important it is to recognise that

---

24. Herman Bavinck, *Reformed Dogmatics*. Vol. 1: *Prolegomena* (Grand Rapids: Baker, 2003), p. 493.

faith begins when reason can go no further. It is faith that enables us to see in the child in the crib, not just a child, but him of whom St John wrote: 'The Word was flesh and dwelt amongst us.' Not to believe is a modern disease.[25]

Although well aired in academic circles, this challenge to the deity of Christ burst upon the British public in 1963. Dr John A. T. Robinson brought together some of the work of Rudolf Bultmann, Paul Tillich and Dietrich Bonhoeffer, publishing it in a popular form in a book entitled *Honest to God*. It is a mark of how radical and provocative this book was seen to be at the time that Robinson, an Anglican bishop, appeared on the front page of many of the daily newspapers when it was published. It is also striking to note that the book, first published in March 1963, was reprinted three times before that month was finished and then reprinted another five times by the end of September 1963, and numerous times since! See how Robinson spells out his argument:

> But suppose the whole notion of 'a God' who 'visits' the earth in the person of 'his Son' is as mythical as the prince in the fairy story? Suppose there is no realm 'out there' from which the 'Man from heaven' arrives? Suppose the Christmas myth (the invasion of 'this side' by 'the other side') – as opposed to the Christmas history (the birth of the man Jesus of Nazareth) – has to go? Are we prepared for that? Or are we to cling here to this last vestige of the mythological or metaphysical world-view as the only garb in which to clothe story with power to touch the imagination? Cannot perhaps the supranaturalist scheme survive at least as part of the 'magic' of Christmas?
>
> Yes, indeed, it can survive – as myth. For myth has its perfectly legitimate, and indeed profoundly important, place. The myth is there to indicate the significance of the events, the divine depth of the history. And we shall be grievously impoverished if our ears cannot tune to the angels' song or our eyes are blind to the wise men's star. But we must be able to read the nativity story without assuming that its truth depends on

---

25. Basil Hume, *The Mystery of The Incarnation* (London: Darton Longman & Todd, 1999), p. 24.

there being a literal interruption of the natural by the supernatural, that Jesus can only be Emmanuel – God with us – if, as it were, he came through from another world. For, as supranaturalism becomes less and less credible, to tie the action of God to such a way of thinking is to banish it for increasing numbers into the preserve of the pagan myths and thereby to sever it from any real connection with history. As Christmas becomes a pretty story, naturalism – the attempt to explain Christ, like everything else, on humanistic presuppositions – is left in possession of the field as the only alternative with any claim to the allegiance of intelligent men.[26]

In the UK this move away from traditional beliefs as to the deity of Christ culminated in the publication of a book entitled *The Myth of God Incarnate*, edited by John Hick and containing essays by senior academics from Oxford, Cambridge and Birmingham. Here is an extract from the preface:

It is clear to the writers of this book – as to a great many other Christians today – that Christianity has throughout its history been a continuously growing and changing movement. As a result its theology has developed an immense range of variation as the church has passed through successive historical periods and responded to widely different cultural circumstances. Indeed, as T. S. Eliot said, 'Christianity is always adapting itself into something which can be believed'.

In the nineteenth century, Western Christianity made two major new adjustments in response to important enlargements of human knowledge: it accepted that man is part of nature and has emerged within the evolution of the forms of life on this earth; and it accepted that the books of the Bible were written by a variety of human beings in a variety of circumstances, and cannot be accorded a verbal divine authority. These two adjustments were not made without much 'kicking against the pricks' of the facts, which caused wounds that have even now not completely healed. Nevertheless, human knowledge continues to grow at an increasing rate, and the pressure upon Christianity is as strong as ever to go on adapting itself into something which can be

---

26. J. A. T. Robinson, *Honest to God* (London: SCM, 1963), pp. 67–68.

believed – believed by honest and thoughtful people who are deeply attracted by the figure of Jesus and by the light which his teaching throws upon the meaning of human life.

The writers of this book are convinced that another major theological development is called for in this last part of the twentieth century. The need arises from growing knowledge of Christian origins, and involves a recognition that Jesus was (as he is presented in Acts 2:21) 'a man approved by God' for a special role within the divine purpose, and that the later conception of him as God incarnate, the Second person of the Holy Trinity living a human life, is a mythological or poetic way of expressing his significance for us. This recognition is called for in the interests of truth; but it also has increasingly important practical implications for our relationship to the peoples of the other great world religions . . .

There is nothing new in the main theme of this book and we make no pretence to originality. A growing number of Christians, both professional theologians and lay people, have been thinking along these lines. But we have written this book in order to place its topic firmly on the agenda of discussion – not least in England, where the traditional doctrine of the incarnation has long been something of a shibboleth, exempt from reasoned scrutiny and treated with unquestioning literalness.[27]

It might be imagined that these books represent a small minority of scholars and that their position does not impact on the everyday life of the church, but this would be untrue. This mythological view has had considerable influence at grass-roots level. Some time ago there was a programme on BBC Radio Four that illustrates the trend. The programme was a recorded diary of a vicar who was leaving his parish to go to India to write a couple of books. As the programme moved on, however, it became clear that the vicar no longer believed in God. The most striking point of the programme was that his parishioners (or at least the ones to whom we were introduced) wanted him to stay. They said he was a 'good vicar'. The fact that he no longer believed in God was not seen as a barrier to his continuing as a Christian minister!

---

27. John Hick (ed.), *The Myth of God Incarnate* (London: SCM, 1977), pp. ix–xi.

Liberal theology

The origins of this type of thinking lie in the Enlightenment, where autonomous human reason became the final arbiter of truth. It was out of this Enlightenment philosophy that liberal theology was born. F. D. E. Schleiermacher, Albrecht Ritschl, Adolf von Harnack and Wilhelm Hermann, although different in many ways, were the key figures in the early development of liberal theology. Believing that Kant's argument about the noumena was well established and realizing that another epistemological basis had to be found for Christian theology, they devised ways of thinking, and criteria for decision-making, that would ultimately lead to the desupernaturalization of Christianity, thus making it agreeable to autonomous human reason.

Christology from below

In terms of Christology, post-Enlightenment liberal scholars began searching for the 'historical Jesus', a Jesus who was not the 'Christ of faith'. Thus began what became known as the Christology 'from below'. Christology 'from below' describes those attempts to understand Jesus Christ in which his humanity is emphasized to the detriment or even the exclusion of his divinity. The exponents of a Christology 'from below', as Gerald Bray writes, 'produced a Jesus who was essentially a prophetic moralist and religious reformer, crucified because his thinking was ahead of his time'.[28] It is not possible to cover all those who have expounded a Christology 'from below', but we might usefully consider Rudolf Bultmann as the classic example of this type of thinking.

Bultmann drew heavily on those who had gone before him, particularly those who had been influenced by Hegel. Two of his predecessors are worthy of special note as they, to some extent, prepared the way. Ferdinand Christian Baur (1792–1860) was a German theologian and founder of what has come to be known as the Tübingen School of biblical criticism. This was the most radical school of thinking in the first half of the nineteenth

---

28. Gerald Bray, 'Christology', in Sinclair B. Ferguson and David F. Wright (eds.), *New Dictionary of Theology* (Leicester: IVP, 1988), pp. 137–140.

century. Baur was a pioneer in developing a non-supernatural method. David Freidrich Strauss (1808–74) was a student of Baur at Tübingen, where he received his doctorate. His book *Life of Jesus, Critically Examined*[29] caused a storm. In that book he argued that, although Jesus of Nazareth did exist, his life story in the Gospels had been so mythologized as to make it useless for historical evidence. All the miracles and so on were mythical additions to the original story. In this respect he anticipated and prepared the ground for the later work of Bultmann.

Rudolf Bultmann (1884–1976) was a New Testament scholar and a leading theologian. His existentialist theology and particularly his attempt to 'demythologize' the New Testament, led to the creation of perhaps the most radical school of New Testament theology in the twentieth century. Although Bultmann was initially part of the group of scholars associated with Karl Barth, he became more and more influenced by existentialist philosophy, particularly due to the influence of his colleague in Marburg, the Professor of Philosophy, Martin Heidegger. He was also a key figure in the development of 'form criticism'. This was the view that the Gospels could be broken down into smaller units that had arisen directly as a result of oral tradition, and that had later been used to build the Gospels. He was essentially a sceptic in respect of the truth and reliability of these oral traditions.

Due to this work in the area of form criticism, Bultmann became quite convinced that no real historical knowledge about Jesus could be obtained. The Gospels were essentially the product of the early church (the post-Easter church) and said more about the faith of those who wrote them than about the historical events they claimed to describe. On this basis Bultmann concluded that historical evidence could not and should not be the basis for faith and theology. Instead, he wanted to speak of an existential encounter with God, an encounter not based upon proving anything historical. Indeed, whether or not the historical events described in the Bible took place or not becomes irrelevant. In

---

29. First published in 1846.

short, Bultmann's Jesus is not an incarnate God but a mere human being, and his Christology was emphatically 'from below'.

Christology from above

The response to this Christology 'from below' was the development of a Christology 'from above'. Having taken Bultmann as our representative of the 'from below' school, we will take Karl Barth as the classic example of a Christology 'from above'. In doing so, it is instructive to consider Barth's early reaction to liberal theology so as to fully understand why he developed his theology in the way he did.

Liberal theology was characterized by an optimism about the future, largely because of a high view of human progress and a supreme confidence in the ability of modern science and technology to solve the problems of the world. The general view was that humankind was progressing towards the day when poverty, war, violence and all the other ills of society would be abolished or defeated, and all would be well. This was inevitably linked to a lack of emphasis upon sin, and a determination to believe in the goodness of man. This whole optimistic view was, however, fatally damaged by the First World War. Alasdair Heron puts it like this:

> It did not only transform the political and military map: by the destruction which it wrought, unparalleled in previous human history in its scale, it hurled a black question mark against the confidence in the onward and upward progress of Christian civilisation which had so strongly characterised liberal theology, and forced the bitter question whether the advanced theological thought of the nineteenth century as a whole had not been far too unaware of the darker side of human nature, too optimistic about innate human capacity for good, too willing to take contemporary culture at its own high evaluation of itself, and overall too disposed to take God for granted, and to assume that he was somehow simply 'given' in what it regarded as the highest ethical, spiritual and religious values of mankind.[30]

---

30. Alasdair Heron, *A Century of Protestant Theology* (Guildford: Lutterworth, 1980), p. 69.

Heron also makes the perceptive point that the tragedy of the war, and the realization of what human nature was really like, forced people to ask whether you could build any kind of theology on the basis provided by the liberals. Could you begin with human experience (albeit religious experience) and then proceed to talk about God? Could you build an ethical system on the basis of human life and then go on to speak about God? In answer to these kinds of questions, people began to believe that theology must be done from the top down rather than from the bottom up.

Barth's entrance on to the scene begins when, at the outbreak of war, ninety-three German intellectuals signed a document supporting the Kaiser's war policy, saying that they believed it to be necessary for the defence of Christian civilization. Some of Barth's own teachers were among those who had signed. Barth had already begun to have considerable difficulties with the liberal theology in which he had been trained, because he was finding it impossible to preach. More and more he turned to the Bible and increasingly saw the emptiness and essentially destructive nature of liberal theology. When his old teachers signed this document supporting the Kaiser's war policy, this was the last straw. As far as Barth was concerned, any theology that led to the conclusion that such a war was necessary for the defence of Christian civilization was morally bankrupt.

All of this led to Karl Barth publishing a commentary on Romans.[31] It was said that this commentary 'fell like a bomb on the playground of the theologians'.[32] In other words, this book spelled the end of liberal theology as the dominant force in Christian theology. A new era was about to dawn, the era of Barth and his associates. Barth himself says that the reaction to the commentary came as a complete surprise to him. He says that he was like a man wandering around in the darkness of a bell tower trying to get his bearings when, by accident, he grabbed hold of the bell rope and alarmed the whole countryside. His commentary on Romans was

---

31. Karl Barth, *The Epistle to the Romans* (Oxford: Oxford University Press, 1975).

32. Karl Adam, 'Die Theologie der Krisis', *Hochland* 23 (1925–26), p. 271.

quite different from any ever written on the epistle before. There was no section dealing with matters of authorship, date and all the usual technical questions. It was rather an attempt to bring to life some of the great themes of the epistle. Barth felt that previous scholars (especially the liberal school) had become so concerned with the technical side that they did not let the Bible speak. They treated it as the word of man and not as the Word of God.

Schleiermacher and those who followed had treated God as if he were simply an aspect of our own experience. They had tried to bring him down to our level. In many ways they thought of God simply as a bigger and better version of man. Barth reacted totally against this. He began to teach that God was 'wholly other', that there was nothing in God about which we could have any real knowledge unless he chose to reveal himself. And so he began to do theology from the top down rather than from the bottom up. He insisted that there is a transcendent God who encounters humankind, because in his sovereign freedom he chose to do so, in the person of Jesus Christ.

Any modern study of Christology must take account of Barth's massive theological project, because in his *Church Dogmatics* he sought to bring a Christological control over all theology.[33] Indeed, he did so to such an extent that he was accused of 'Christomonism'. Every single doctrine was interpreted Christologically. For example, in his doctrine of election, it is Christ who is elect and we are elect only in so far as we are 'in Christ'. Similarly, our faith is a participation in Christ's faith; our repentance is a participation in Christ's repentance; our baptism a participation in his baptism and so on. This is all grounded theologically in the conviction that there is no God lying behind Jesus Christ and that the only God we know is the God who has revealed himself in the person of Jesus Christ. If we have seen him, we have seen the Father. If we want to know what God is like, we must focus upon Jesus Christ.

Much as Barth's position is to be preferred to that of Bultmann, there are problems with his position. To give just one example, the present writer rejects Barth's notion that Christ took 'fallen

---

33. Karl Barth, *Church Dogmatics*, 14 vols. (Edinburgh: T. & T. Clark, 1936–69).

humanity', not least because of its implications for the Adam/ Christ parallel in Romans 5 and 1 Corinthians 1:15.[34] In order to develop a truly evangelical Christology we must avoid being held too closely to this below/above dichotomy. If we are truly to hold to the Chalcedonian emphasis that Christ is God and man, one person with two natures, we shall want to develop a Christology that takes seriously both Christ's humanity and his deity.

The theological significance of Chalcedon

We have argued that the Christological teaching found in the Chalcedonian Definition (Jesus Christ was one person with two natures) is true to Scripture and presents a biblical picture of Jesus Christ, as opposed to the liberal Christology 'from below'. We must now conclude by making three further points, to highlight the theological significance of the Definition.

The person of the Logos

We must begin by noting that the one person of Jesus Christ is the person of the Logos. It is the Logos, the second person of the Trinity, who is the subject of the incarnation. The human nature of Christ is not a person. Rather the divine Logos, who already had a divine nature, took to himself a human nature and united the two natures in his one person. That is to say, the Logos did not take to himself a human 'person' but a human nature. The human nature of Christ does not have an independent 'subject' controlling it other than the Logos.

This led theologians to say that the human nature of Christ was 'impersonal'. They called this the *anhypostasia*. By this means, they were arguing that the human nature of Christ does not have a 'human person' as its subject (only the person of the Logos) and therefore it is impersonal. Some were unhappy with this notion, believing that it did not do full justice to the human nature in its

---

34. A. T. B. McGowan, *The Federal Theology of Thomas Boston* (Carlisle: Paternoster, 1997), pp. 24–33. Cf. Barth, *Church Dogmatics* 1/2, p. 151.

relation to the Logos. For that reason, some have used the term *enhypostasia*. Donald Macleod sums up the way in which this term is used:

> The import of *enhypostatos* is that the human nature of Christ, although not itself an individual, is individualised as the human nature of the Son of God. It does not, for a single instant, exist as *anhypostatos* or non-personal. As embryo, foetus, infant, child and man it is *hypostatos* in the Second person of the Trinity.[35]

The communio idiomatum

Practical issues also flow out of the Chalcedonian Definition. For example, can we say that in his divine nature Christ is omniscent but in his human nature he is not? Different solutions have been proposed to solve this problem. The Lutheran Church has always held to what is called the *communicatio idiomatum*. This means that the properties of the divine nature are transferred (communicated) to the human nature. John Murray affirms the truth that the Lutherans are anxious to preserve, namely, that 'whatever can be predicated of either nature can be predicated of the person',[36] but rejects the Lutheran way of expressing this. Rather, he argues for a *communio idiomatum*. He writes, 'The Reformed view is rather that what is true of either nature is true of the person, and the person may be *designated* in terms of one nature when what is predicated is true only in virtue of the other.'[37]

The last Adam

These last two points may seem somewhat abstruse and purely technical; yet they are important. We must conclude, however, with a matter that takes us to the very heart of the significance of the hypostatic union, namely, the affirmation that because Christ was both God and man, he was able to serve as Mediator and Saviour.

---

35. Donald Macleod, *The Person of Christ* (Leicester: IVP, 1998), p. 202.
36. John Murray, *Collected Writings of John Murray*. Vol. 2: *Systematic Theology* (Edinburgh: Banner of Truth, 1977), p. 140.
37. Ibid.

In Genesis 2:16–17 we read of how God entered into a relationship with Adam, to the effect that if he disobeyed God's clear and firm instructions, and thus broke God's law, then death would result and a perfect world would be spoiled. Despite this clear statement from God, our first parents succumbed to temptation, disobeyed him, and began a life that was self-centred instead of God-centred.

The key point here is that when God entered into that relationship with Adam, he did so, not with Adam as a private individual but as representative of the human race. If the Prime Minister signs an international treaty, he does so in a representative capacity and not as a private individual. Similarly, when Adam sinned, it was as representative of the human race and so his sin affected the whole human race. In other words, the consequences of Adam's disobedience fell upon all humanity yet unborn. For this reason we are born as sinners and will eventually die.

This means, of course, that death is an enemy (the 'last enemy' says Paul in 1 Cor. 15:26), an intruder into God's world. This intrusion, however, is only temporary. When we come to the last book of the Bible, we find a picture being drawn of the new Jerusalem, the new heaven and the new earth in which 'He will wipe away every tear from their eyes, and death shall be no more, neither shall there be mourning nor crying nor pain anymore, for the former things have passed away' (Rev. 21:4). But how is this to be accomplished? The answer is found in 1 Corinthians 15:21–22, where we read, 'For as by a man came death, by a man has come also the resurrection of the dead. For as in Adam all die, so also in Christ shall all be made alive.' This parallel between Adam and Christ is vital to our understanding of sin and salvation. The same parallel is also found in Romans 5:12–21. It is the axis around which the whole Bible revolves.

God, as we saw, entered into a relationship with Adam, and Adam failed to obey, bringing death upon himself and the entire human race. God, however, entered into another relationship with the human race, this time in Jesus Christ. Since Jesus Christ is man, he could be our representative; since he is God, he was not subject to sin and could offer a worthy sacrifice. Here, then, is the ultimate significance of the hypostatic union: the death of the God-man as our representative. In affirming the hypostatic union, we bear witness to the triumph of Christ, the last Adam, who has accomplished salvation on our behalf. This was well expressed by Cardinal John Henry Newman, in his great hymn 'Praise to the Holiest in the Height':

O loving wisdom of our God,
When all was sin and shame,
a second Adam to the fight
and to the rescue came.

O wisest love! that flesh and blood,
Which did in Adam fail,
Should strive afresh against the foe,
Should strive and should prevail.

Conclusion

This doctrine of the hypostatic union is complex and requires us to walk very carefully in a minefield of potential errors and heresies. In one sense, this is a mystery we will never fully comprehend, but nevertheless we are required to state what we believe God has revealed to us of this mystery. The Council of Chalcedon did not claim to have fully understood or 'settled' the mystery of the hypostatic union, but, in seeking to understand and expound the Scriptures, it laid down parameters for the church. We can do no more than that.

© A. T. B. McGowan, 2007

2. THE INNER OR PSYCHOLOGICAL LIFE OF CHRIST

Philip H. Eveson

Paul introduces the universally acclaimed belief concerning the one who 'was manifested in the flesh', with the words 'Great indeed, we confess, is the mystery of godliness' (1 Tim. 3:16). It is very tempting to use this phraseology when describing the complex nature of the subject under discussion. As in so many aspects of the Christian faith, human understanding is left floundering as it seeks to come to terms with the revelation of God in Christ. The New Testament itself speaks of comprehending the unknowable, expressing the inexpressible and praising the unsearchable judgments of God and his inscrutable ways (see 2 Cor. 9:15; Eph. 3:18–19; Rom. 11:33).

Care must be taken, however, in the use of the term 'mystery'. It would be inappropriate to apply Paul's employment of the word to our inability to comprehend the incarnation. 'Mystery' as used in the New Testament is associated with the term 'revelation'. It describes something that was hidden but is now revealed (1 Cor. 2:7–10; Eph. 3:1–6; Col. 4:3). At the heart of the Christian proclamation is the truth that what was hidden in times past, though preordained and prophesied, is now disclosed. This disclosure has to do with the proclamation of the good news that centres on the incarnate Son of God who died on a cross and rose from the dead that all nations might be blessed through him.[1] It is one aspect of this revealed truth that we shall consider in this chapter.

The fact that the incarnation is now a secret for all the world to know does not make it any easier to understand. From the start we acknowledge the inability of our finite minds to grasp the truth of 'Our God contracted to a span, / incomprehensibly made man'.[2] It is not, however, a discovery that our faith has produced but a divine disclosure that faith embraces. In our approach and attitude to this sacred subject we must have a reverent and worshipful spirit:

> Where reason fails,
>   with all her powers,
> There faith prevails,
>   and love adores.[3]

The person considered

Who is the person into whose human psychological life we are seeking to probe? The focus is on a person who already had an existence before he was born of the virgin Mary. This existence is nothing remotely like reincarnation teaching. The New Testament presents us with this given position that the person named as Jesus of Nazareth, the Messiah, had a glorious life in eternity past before he was seen on earth in his human existence.

It was not the entire Godhead, the triune God, that became flesh. Neither was it the Father or the Holy Spirit who assumed human nature. The person who was born of a woman and suffered under Pontius Pilate is God the Son, the second person of

---

1. See D. A. Carson, 'Mystery and Fulfillment', in D. A. Carson, P. T. O'Brien and M. A. Seifrid (eds.), *Justification and Variegated Nomism*. Vol. 2: *The Paradoxes of Paul* (Tübingen: Mohr Siebeck, 2004), pp. 412–425.
2. From Charles Wesley's hymn 'Let Earth and Heaven Combine'.
3. From Isaac Watts's hymn 'We Give Immortal Praise'.

the holy Trinity, the Logos, the Lord of glory (John 1:1–18; 17:5; Gal. 4:4; Phil. 2:6–7; Heb. 1:1–3; 2:10, 14; 1 John 1:1–2).

Calvin's extra

When the Son became incarnate in Jesus of Nazareth, there was no change in God's being. There was no alteration of his essence, no reduction in what God has always been and will be. The person who was seen in the flesh remained the one who is with God and is God. There was therefore no diminution in his being as God so that the person of the Godhead who became human did not cease to be what he was. The Logos did not become something or somebody else at the incarnation.

This assertion that the divine Logos underwent no change when the Word became flesh is often referred to as the *extra Calvinisticum*. It was fundamental to Calvin's view of God that the Son of God who was born of a virgin and hung upon a cross 'continuously filled the world even as he had done from the beginning'.[4] In this Calvin was following the position of one of the early church leaders, Cyril of Alexandria (d. AD 444), who wrote concerning Christ what could be termed the *extra Cyrillianum*: 'While visible as a babe in swaddling clothes, and yet in the bosom of the Virgin who bare Him, He was filling all creation as God.'[5] Joseph Hart, the hymn writer, placed the same truth into verse:

> No less almighty at his birth,
> Than on his throne supreme;
> His shoulders held up heaven and earth,
> When Mary held up him.[6]

But though the Son did not become something or someone else, he did become what he had never been before. In this sense

---

4. John Calvin, *Institutes of the Christian Religion*, trans. Ford Lewis Battles (Philadelphia: Westminster, 1960), 2.13.4.

5. Cyril's works as quoted by T. H. Bindley (ed.), *The Oecumenical Documents of the Faith* (London: Methuen, 1925), p. 214.

6. From his hymn 'The Lord That Made Both Heaven and Earth'.

only was there change, for he became the man Christ Jesus. While he was always God he was not always flesh. He 'assumed' human nature, taking up humanity into union with himself at the incarnation. The immutable God is immutably free and able to become what he wills to become in order to fulfil his redemptive purposes, and we can say, as Donald Macleod helpfully suggests, that 'only God could have undergone becoming on the scale implied in the incarnation. God was the only being who could have become man.'[7]

'Behold the man!'

Pannenberg remarks that for us today, in comparison with Gnostic and early heresies, 'it no longer seems particularly remarkable that Jesus was a real man'.[8] This may be true among those who embrace liberal theology, who have difficulties with Christ's deity. For those, however, who confess the orthodox position the danger exists of so emphasizing Christ's divine nature that his human nature is undervalued and misunderstood. This danger is not confined to traditional Roman Catholicism where Mary is often considered to be more approachable than Jesus. Some evangelicals too can have a less than biblical view of the humanity of our Lord.

Flesh

The New Testament is adamant that God's unique Son was a real flesh-and-blood person, living in this present age under the curse, subject to the experiences of life in a fallen world. 'Flesh' in such passages as 'manifested in the flesh' and 'became flesh' (1 Tim. 3:16; John 1:14) denotes human nature in its entirety – body, mind and spirit. Besides all the bodily parts and functions, human nature possesses a psyche that includes temperament, will, emotions and spirituality. The apostle John, the one who emphasizes Jesus' divine nature, far from presenting a Docetic Christ, makes a point of stressing his full humanity. He did not 'appear' to be human; he *was* human. God's self-expression, the Logos, became 'flesh' and

---

7. Donald Macleod, *The Person of Christ* (Leicester: IVP, 1998), p. 186.
8. Wolfhart Pannenberg, *Jesus – God and Man* (London: SCM, 1968), p. 189.

lived among us (John 1:14).[9] Though he was *vere Deus*, 'very God',
he was also *vere homo*, 'very man'.

Unsullied humanity

When Paul wrote that God sent his own Son 'in the likeness
(*homoioma*) of sinful flesh' (Rom. 8:3) he was not presenting a
Docetic view, where the Son only appeared to be human but was
not really, nor was he suggesting that Jesus was so much like
humans that he was sinful as the rest of humanity. The word 'likeness' is 'meant to indicate that Jesus' humanity was indeed the
genuine article'.[10] Similarly, when Paul writes to the Philippians, he
refers to our Lord 'being in the likeness (*homoioma*) of men' (Phil.
2:7). He is a true human experiencing the same conditions of
human life as the rest of us. As our older brother he was 'flesh and
blood', 'made like his brothers in every respect' (Heb. 2:14, 17).

The same truth is taught in the phrase 'being found in human
form' (Phil. 2:8a). Again, Paul is not presenting a Docetic view of
Jesus. What the phrase expresses is that when people saw him,
there was nothing out of the ordinary about him. When fellow
humans saw him, brushed past him in the street or confronted
him, he looked like any other human being. He was no superman.
There were no physical distinguishing marks of divinity. His
appearance would not have merited a second glance. 'He had no
form or majesty that we should look at him' (Isa. 53:2b).

What Paul is seeking to preserve by the addition of the word
'likeness' is our Lord's sinlessness. He does not simply say that
God sent his Son 'in sinful flesh' for that would undermine what
he has taught in Romans 5:12–21. The Son is not guilty of sin and
does not come under the condemnation that all 'in Adam' deserve,
a point I shall return to later. The sinlessness of Christ is an
amazing exception in the light of the universal sinfulness of

---

9. Käsemann is one of a number who have claimed that John's Gospel is
   Docetic; see D. A. Carson, *The Gospel According to John* (Leicester: IVP;
   Grand Rapids: Eerdmans, 1991), p. 127.
10. N. T. Wright, 'Romans', in Leander E. Keck (ed.), *The New Interpreter's
   Bible*, vol. 10 (Nashville: Abingdon, 2002), p. 579.

humanity. In him there was no falsehood (John 7:18). He 'knew no sin' and though he was 'in every respect' tempted as we are, he was 'without sin', being 'holy, innocent, unstained, separated from sinners' (2 Cor. 5:21; Heb. 4:15; 7:26). He 'committed no sin', was not deceitful (1 Pet. 2:22) and was able to confront his enemies directly with the question 'Which one of you convicts me of sin?' (John 8:46). Sin is not part and parcel of what it is to be human. Our first parents were truly human before they sinned. Sin spoiled their humanity. In Jesus Christ we have unspoiled humanity.

One person, two natures

Confessing that the Christ is truly God and truly man is one thing; understanding how the divine and human natures can exist in the one person is quite another. The question that concerns us is how it is possible for the Christ of God to have a genuine experience of human life on earth as a real man and still be the divine Logos? How can this divine person have a developing inner psychological life as a human without the divine influencing it in some way?

Various approaches have been suggested to take account of these concerns, but they run into error by either neglecting Christ's true humanity or undermining his deity. Chalcedon rejected Arianism (the denial of Christ's deity), Apollinarianism (the denial of Christ's full humanity), Nestorianism (the denial of the unity of Christ's person) and Eutychianism (the denial of Christ's two distinct natures) and encouraged the church to hold in tension the biblical evidence concerning the two natures of Christ in the unity of his person. However, this has not stopped theologians from seeking to break that tension in their endeavour to understand the profundity of the subject.

The communication of attributes

In the early period following Chalcedon discussions continued as to how the two natures of our Lord could be united in the one person without damaging the distinctiveness of each. How could people touch the body of Jesus and be healed unless his flesh was in some way divinized, and how could he at other times show weakness of body? The solution to this dilemma proposed by some theologians (e.g. the Cappadocian Fathers) was to suggest a 'transfer of properties' or 'communication of attributes' (*communi-catio idiomatum*). On this view Jesus borrowed divine attributes as and when he needed them. Such a mutual interpenetration (*perichoresis*) of the natures in Christ seemed necessary in order to maintain the unity of Christ's person, without conveying the erroneous idea of Eutychianism that the two natures were blended to form a third. The difficulty with this Alexandrian and Cappadocian Christology was that the divine nature tended to dominate the human. It gave rise to the absurd notion that Jesus only pretended to be ignorant of the future in order to convince his disciples that he really was human and that he did not really need to pray but did so to set a good example to his followers.[11] This Docetic type of teaching would make our Lord's life on earth a sham and charade.

In the Reformation period Luther revived the *communicatio idiomatum* teaching, believing in the idea of the real mutual inter-penetration of the two natures (*perichoresis*), all in the interests of his doctrine of the Lord's Supper. He maintained that the Lord's glorified human body in heaven so participated in the attributes of his divinity that it could be present wherever the Lord's Supper was celebrated on earth. This led later to further controversies within Lutheranism.

A modern example of this same tendency is found in Grudem's *Systematic Theology*. He suggests that some qualities or abilities 'were given (or "communicated") from one nature to the other'. Jesus' 'worthiness to be worshiped' and his inability to sin, he believes, are illustrations of a communication of qualities from Christ's divine to his human nature, while Jesus' experience of suffering and death and his ability to understand our experiences and to be our substitute sacrifice is an instance of a communication of qual-ities from Christ's human to his divine nature.[12]

---

11. See G. L. Bray, *Creeds, Councils and Christ* (Leicester: IVP, 1984), p. 152; G. L. Bray, 'Christology', in S. Ferguson and D. Wright (eds.), *New Dictionary of Theology* (Leicester: IVP, 1988), p. 139.

12. Wayne Grudem, *Systematic Theology* (Leicester: IVP; Grand Rapids: Zondervan, 1994), p. 563.

The Reformed view has been succinctly presented by John Murray. He stresses that the two natures find their union in the one divine person so that what is true of the divine nature and the human nature is true of the person without there being any transfer of properties from one nature to the other. Instead of speaking of *communicatio idiomatum* (communicating of properties/attributes) with its attendant dangers and misapplications, Murray expresses what is involved as *communio idiomatum* (mutual participation of properties/attributes), meaning that the interchange of attributes takes place at the level of the person and not between the two natures of Christ. We are not to think of a transfer of attributes from the divine to the human nature of Christ or vice versa, but of the mutual participation of attributes in Christ's person.[13] What is true of the Christ either as human or divine is true of him as a person. It is this person, the divine Logos, who slept, wept, suffered and died, whether one speaks of him as Jesus of Nazareth or the Lord of glory. It is this person, the divine Logos, who spoke of his pre-existent glory and forgave sins, whether one speaks of him as the unique Son of the Father or as the man, Christ Jesus. This means that when we consider Christ's human inner life, we are considering the one who is the God-man. In all his experiences as a man they are at one and the same time the experiences of God in Christ.[14]

The communication of graces

It has been traditionally understood that the union of the two natures in the person of the Son also meant that there was a 'communication of graces' (*communicatio gratiarum*), sometimes called a 'communication of gifts' (*communicatio charismatum*), from

---

13. *Collected Writings of John Murray*. Vol. 2: *Systematic Theology* (Edinburgh: Banner of Truth, 1977), pp. 140–141.

14. This is referred to as *communicatio apotelesmaton* or the communication of Christ's mediatorial accomplishments. See H. Bavinck, *Reformed Dogmatics*. Vol. 3: *Sin and Salvation in Christ* (Grand Rapids: Baker Academic, 2006), pp. 308ff.; Macleod, *Person of Christ*, pp. 194–195; P. Helm, *John Calvin's Ideas* (Oxford: Oxford University Press, 2004), pp. 58–92.

the divine to the human nature of Christ so that the humanity of
Jesus was raised above all other human beings. This position,
however, is also in danger of merging the natures, and a much
more satisfying and biblical approach is that set out by John
Owen. He argues that the graces and gifts undoubtedly seen in
our Lord during his earthly ministry were communicated to him
by the Holy Spirit. Jesus was not only conceived by the Holy Spirit
but given the Spirit without measure to produce the graces of
faith, hope and love (John 3:35) and the baptism of the Spirit to
accomplish his public ministry (Mark 1:10–12; Luke 3:22; 4:1, 14,
18–21). This indwelling and anointing of the Holy Spirit explains
Christ's supernatural abilities as well as his moral and spiritual
pre-eminence.[15]

One will or two?

Another controversy arose in the period immediately following
Chalcedon over the issue of whether Christ had two wills, one
divine and one human, or whether in the unity of his person he
had only one. It is conceivable that many evangelicals today who
pride themselves on their orthodoxy and agree with Chalcedon
that our Lord has two natures, hold to the view that he has one
will, opting either toward an Apollinarian position where our
Lord's will is a divine will or, more likely, a Eutychian view, with a
merging of the divine and human wills into one. Over against the
various brands of Monothelites (the one willers) it was agreed at
the Council of Constantinople (AD 680) that Christ had two wills
(dyothelitism). This was in accord with the Chalcedon Definition,
and of course the New Testament witnesses to Christ's human as
distinct from his divine will when, for instance, in the Garden of
Gethsemane Jesus prayed, 'not as I will, but as you will' (Matt.
26:39; see also John 5:30).

Kenotic conclusions

The conundrum of how the divine Logos could experience a real

---

15. *The Works of John Owen*, ed. William H. Goold (London: Banner of Truth,
     repr. 1965 [1850–53]), vol. 1, p. 93; vol. 3, pp. 168–188.

human life has led some scholars from the tendency to minimize Christ's humanity to the opposite conclusion that the Son of God laid aside his divine attributes of omnipotence, omniscience and omnipresence.[16] Scriptural evidence for such notions comes principally from the hymnic passage in Philippians 2:6–7, which states that Christ 'emptied himself'. Various kenotic[17] theories have been advanced, and they all assume that Christ could not be fully God and fully man at the same time, that he divested himself, at least for a time, of his distinctively divine attributes. If this were the meaning of Christ's self-emptying, it would imply a change in the being of God. It would mean that this person who is God the Son ceased to be fully God when he became a human. It would also seem to leave no room, as D. M. Baillie writes, for the traditional teaching concerning 'the permanence of the manhood of Christ'.[18] On this understanding, Christ leaves his deity aside while on earth and assumes it again when he has finished his earthly mission. But that is not the biblical position. He remains the God-man to all eternity. The mediator we have at God's right hand is still the man Christ Jesus (1 Tim. 2:5).

Furthermore, as various commentators have pointed out, the words of the hymn do not demand some genitive of content, suggesting that Christ emptied himself of 'the form of God'. He did not empty himself of anything, but simply emptied himself. The expression, in fact, is defined more precisely by the phrases that follow – 'taking the form of a slave', 'being in the likeness of men' and 'being found in human form'. This kenosis is not by subtraction but addition. The paradox in Christ's selflessness is accomplished by 'taking', by becoming what he was not before. F. F. Bruce writes, 'The implication is not that Christ, by becoming incarnate, exchanged the form of God for the form of a slave, but

---

16. For the kenotic theory, see Macleod, *Person of Christ*, pp. 205–212. For a recent attempt to revive the theory, see C. S. Evans (ed.), *Exploring Kenotic Christology: The Self-Emptying of God* (Oxford: Oxford University Press, 2006).

17. From *kenōsis* (emptying). The verb used in Phil. 2:7 is *kenoun*.

18. D. M. Baillie, *God was in Christ* (London: Faber & Faber, 1948), p. 96.

that he manifested the form of God in the form of a slave.'[19] The kenotic theories 'do not do justice to the biblical and historic doctrine as defined at Chalcedon'.[20]

The personality of Christ's human nature

Chalcedon has been criticized for encouraging the view that Christ's human nature is impersonal. It was agreed at Chalcedon that Christ had two distinct natures, human and divine, but only one person or hypostasis, and that that one person is the divine Logos. This would seem to imply that our Lord's humanity is impersonal (anhypostatic). If that is so, is there any reality to Christ's human nature? Moberley bluntly states that 'Human nature which is not personal is not human nature.'[21] John Murray also raises the question as to whether the *anhypostasia* does justice to the New Testament's emphasis on the manhood of Christ.[22]

Tony Lane has helpfully shown that this criticism is the result of a misunderstanding over the meaning of 'person' and illustrates the need to translate Chalcedon into contemporary terms.[23] In modern parlance 'person' is concerned with those personable elements associated with our psychological make-up. This was not how the early Fathers of the church used the word. 'Person' was essentially a metaphysical term associated with the very essence of existence. It was particularly used to counteract adoptionist

19. F. F. Bruce, 'Paul in Macedonia. 3. The Philippian Correspondence', *Bulletin of John Rylands Library* 63 (1980–81), p. 270, quoted in Peter T. O'Brien, *Commentary on Philippians*, New International Greek Testament Commentary (Grand Rapids: Eerdmans, 1991), p. 218.

20. Alan M. Stibbs, *God Became Man* (London: Tyndale, 1957), pp. 9–10.

21. R. C. Moberley, *Atonement and Personality* (London: John Murray, 1901), p. 93, cited in Baillie, *God was in Christ*, p. 86.

22. Murray, *Collected Writings*, vol. 2, p. 137.

23. A. N. S. Lane, 'Christology Beyond Chalcedon', in H. H. Rowdon (ed.), *Christ the Lord: Studies in Christology Presented to Donald Guthrie* (Leicester: IVP, 1982), pp. 272–273.

tendencies that suggested Jesus was merely a human being who was indwelt by God. On the other hand, the supporters of Chalcedon who spoke in terms of impersonal human nature (*anhypostasis*) had no intention of introducing another form of Docetism by denying the full humanity of Christ, including the development of his inner psychological life. Christ had a full human existence in his human nature, as I shall demonstrate, but when it is asked who the subject is of these human experiences and developments, the answer is the divine Logos. Christ did and does not have an independent human existence separate from the divine being he is. In this sense Christ's human nature is impersonal. At the incarnation, the second person of the Godhead was not joined to an already existing human being. Christ's human nature belongs to the person he is, the divine Logos. This, however, does not in any way make him less human. He took human nature into personal union with himself.

Enhypostasia

Even before the rise of modern psychology and the confusion over 'person' and 'personality', as Macleod observes, 'there were suspicions that anhypostasia was not the best term to apply to the humanity of Christ'.[24] To indicate that Christ's human nature must not be thought of as impersonal the term *enhypostasia* (in-personal) was introduced at an early date.[25] It made it clear that there was never a time when Christ's human nature existed as non-personal. It was always personal in the person of the Son of God. 'The human nature has its personal existence in the person of the Logos. It is in-personal rather than impersonal.'[26]

The human nature of Christ, therefore, is complete, deficient in nothing common to all humans, displaying all the personable aspects of human nature. It does not lack individuality, having a

---

24. Macleod, *Person of Christ*, p. 201.

25. It was used by Leontius of Byzantium (c. 485 to c. 543) and then by John of Damascus (c. 675 to c. 749) to emphasize that the humanity of Christ derived its personality from the person of the Son.

26. L. Berkhof, *Systematic Theology* (London: Banner of Truth, 1958), p. 322.

mind and will of its own. However, with regard to existence, the human nature of Christ has no existence of its own. When the Scriptures seek to define who this man Jesus is, they point to a divine person. It is the divine person that gives Christ's human nature the existence it has.

Two consciousnesses, one self-consciousness

In insisting that Christ's human nature belongs to him who is the second person of the holy Trinity it must not be thought that our Lord's human consciousness is lost in the divine. He has two centres of consciousness, a human and a divine. As man he possessed a finite mode of consciousness so that his knowledge, power and other divine perfections were limited; nevertheless, at the same time, he retained as God an infinite mode of consciousness, so that he knew all things and was all powerful. On the other hand, as John Murray helpfully argues, there are not two centres of self-consciousness. He is not God and man in the sense that he has two selves, human and divine. That would suggest two beings or persons. On the contrary, Jesus has one self. He is the God-man. That self-identity and self-consciousness 'can never be thought of in terms of human nature alone'. When he became incarnate, 'there was no suspension of his divine self-identity'. His self must always be defined in terms that include the fact that he is God's unique Son.[27]

How his finite human consciousness could coexist with the divine consciousness in the single self of the God-man is impossible for us to grasp. Nevertheless, it is an essential element of revealed truth concerning the incarnation that faith is called to confess. The most impressive human analogy that has been proposed to help us appreciate how the two modes of consciousness could remain distinct in the one person is taken from the amazing world of the human mind. Charles Harris seems to have been the first to suggest the analogy.[28] Buswell later used it in his

---

27. Murray, *Collected Writings*, pp. 136–139.
28. See Stibbs, *God Became Man*, p. 12, who quotes C. Harris, *Pro Fide*, 4th ed. (1930).

systematic theology,[29] and more recently Andrew Hodges has developed it.[30]

Human beings possess minds that are incredibly complex. Hodges informs us that the human mind can process 'incoming information simultaneously on two tracks, conscious and unconscious', with the unconscious, 'subliminal track possessing, for the most part, by far the greater abilities'.[31] It can record in remarkable detail every moment of a person's life, beyond anything that a present-day computer or video camera can do. One psychoanalyst, after viewing a patient's unconscious mind, described it as 'like being in the room with an almost omniscient being'.[32] Hodges suggests that this is a very impressive analogy of how the human and divine natures might operate in Jesus, the incarnate God. Harris had come to a similar conclusion, arguing that 'the finite or human consciousness of the Redeemer was compassed about by an infinite ocean of divine consciousness, belonging to the same personality'.[33] Of course, our Lord's state was infinitely more complex, for he possessed a divine mind that was omniscient and a finite human mind that consisted of the conscious and the subliminal.[34]

The formation of Christ's human nature

To appreciate the development of Christ's human psychological life, we need to ask some specific questions about his human nature. In Hebrews 10:5 the writer introduces a quotation from the Septuagint text of Psalm 40:6–8 and introduces it as coming

---

29. J. O. Buswell, *A Systematic Theology of the Christian Religion* (Grand Rapids: Zondervan, 1962–3), vol. 2, p. 406.

30. Andrew G. Hodges, *Jesus, an Interview Across Time: A Psychiatrist Looks at Christ's Humanity* (London: Monarch, 2004), pp. 17–22.

31. Ibid., p. 19.

32. Ibid.

33. Harris, *Pro Fide*, pp. 590–591.

34. For a different approach, see R. L. Sturch, 'The Metaphysics of the Incarnation', *Vox Evangelica* 10 (1977), pp. 65–76.

from the lips of Christ: 'when Christ came into the world, he said, ". . . a body you have prepared for me"'.[35] In order to redeem his people it was necessary for him to assume a physical body with a human mind, emotions and will, and an immaterial soul or spirit like the rest of humanity.[36] As John of Damascus succinctly put it, 'For the whole Christ assumed the whole me that he might grant salvation to the whole me, for what is unassumable is incurable.'[37]

Origin and composition

From where did this body originate and of what was it composed? Is it a special creation or did God use already existing material? In other words, is Christ's human nature a special creation in the womb of Mary or is his human nature the result of supernatural activity using Mary's ovum? To both questions the answer is in the affirmative. Providing 'a body' for the Son was a creative act but, as in the formation of the original couple, means were used. The formation of Christ's body was, as Owen explains, 'an act of infinite creating power, yet it was formed or made of "the substance" of the blessed Virgin'.[38]

It was not heavenly flesh as the Valentinians of the early period taught and which has been perpetuated in some Anabaptist, Quaker and Brethren circles.[39] Mary is not to be thought of as a

---

35. While the Hebrew has 'ear' instead of the Greek 'body', clearly, as Owen reminds us, we have an example of synecdoche, the use of a part for the whole. The Greek is making clear what lies behind the Hebrew poetic form. See J. Owen, *An Exposition of the Epistle to the Hebrews*, vol. 4 (London: Thomas Tegg, 1840), pp. 242–243.

36. For a helpful treatment of the essential nature of human beings, see Grudem, *Systematic Theology*, pp. 472–489. On Christ's will, see Richard Sturch, *The Word and the Christ* (Oxford: Oxford University Press, 1991), pp. 161–169.

37. Quoted by Bavinck, *Reformed Dogmatics*, vol. 3, p. 297.

38. Owen, *Works of John Owen*, vol. 3, p. 164. In this, Owen was following the teaching of the Westminster Confession of Faith.

39. G. Smeaton, *The Doctrine of the Holy Spirit* (London: Banner of Truth, 1958), p. 123; Bavinck, *Reformed Dogmatics*, vol. 3, p. 295.

mere channel for a specially created heavenly foetus to be brought into the world. 'Christ's human nature was not begotten from the essence of God, but created from the substance of the Virgin.'[40] Without evidence to the contrary, it would not be going too far to say that Jesus would have had features resembling his mother.

While it is necessary to emphasize that the whole Trinity is the author of every work of God and is involved in every work, the Scripture also teaches us that the persons of the Trinity each have their special roles to play. It was the act of the Son to become incarnate to redeem us humans. But it was not the Son's special work to prepare for the incarnation, nor was it the Father's. God acted by the Holy Spirit in the miraculous conception. Mary 'was found to be with child from the Holy Spirit' (Matt. 1:18). The Holy Spirit is the special agent of both Father and Son in preparing and applying God's designs. Thus Christ's human nature was the supernatural activity of the Holy Spirit. God the Father did not father the man Jesus the Messiah, nor did the Holy Spirit. Any suggestion that Christ's conception is due to sexual union between Mary and a member of the Trinity is alien to the text of Scripture. As in the original creation of the first man when God created using the dust of the earth so he created Christ's human nature from earthly female tissue.[41]

Sinless

The virgin conception is a reminder that our salvation is due solely to the action of almighty God. It also emphasizes our Lord's full deity and true humanity in the one person. But it does more. The virgin conception declares a break in the line of descent from Adam. Jesus did not inherit the legal guilt of Adam and is therefore not by nature subject to death (cf. Rom. 5:12–14). But what about Adam's sinful nature and the bodily imperfections that have

---

40. Macleod, *Person of Christ*, p. 42. He also points out that Mary contributed to her son 'what any human mother contributes to her child: ovum, genes, ordinary foetal development and ordinary parturition'.

41. Another parallel between the initial creation and the virginal conception is suggested by the reference to the Spirit (Gen. 1:2; Luke 1:35).

afflicted everyone since the fall? While it is true that the stuff of which our bodies are composed is not evil, there is an inherited corruption that has resulted from Adam's initial sin. Human beings have a sinful nature and all humans have this tendency to sin from birth.

The virgin conception proclaims the moral purity of Jesus both by showing there was no male involved and by emphasizing the Spirit's work. Jesus had no inherited sin through the male line, for he had no human father, but how is it he did not inherit a sinful nature through his mother? David confesses that 'in sin did my mother conceive me' (Ps. 51:5). The Roman Church answers this with their unbiblical doctrine of Mary's immaculate conception, whereas Mary herself indicates her own sinfulness by confessing her need of a Saviour (Luke 1:47).

The Bible's answer to the non-transmission of a sinful nature through Mary to our Saviour is that it was due to the supernatural work of the Spirit. The human nature of Christ was free from original sin or corruption because of the creative work of the Holy Spirit using the ovum of Mary (Luke 1:35). Calvin writes, 'We make Christ free of all stain not just because he was begotten of his mother without copulation with man, but because he was sanctified by the Spirit that the generation might be pure and undefiled as would have been true before Adam's fall.'[42] Similarly, Owen teaches that Christ's human nature 'being thus formed in the womb by a creating act of the Holy Spirit, was in the instant of its conception sanctified'.[43]

---

42. Calvin, *Institutes* 2.13.4.

43. Owen, *Works of John Owen*, vol. 3, p. 168. See also Smeaton, *Doctrine of the Holy Spirit*, p. 125: 'everything required for the sanctification of the Lord's humanity was plentifully supplied by the agency of the Holy Spirit, who warded off every taint from whatever quarter it could possibly approach Him'. William Shedd, misusing biblical texts, goes further. Following the teaching of Augustine and Athanasius, he argues that Christ's human nature needed not only sanctification but justification before the Logos could unite with it. 'Any nature that requires sanctification requires justification; because sin is guilt as well as pollution.' In the formation of a

Pristine condition

Because Christ is without original guilt and sin this does not make him less human. He is as fully human as Adam was before the fall. But does Christ's human nature created by the Spirit from the substance of the virgin mean that his bodily make-up was in a better condition than is true of humans since the fall? There are differing opinions on this point. Herman Bavinck believes that Christ's 'was not the human nature of Adam before the fall; rather, God sent his Son in the likeness of sinful flesh, that is, in flesh that was the same in form and appearance as sinful flesh (Rom. 8:3)'.[44] Warfield, on the other hand, referring to the same verse in Romans, believes that Christ 'assumed the flesh of unfallen man'.[45]

There is some truth in both positions. It would be a fair deduction from Gabriel's words to Mary concerning the activity of the Holy Spirit and also from the use of the word 'holy' to describe the Christ child (Luke 1:35), that his body was more like humanity before the fall than after. In the Mosaic legislation 'holy' means physical wholeness as well as moral purity. The child born to Mary is 'holy' not only in the sense that his human nature is free from moral pollution but that his bodily parts and functions were in a wholesome, pristine condition. Like the Mosaic sacrificial animals, Jesus had no obvious physical defects. The development of the foetus was normal, so that when he was born, he had a healthy body and mind and a balanced temperament. If baby Moses, one of the Old Testament types of Christ, could be described as 'good' or 'beautiful' in appearance (Exod. 2:2; Acts 7:20; Heb. 11:23),[46] how much more the babe in Bethlehem's manger?

---

human nature taken from the Virgin Mary, Christ's future redemptive work was applied by the Holy Spirit to Christ's own humanity. See William T. T. Shedd, *Dogmatic Theology*, vol. 2 (Nashville: Thomas Nelson, 1980), p. 82.

44. Bavinck, *Reformed Dogmatics*, vol. 3, pp. 309–310.

45. See B. B. Warfield, *The Person and Work of Christ* (Philadelphia: Presbyterian & Reformed, 1950), ch. 4, 'The Emotional Life of Our Lord', p. 144, where he states that Christ 'assumed the flesh of unfallen man'.

46. The word 'good' in Exod. 2:2 is the adjective used to describe God's approval of his initial creation; cf. Gen. 1:10, 12, 18, 25, 31.

On the other hand, with the exception of sin, Jesus was made 'like his brothers in every respect' (Heb. 2:17). He experienced life as we know it since the fall. Like us but unlike Adam who was created a fully grown man, Jesus' human existence began as 'the fruit' of his mother's womb (Luke 1:42; cf. Matt. 1:25; Luke 2:7). Again, like us but unlike Adam, who began life on an earth that was pronounced very good, Jesus entered a world full of trouble and under the curse of God. From his very birth he was treated as an intrusion. No sooner was he born than 'the powers that be' conspired to kill him (Matt. 2:13). He was susceptible to attack from all that Satan could throw at him. Unlike us, who fall under the curse of Adam's sin, he was not under that curse by nature; nevertheless, for the sake of others, he became 'a curse for us' (Gal. 3:13). Warfield writes, 'he suffered and died not because of the flesh he took but because of the sins he took'.[47]

Christ's human development

Jesus was no freak. The so-called apocryphal gospels, written well after the New Testament era, are fraudulent accounts of Jesus' life. They fill in the silent years of his childhood with fanciful stories of Jesus using miraculous powers, like some childish magician bent on gratifying his selfish desires. In contrast, the biblical record is sparse, sober but nonetheless significant. It portrays Jesus' growth as it would any normal, healthy child.

The Gospel accounts present the various stages in the early life of Jesus from infancy (Luke 2:16), through childhood (Matt. 2:11, 14, 16, 19–23; Luke 2:39) to a boy about to enter his teenage years (Luke 2:42–43) and then to a fully grown adult of about thirty years of age (Luke 3:23). Our Lord's development matches in many respects the development of his cousin. As John the Baptist 'grew and became strong in spirit' (Luke 1:80), so the child Jesus 'grew and became strong, filled with wisdom. And the favour of God was upon him' (Luke 2:40). Then, as he grew from boyhood

---

47. Warfield, *Person and Work of Christ*, p. 144.

to manhood, he 'increased in wisdom and in stature and in favour with God and man' (Luke 2:52).

Not only so, but Luke's presentation is very reminiscent of the descriptions of the growth of Old Testament figures such as Isaac and Ishmael (Gen. 21:8, 20), Samson (Judg. 13:24), and particularly Samuel, who also grew 'both in stature and in favour with the LORD and also with man' (1 Sam. 2:26). It would, however, be correct to say with Warfield that Jesus' human progress was 'the only strictly normal human development, from birth to manhood, the world has ever seen'. He is the only child who has ever grown up without having his life and lip 'marred at every step by the destructive influences of sin and error'.[48]

We turn now to consider our Lord's mental, moral, emotional and spiritual development.

Christ's mental development

As a newborn baby, Jesus was completely helpless and lacking in knowledge of the very basic kind. Just as he needed to grow in stature, so he grew in knowledge and understanding. His mental kept pace with his bodily development. If Jesus had been given free access to his divine knowledge, he would not have experienced true human development. All he could do at birth was to give expression to those instinctive responses common to all infants, such as crying for food, sucking at his mother's breast and clasping his little hand around his father's finger. Like every human he learnt to eat and drink, to talk and walk, and to read and write – he possessed the normal mental processes for acquiring information. Children develop by asking questions. This we find Jesus doing as a lad in the Jerusalem temple (Luke 2:46–47).

It should not be assumed that our Lord's abilities as a boy of twelve that astonished those who heard him were due to his drawing on his divine nature. Mozart, at the age of six, amazed

---

48. B. B. Warfield, 'The Human Development of Jesus', *Bible Student* NS 6 (January 1900), p. 13.

audiences throughout Europe with his musical skills. Jesus would have had a mind in top condition and uncluttered with sinful thoughts and influences. This does not make him less human. It is we humans under the effects of the fall who are less than perfect when it comes to the use of our minds. For Luke the incident in the temple is a further indication of Jesus' steady but remarkable growth in wisdom. In fact, Luke draws a contrast between the insight of Jesus that amazed the Jewish teachers and the complete lack of understanding by Jesus' parents (Luke 2:47, 50).

Learning

Following Jewish practice (Prov. 1:8; 31:1; 2 Tim. 1:5; 3:15), our Lord would first have been taught at his mother's knee. Both his pious parents would have instructed him in the redemptive history of Israel (see Exod. 12:26–27; 13:8, 14; Deut. 6:4–7, 20–25). Later, the synagogue school at Nazareth would have been a further place of instruction for young Jewish boys. Unlike Saul of Tarsus, however, our Lord never sat at the feet of rabbis like Gamaliel (John 7:15).

His growing in wisdom would have included learning to be of help around the house and in the carpenter's shop. He may well have been a quick learner, but still needed to put his mind to acquiring skills and doing jobs properly. Like Saul of Tarsus (Acts 18:3), Jesus acquired a trade and was known as 'the carpenter, the son of Mary' (Mark 6:3) or 'the carpenter's son' (Matt. 13:55). No doubt Joseph taught Jesus the trade.[49] Unlike the apostle Paul (Acts 20:34; 1 Cor. 4:12; 1 Thess. 2:9) and well-known Jewish rabbis such as Shammai (who was also a carpenter), there is nothing to indicate that Jesus later combined his itinerant ministry with working for a living. The impression is that he gave himself fully to the work of preaching the gospel and healing the sick and that his material needs and those of his twelve disciples were met by some of the women folk of Galilee or his friends at Bethany (see Mark 15:41; Luke 8:3; 10:38; Matt. 21:17).

---

49. The term 'carpenter' (*tektōn*) was applied to those who worked in stone or metal as well as wood. A late second-century tradition suggests that Jesus made ploughs, yokes and other farm equipment.

Ignorance

Jesus' admission during his teaching ministry that he was ignorant of the time of his second coming and of the end of the age only confirms Luke's inference concerning his growth in wisdom. Many early copyists of the text of Matthew 24:36 and Mark 13:32 omit this reference to the ignorance of the Son, assuming that such verses detract from Christ's deity.[50] In his human nature he was not omniscient. Though our Lord still possessed his divine omniscience as God, it was deliberately kept, as Alan Stibbs suggests, 'below the threshold of his human consciousness' in perhaps a way similar to the workings of the human subliminal, unconscious mind, as suggested above.[51] Even now in his glorified human nature, we must conclude that Jesus does not possess infinite knowledge, despite having all authority given to him by the Father.

Liberal scholarship has used the example of Jesus' ignorance to argue that Jesus was a child of his age and that we must reckon with the thought that there were items he believed and taught that are now known to be incorrect.[52] His view of the Old Testament, for instance, we are led to understand, was according

---

50. Though it may be thought that the absolute use of 'Son' in both passages followed by 'Father' suggests Christ's eternal sonship as the unique 'Son of God' (see Matt. 11:27, where it certainly means that), the linking of 'the Son of Man' and 'his angels' in Matthew 24:30–31 suggests, as John Nolland indicates in his commentary on Matthew (Grand Rapids: Eerdmans; Milton Keynes: Paternoster, 2005), p. 991, that 'the Son' here 'is likely to be the Son of Man rather than the normally assumed Son of God'. This is confirmed by a similar combination of Father, Son and angels in Matt. 16:27, where the reference is clearly to 'Son of Man'. Furthermore, in Mark 13:26 prior to the mention of the Son's ignorance, Jesus refers to himself as the 'Son of Man'.

51. Stibbs, *God Became Man*, p. 13.

52. John Owen, in answering those who objected to the thought of ascribing ignorance to the human soul of Christ, distinguishes between *ignorance* and *nescience*. If ignorance is taken to mean a moral defect, then clearly that cannot be applied to Christ. But if it means no more than nescience, then

to the thinking of the day and cannot be taken as infallible. However, because he was the Son of God it could be argued with Stibbs that his finite human consciousness was completely guided by his divine consciousness so that in all that he taught as a human he did not lead people astray but spoke only what was true.[53]

Macleod is of the opinion that our Lord's infallibility as a human is not to be thought of as the direct action of his divine nature on his human nature. The real reason for our Saviour's infallibility as a man is that he was a prophet, indeed, the great prophet promised by Moses, and as such was 'especially endowed with the Holy Spirit'. He adds the rider that, unlike other prophets, Jesus also had a relationship with the Father and Spirit that was unique.[54] This solution avoids the difficulties surrounding the communication of attributes.[55]

During his public ministry the same quick-witted ability to answer his critics and call to mind the right biblical text for the occasion that was noted when he was twelve continued to amaze both friend and foe alike (Matt. 7:28–29; John 7:15). The hard graft of learning the text came before using the text appropriately. He learnt the Jewish Scriptures in such a way that he was able to call to mind different parts of the canon when need arose. Three times he quoted the Torah during his temptations in the wilderness, and in reply to those who criticized his actions on the Sabbath he referred them to the former prophets and used the Psalms to counteract those who sought 'to trap him in his talk'. So well did he know the Scriptures that even when he was experiencing great physical, mental and spiritual torment he was able to quote the opening words of Psalm 22 and committed himself to the Father in the words of Psalm 31:5. In his resurrection state he continued

---

Footnote 52 (cont.)

    Owen states, 'there is no more in it but a denial of infinite omniscience'.

    See Owen, *Works of John Owen*, vol. 3, p. 170.

53. See Stibbs, *God Became Man*, p. 13.

54. Macleod, *Person of Christ*, p. 170.

55. See above on 'the communication of graces'.

to instruct his disciples from all parts of the Jewish Scriptures the things concerning himself (Luke 24:27).

Supernatural knowledge

But what are we to make of those passages where he astounded people with knowledge that did not come through normal human channels? John recounts numerous incidents where Jesus' knowledge can only be described as miraculous. Nathaniel and the woman of Samaria were taken aback by his intimate knowledge of them (John 1:47–49; 4:16–19, 29). John also records that 'Jesus knew from the beginning who those were who did not believe, and who it was who would betray him' (John 6:64). This same uncanny knowledge appears in the Synoptic Gospels when Jesus told his disciples what to expect when they were sent to prepare a room for celebrating the Passover (Mark 14:13; Luke 22:7–13), or when he informed Peter where to find the shekel to pay the temple tax (Matt. 17:27).

Do these examples give evidence of Jesus drawing directly on his own divine knowledge as Son of God? Perhaps, but not necessarily. We should consider the possibility that supernatural knowledge was revealed to him by his Father, as some of the Old Testament prophets experienced. This is how the prophet Elisha was able to inform the king of Israel what the Syrian king was planning in the privacy of his own bedroom (2 Kgs 6:12). Another possibility is that supernatural knowledge was conveyed to him by the Holy Spirit from his own divine nature as the Son of God. What must always be borne in mind is that although the humanity of Jesus could receive supernatural knowledge, in no way could his human finite mind contain infinite knowledge.

Christ's moral development

Like us but unlike Adam, who was created as an adult with the ability to receive and appreciate a divine command and either to act upon it or to ignore and disobey it, our Lord came into this world in no position to make moral choices. The infant Immanuel was unable at first 'to refuse the evil and choose the good' (Isa. 7:15; Matt. 1:22–23). This expression of Isaiah is best treated as a reference to moral discrimination. The son born of a virgin was to be no superbaby but a normal child needing time to develop an appreciation of right and wrong.

The summary statements of Luke indicate that there was perfect moral as well as physical growth from infant to boy and from boy to adult so that at every stage of his early life the divine favour rested upon him (Luke 2:40, 52). Before people began to take exception to his ministry, his life was also pleasing to all the people who knew him. Luke's references to his wisdom remind us of the Old Testament sapiential literature with its emphasis on fearing God and turning away from evil.

The age of accountability within Judaism has been variously calculated, with the earliest often set at twelve. Some rabbis considered this to be the time when vows became binding and when parents could punish their offspring more severely.[56] It is therefore significant that Luke presents a glimpse of Jesus at this particular age. The account brings to our attention the tension that often exists between parents and children. Jesus' response to his mother's natural anxieties conveys genuine surprise and implies that he was upset that they were in such distress. In as respectful a way as possible his reply also carries the mildest of rebukes that a boy of his age could deliver to parents who were feeling that he had been disloyal toward them. Mary received a further firm rebuke from her son that was neither rude nor discourteous at the time when Jesus began his public ministry and performed his first miracle (John 2:4). It must have been as difficult for Jesus to have distanced himself from his mother in this way as it was for Mary to accept her son's rebuke. However, at the point where Jesus began to make that transition into adult life, both boy and parents were brought to acknowledge a distinction between Jesus' commitment to his heavenly Father and his obligations toward his earthly parents.

---

56. John Nolland, *Luke 1–9:20*, Word Biblical Commentary (Dallas: Word, 1989), p. 129.

Whatever his parents may have thought about the incident in Jerusalem, his subsequent impeccable behaviour assured Mary and Joseph that on that occasion his conduct did not flow from any insubordinate attitude. Luke encourages us to believe that he continued to obey them during his adolescent years, the period that parents and children often find so difficult to manage (Luke 2:51).

Jesus began his ministry when he was about thirty, the age when a number of Old Testament figures gained office (Gen. 41:46; Num. 4:3; 2 Sam. 5:4). The first words of Jesus that Matthew records were in response to his cousin John's reluctance to baptize him: 'thus it is fitting for us to fulfill all righteousness' (Matt. 3:15). They indicate Jesus' commitment to do all that God required of him. Jesus humbled himself by identifying himself with his sinful people right from the beginning of his public ministry.

Temptation

The temptations of Jesus in the wilderness (Matt. 4:1–11; Luke 4:1–13) provide another glimpse into his inner life. If Jesus had allowed his divine omniscience to dominate, then the temptations would not have been real. Furthermore, as to his human nature, Jesus, as discussed above, possessed the same moral standing Adam enjoyed before he sinned. Like Adam he had a choice to make, either to believe the devil or to trust God, which would suggest that theoretically Christ's pre-fallen human nature had the ability to sin and the ability not to sin. This is the position of R. C. Sproul, who writes, 'We must insist that the human nature of Christ had the ability to sin just as Adam did . . . The temptation of Christ was not an empty charade.'[57] He follows Charles Hodge, who argues that though our Lord was sinless this 'does not amount to absolute impeccability. It was not a *non potest peccare*. If He was a true man He must have been capable of sinning.'[58] On the other hand, we must also hold to the fact that his human nature was not independent of the person he was, the holy Son of God who cannot be tempted and cannot sin.

---

57. R. C. Sproul, *The Glory of Christ* (Wheaton: Tyndale House, 1990), p. 71.
58. C. Hodge, *Systematic Theology*, vol. 2 (London: James Clarke, 1960), p. 457.

Thus, just as in his divine nature he could not suffer hunger or thirst but in his human nature was both hungry and thirsty, so also in his divine nature the Son of God could not be tempted and could not sin; nevertheless, as the man, Christ Jesus, 'he was vulnerable to temptation on every side',[59] and had real choices to make. His temptations came through the old serpent, the devil, and he felt the full force of each temptation. But whereas our first parents succumbed even though they were in a place of life and plenty, Jesus stood firm in a desert place and when he was in great physical need. As he faced the tempter both in the wilderness and later, we do not read of his deriving comfort from his own sinlessness and his divine inability to sin. In his human nature there is no hint that Jesus knew the outcome of the devil's attacks. He was dependent on the same spiritual weapons available to all his followers, namely, the Scriptures (Matt. 4:4, 7, 10), fellowship (Mark 14:33) and prayer (Mark 14:35).

When the writer to the Hebrews informs us that 'he learned obedience through what he suffered' (Heb. 5:8), this does not mean that Jesus did wrong, suffered the consequences and learnt the hard way to do what was right. Rather, in all his temptations and the suffering that these testing experiences entailed, Jesus learnt to say 'no' to the devil and 'yes' to God. Even when his enemies taunted him to come down from the cross if he were the Son of God, he continued to stand firm. 'It is part of the evidence of man's maturity that He would have faced and fought temptation: that he should have learned to deal with the subtleties and stratagems of the devil.'[60]

He learnt to obey his Father and to resist the devil without knowing all the facts and to trust without his infinite divine knowledge. He freely and willingly chose to forgo his omniscience. 'Christ had to submit to knowing dependently and to knowing partially.'[61] In the same way he did not fall back on his divine omnipotence.

---

59. Bavinck, *Reformed Dogmatics*, vol. 3, p. 309.

60. H. D. McDonald, *Jesus – Human and Divine* (London: Pickering & Inglis, 1968), p. 30.

61. Macleod, *Person of Christ*, p. 169.

Christ's emotional development

Our Lord's human emotions would have consisted of instinctive sensitivities as well as feelings and reactions that arose from the ever-increasing awareness of other people and situations, his moral and spiritual growth and his sense of mission. Psychologists consider three aspects to emotion. There is, first, the behavioural, where the emotion is expressed very clearly in some action or other. The little child expresses her joy by skipping and dancing. Then, second, there is the physiological, where the emotion is displayed more discreetly or may not be detected through normal observation. The most obvious examples include heart-rate increase, breathing irregularities, blushing or blanching and muscle tension. The third is the psychological, which refers to the state of mind of the person. This cannot be directly sensed by others, who must rely on the person to report on how he or she feels. We detect within the New Testament all three elements within our Lord's emotional life.

Benjamin Warfield, who was at Princeton Theological Seminary from 1887 to 1921, has a fine essay on our Lord's emotional life.[62] Before examining the various texts of Scripture that bear upon the subject, he highlights two opposite tendencies that revealed themselves in the early church period, but which subsequent generations have also been tempted to adopt. The one tendency, derived originally from the Stoic ideal of a passionless humanity, has served to minimize Jesus' emotional life in the interests of his perfect manhood, while the other, in the interests of presenting a Redeemer who can sympathize with and deliver from every human weakness, has been inclined to magnify his emotional life to the point where his sinlessness might be called into question. We must guard as much against a cold and remote Jesus as against a Jesus who is unworthy of the highest reverence. On the other hand, Warfield does not want to be left with some vague figure but to present as full an appreciation of his emotional life as

---

62. 'The Emotional Life of Our Lord', in Warfield, *Person and Work of Christ*, pp. 93–145.

the evidence allows. Reviewing the various emotions displayed by Jesus in the Gospel records provides for him the starting point for a study of this aspect of our Lord's humanity. His conclusions reveal not only the strength and reality of our Lord's emotional reactions but their purity and perfection and how fitting Jesus is to be our High Priest and Saviour.

Calvin comments, 'Those who pretend the Son of God was immune from human passions do not truly and seriously acknowledge Him as a man', and the Gospel accounts present us with much evidence that he experienced a wide variety of emotions. However, Calvin makes it clear that whereas none of our feelings is free of sin, the emotions Christ displayed were unsullied.[63] While sinful human beings have difficulty controlling their emotions, Jesus did not allow his feelings to rule him or to exceed their proper limits. His emotions were under the control of a will that was one with the divine will.[64]

C. F. Alexander's lines 'He was little, weak, and helpless; / Tears and smiles like us He knew'[65] are nearer the biblical picture of Jesus as a baby than the sentimental verse often attributed wrongly to Luther, which suggests that the little Lord Jesus 'no crying He makes'.[66] Loud lowing of the cattle would have startled him as it would have startled any baby, and he would have cried instinctively as he would have cried for his mother's milk. He was a real human baby and expressed the feelings typical of an infant. But he was a perfect baby and that meant he never got out of control.

Troubled and sorrowful

As the prophecies of the Suffering Servant suggest, Jesus was 'a man of sorrows and acquainted with grief' (Isa. 53:3). The books

---

63. John Calvin, *A Harmony of the Gospels Matthew, Mark and Luke*, trans. T. H. L. Parker, ed. D. W. Torrance and T. F. Torrance, vol. 3 (Edinburgh: St Andrew Press, 1972), pp. 147–148.

64. See T. B. Kilpatrick, 'Character of Christ', in J. Hastings (ed.), *Dictionary of Christ and the Gospels*, vol. 1 (Edinburgh: T. & T. Clark, 1906), p. 295a.

65. From the carol 'Once in Royal David's City'.

66. From the carol 'Away in a Manger'.

of Psalms and Lamentations also impress upon us the overwhelming trouble and suffering experienced by the One whom the Old Testament individuals typified. During his earthly ministry, we hear of him weeping over his friend's death (John 11:35), wailing over Jerusalem (Luke 19:41), grieving at the Pharisees' hardness of heart (Mark 3:5), groaning deeply with dismay as he responded to their demands (Mark 8:12), sighing as he healed the deaf and dumb man (Mark 7:34), being profoundly disturbed over the death of Lazarus and its effects (John 11:33), intensely troubled with revulsion as he contemplated the cross and his betrayer (John 12:27; 13:21), being astonished, distressed and very sad as he prepared to pray in the Garden of Gethsemane (Mark 14:33–34; Matt. 26:37–38), sweating profusely through the agonizing ordeal of his prayer (Luke 22:44), loudly voicing his desolate state after three hours of hell on the cross (Mark 15:34), and then, before handing over his spirit to the Father, loudly giving vent to a new mood of satisfaction and triumph that impressed the centurion who stood facing him (Mark 15:37, 39; Luke 23:46–47; see also John 19:30).

Zealous

From the time he first became aware of it through his own meditation on the Scriptures and the Spirit's illumination, the prospect of his sufferings on the cross dominated his thinking. He spoke of his death as a baptism and that he was totally consumed by it until it was finally accomplished (Luke 12:50). This consuming passion that the disciples saw displayed when Jesus cleansed the temple reminded them of Psalm 69:9: 'Zeal for your house will consume me' (John 2:17). Carson comments, 'If his disciples remembered these words at the time, they probably focused on the zeal, not the manner of the "consumption". Only later would they detect in these words a reference to his death (cf. 2:22).'[67]

The one great desire of Jesus was to do the will of his heavenly Father (Ps. 40:8; Heb. 10:7–9). In part fulfilment of that wish he 'earnestly desired' to share the Passover meal with his disciples (Luke 22:15) and used the occasion to point to the significance of his own

---

67. Carson, *John*, p. 180.

atoning death and the inauguration of a new era. This burning desire
and zeal could be said to be his one great obsession. An obsession is
considered to be a fault, for it so controls the mind that it prevents
the person from engaging in the normal activities of life. Yet, despite
the deprivations involved, our Lord was no psychopath but one who
mixed freely and easily with people and enjoyed the company of
friends. 'Single-mindedness' rather than 'obsession' would be a better
term to describe our Lord's commitment.

Fearful

While he set his face like flint to accomplish God's will, he shrank
from his awesome destiny and was greatly agitated and disturbed
by it. He feared and trembled at the thought of tasting the bitter
cup of God's wrath. John does not record the agony of Jesus in
Gethsemane but does reveal that it was a growing concern prior to
that dreadful experience (John 12:27). With turmoil of soul he
questioned in his mind whether he should pray the Father to save
him from that hour. But then he considered his commitment to
doing God's will: 'for this purpose I have come to this hour', and
so he did not pray against God's will.

Anger and outrage

It is possible for humans to be angry and not sin (Eph. 4:26).
Often what we call 'anger' is merely bad temper, an irrational outburst that erupts from an irritable spirit.[68] The emotions of anger
and displeasure arose out of Jesus' moral consciousness. Strong
language is used at times to express his outrage both at the sinful
attitudes of those who should have known better and at the
misery of human suffering and its deep causes. This is probably
the reason for the strong emotion that gripped Jesus in connection
with the death of Lazarus. Jesus' reaction to the wailing of Mary
and the people who accompanied her is somewhat muted in the
English versions (John 11:33). The same Greek word for 'deeply
moved' (*embrimaomai*) is found a few verses later to describe the

---

68. See Robert Law, *The Emotions of Jesus* (Tipperary: Tentmaker, repr. 1995
    [1915]), ch. 5.

deep emotion of Jesus as he approached the tomb of Lazarus (John 11:38). The verb is used in Classical Greek for the snorting of horses, and when applied to humans suggests strong indignation that was audibly expressed. The Septuagint usage would also support the note of anger. Morris suggests that it refers to his anger at the attitude of the mourners.[69] Carson agrees but also believes that this understanding is compatible with the more traditional view[70] that Jesus was angry 'with the sin, sickness and death in this fallen world that wreaks so much havoc and generates so much sorrow'. Jesus displayed both anger and sympathy, for 'the same sin and death, the same unbelief, that prompted his outrage, also generated his grief'.[71]

This same strong emotion is also evident in situations where we would not expect Jesus to react in such a way. Having made a leper whole (Mark 1:43) and given sight to two blind men (Matt. 9:30), Jesus angrily sent the men away with orders not to make the miracles known. His compassion was there from the start and he showed mercy on those who asked for it (Mark 1:41; Matt. 9:27).[72] Yet, he burned with anger and that anger must again be on account of sin and the prince of this age.[73] Jesus showed compassion but he

---

69. L. Morris, *The Gospel According to John* (Grand Rapids: Eerdmans, 1971), pp. 557–558.

70. See e.g. Warfield, *Person and Work of Christ*, p. 117: 'It is death that is the object of his wrath, and behind death him who has the power of death, and whom he has come into the world to destroy.' See also Judg. 10:16, where God is indignant over Israel's misery.

71. Carson, *John*, p. 416.

72. There is some textual evidence for the more difficult reading that Jesus was 'filled with anger' than with compassion. In this case the anger will be the result of Jesus' appreciation of the misery that sin and Satan have caused. This reading would only underline our Lord's compassion that led to him healing the men.

73. See Warfield, *Person and Work of Christ*, pp. 110–114, for the various scholarly views concerning our Lord's anger on these occasions. He considers that its cause 'lay outside the objects of his compassion', and uses other examples to show that the object of his wrath was the devil and his works.

also had that sense of outrage. Nothing was to hinder the ultimate work he had come to do. Only through the cross would the new age dawn and people rightly acknowledge Jesus as the true Messiah.

There are many other examples where Christ's anger is revealed, but not in such strongly expressed language. As he surveyed the callousness of his opponents, his wrath (*orgē*) was stirred and he was 'grieved' at their 'hardness of heart' (Mark 3:5). When his disciples prevented mothers bringing their babies and young children to Jesus (Mark 10:14; Luke 18:15), his anger was aroused (*aganaktein*). Both incidents reveal his strong reaction to all forms of inhumanity.

Our Lord's indignation is also expressed by his rebukes. He was forced to 'rebuke' James and John when they wished to call down fire on a Samaritan village for not receiving him (Luke 9:51–56). He censured them for failing to appreciate his present mission, for he had not come to usher in the day of judgment but of salvation for all races (Luke 4:18–19; Isa. 61:1–2). He also rebuked the cries of the demon possessed and the restless waves of the sea (Mark 1:25; 4:39). Behind all these references Jesus perceived, as at the tomb of Lazarus, the destructive activity of the prince of the power of the air (see Job 1:6 – 2:8). When Peter started to rebuke Jesus for informing them of his death and resurrection, he was in turn sharply rebuked with the words 'Get behind me, Satan!' (Mark 8:31–33).

Reference has already been made to the zeal of our Lord in cleansing the temple. That zeal can be described as a 'wrathful zeal' toward those who polluted his Father's house. Jesus drew attention to the kind of Messiah he was by first displaying a majestic meekness as he rode into Jerusalem on a donkey and then as a royal reformer giving expression to his righteous anger. That same indignation was expressed in his denunciations. Jesus called Herod 'that fox' (Luke 13:32) and pronounced woes upon hypocrites, calling them blind guides, whited sepulchres, a brood of vipers and children of the devil. He hated all falsehood and selfishness, especially as it was seen in those who claimed to represent his God and Father.

Amazement

Amazement is what is so often associated with the crowds as they saw the miracles of Jesus and heard his teaching. It is applied to

Jesus on two occasions. He expressed amazement and surprise at the centurion's faith (Matt. 8:10; Luke 7:9) and at the unbelief of the citizens of his home town of Nazareth and his close relatives (Mark 6:6). Members of his own family had turned against him. Remembering that Jesus' human knowledge was limited, it is perfectly understandable that he should be astonished, for without special revelation he could not predict who would be among his followers and who would remain stubbornly unbelieving. We can sense the hurt of rejection by the proverb he quoted, 'A prophet is not without honour, except in his home town and among his relatives and in his own household' (Mark 6:4; see John 1:11). Through the Scriptures he probably learnt from an early period that one of his close followers would betray him (Ps. 55:12–14; Zech. 11:13). Knowing what would happen and who would be involved would in no way have lessened the hurt. What David felt when his trusted counsellor defected was the experience of our Lord:

> Even my close friend in whom I trusted,
> who ate my bread, has lifted his heel against me.
> (Ps. 41:9; see Ps. 55:12–14)

Shame

Even before the crucifixion, we shall never know his pain of being misunderstood by family, friend and foe, and treated as a glutton and drunkard, a madman, a blasphemer, a Sabbath breaker and a pawn of the devil. What shame and ignominy he faced at the hands of the Romans who spat in his face, mocked and ridiculed him and hung his naked body on the cross. Yet this was nothing to the anguish of soul as he bore the sicknesses and sins of the world (Matt. 8:17; 1 Pet. 2:24; Isa. 53:4–5).[74] The words of the psalmist he would have made his own:

> You know my reproach,
> and my shame and my dishonour;

---

74. See further James Stalker, *Imago Christi: The Example of Jesus Christ* (London: Hodder & Stoughton, 1905).

my foes are all known to you.
  (Ps. 69:19)

Joy and contentment

The observation that the Gospel writers record Jesus only weeping, not laughing or smiling, is in itself no more significant than the fact that Peter is never depicted as laughing and smiling, only weeping (Luke 22:62). Is it wrong to imagine him as a young lad playing and laughing with other children? His attendance at the wedding in Cana of Galilee and how he transformed an embarrassing moment into one of joy and satisfaction again suggests that he could enter into the enjoyment of the occasion. That in no way takes away from the deeper significance of the event (John 2:4, 11). He was often invited to recline at table both with the religious and the sinners (Luke 7:36; 11:37; 14:1; Matt. 9:10; 11:19). He enjoyed the delights of human association and at the same time used the occasions to teach valuable lessons.

The apostle Paul encourages believers to rejoice with those who rejoice and weep with those who weep (Rom. 12:15) and that is precisely the picture we have of the Lord Jesus. While Paul became an example to the churches of a joyful, contented Christian (Phil. 4:4–12), the perfect example is Jesus. Our Lord was the happiest and most fulfilled person ever to have lived on this earth. He found contentment in carrying out his Father's will (John 4:34; 5:30; 6:38). He was full of joy and his desire was that his disciples would know his joy and that their joy would be full. (John 15:11; 17:13). He openly expressed his joy when the disciples 'returned with joy' from their mission (Luke 10:17–21). Such joys relating to his mission, which enabled him to endure the cross (Heb. 12:2), though paramount, must not be allowed to detract from the human pleasures and delights he experienced as he interacted with people and close friends.

Love

Jesus loved people and out of that heart of love flowed affection, sympathy, concern, pity, mercy, tenderness and sensitivity toward others. The human emotion of love expressed itself at first for his earthly parents as he sought to live in submission to them. It was

demonstrated toward his mother very poignantly at the cross
when he committed her into the care of his closest disciple (John
19:26–27). This was the disciple who had the privilege of being
called the disciple 'whom Jesus loved' (John 13:23; 19:26–27;
20:2–9; 21:7, 20–23, 24–25). By a process of elimination it is clear
that the reference is to the apostle John. Jesus chose twelve apostles to be with him and of these Peter, James and John belonged to
the more intimate circle (Mark 5:37; 9:2; 14:33). Even so, John had
a special place in Jesus' affections. With Calvin we can say that
having a fondness for some more than others is not always incon-
sistent with Christian love.[75]

Outside the circle of the Twelve Jesus also had a special attach-
ment for the family at Bethany (John 11:5). He was especially close to
Lazarus, as the message that Mary and Martha sent to Jesus reveals:
'Lord, he whom you love is ill' (John 11:3). When later the onlookers
saw Jesus weeping, they said, 'See how he loved him!' (John 11:36).
Here was clean, wholesome friendship (John 11:11). Significantly, it
is the disciple whom Jesus loved who alone gives us this insight into
Jesus' special relationship with the Bethany household.

Whereas we have these numerous references in the Fourth
Gospel, love is attributed to Jesus only once in the Synoptics. Mark
records that Jesus, as he looked on the rich young ruler, 'loved him'
(Mark 10:21). There is a suggestion that the verb refers to an
outward action, such as a hug, and not simply to the inner
emotion.[76] But this is not the love of warm affection such as we
have found in John's Gospel. The searching look of Jesus goes
with his love for the young man and indicates that Jesus longed to
do him some good. It is similar to Jesus seeing the crowd and
having compassion on them (Mark 6:34). This emotion of love is,
as Warfield puts it, 'not far from simple compassion'.[77]

75. John Calvin, *The Gospel according to St John 11–21 and The First Epistle of John*,
    trans. T. H. L. Parker, ed. D. W. Torrance and T. F. Torrance (Edinburgh:
    St Andrew Press, 1961), p. 66.

76. See Craig A. Evans, *Mark 8:27–16:20*, Word Biblical Commentary
    (Nashville: Thomas Nelson, 2001), p. 98.

77. Warfield, *Person and Work of Christ*, p. 102.

Compassion

This brings us to consider the most memorable expression that the Synoptics use in relation to Jesus' ministry of doing good to people. While the Fourth Gospel simply uses the word 'love' (e.g. John 15:13),[78] the other Gospel writers speak of Jesus being moved with 'compassion' (Matt. 9:36; 14:14; 15:32; 20:34; Mark 1:41; 6:34; 8:2; Luke 7:13; see also Matt. 18:27; Mark 9:22). It is a powerful word.[79] 'Compassion', comments Nolland, 'involves so identifying with the situation of others that one is prepared to act for their benefit.'[80] While the action of Jesus in feeding the crowds or healing the sick displayed his feeling of pity toward people in need, no-one would have known his state of mind if he had not indicated how he felt. Only on one occasion, at the feeding of the four thousand, is it recorded that Jesus made known his feelings to his disciples (Matt. 15:32; Mark 8:2).

Many were the earnest pleas for mercy or pity by people in need as Jesus passed by, and these appeals were met with a heartfelt response. Whereas a Jewish rabbi would normally recoil from a leper's cry for help, Jesus showed his compassion by touching the untouchable and making him whole and clean (Mark 1:41).[81] When Mark next draws our attention to Jesus' compassion, it is at a point where Jesus and his disciples were seeking to spend time alone for rest and relaxation away from the swirling crowds. Yet we are told that when Jesus saw the great crowd, 'he had compassion on them, because they were like sheep without a shepherd' (Mark 6:34; see also Matt. 9:36; 14:14; Num. 27:17; 1 Kgs 22:17; 2 Chron. 18:16; Ezek. 34:5). He did not react with an irritable spirit at not being

---

78. In Greek, John, without any appreciable difference in meaning, uses two words for love: *phileō* and *agapaō*.

79. The Greek verb is *splanchnizomai*.

80. John Nolland, *The Gospel of Matthew*, New International Greek Testament Commentary (Grand Rapids: Eerdmans; Milton Keynes: Paternoster, 2005), p. 407.

81. The Western reading 'filled with anger' replaces 'compassion' at this point. This reading is unlikely to be the original; but, for the idea of Jesus being moved by anger as by compassion, see John 11:33–38 above.

able to get away from them, but with a sympathy that arose out of seeing their spiritual state.

He was just as concerned over the crowd's physical need for sustenance, especially when they had been listening to his teaching for three days in a desert place (Mark 8:2–3; Matt. 15:32). His compassion for the people arose out of a deep interest in them as human beings. He had a pastor's heart and loved the people. He felt for them and was not dismissive of their physical needs. Whether it was the sight of thousands of destitute souls or the desperate plight of individuals like the weeping widow of Nain (Luke 7:13) and the blind beggars on the Jericho road (Matt. 20:34), the heart of Jesus went out to such people, and it was from such a heart that he acted to alleviate their wretched conditions. This is the love that took him to the cross of Calvary to give his life as a ransom for peoples of all nations.

The emotional life of our sinless Saviour indicates that we should not be afraid of our emotions or seek to suppress them. There is still too much of the stoic, stiff-upper-lip mentality among many Christians. In addition, it is clear from our Lord's example that there is no sin in having a liking for some people more than others. This, of course, puts us in a vulnerable position, as it did Jesus, and makes it all the harder to bear when intimate friends betray and abandon us.

Christ's spiritual development

As many who are brought up in Christian homes can testify, our Lord would never have known a time when he did not love and trust his heavenly Father, pray to him or appreciate his Word. At every moment of his life from the time he could begin to think he sought to glorify God and enjoy him. His maturing in wisdom and being in favour with God would suggest this. Because he was by nature spiritually alive and had a perfect mind unaffected by the fall his thinking never became futile (Rom. 1:21–22).

Communal worship
During his developing years he would have attended synagogue

with his parents, something he continued to do as an adult, often preaching and performing miracles there (see Luke 4:15, 16–28, 31–37). His parents were also regular in their attendance at the annual Passover festival in Jerusalem. After his own early experience we find him a frequent visitor to the temple during his public ministry, attending the festivals and preaching in the temple courts. He could have said with David:

> How lovely is your dwelling place,
>   O LORD of hosts!
> My soul longs, yes, faints for the courts of the LORD;
> my heart and flesh sing for joy
>   to the living God . . .
> (Ps. 84:1–2)

Scripture

When he heard the Scriptures read, he received them as the Word of God, memorized them and was quick to see their implications. His mind was full of the Scriptures as he lived his life, taught the people, replied to the devil's temptations and suffered on the cross. The Scriptures were for him not only a textbook but his spiritual food and drink. Jesus could say of himself, 'Man shall not live by bread alone, but by every word that comes from the mouth of God' (Matt. 4:4: Deut. 8:3).

He studied and delighted in God's Word so that what the psalmists wrote would have applied even more to David's greater son:

> Oh how I love your law!
>   It is my meditation all the day.
> (Ps. 119:97)

> How sweet are your words to my taste,
>   sweeter than honey to my mouth! (Ps. 119:103)

> Your word is a lamp to my feet
>   and a light to my path
> (Ps. 119:105)

More to be desired are they than gold,
    even much fine gold;
sweeter also than honey
    and drippings of the honeycomb.
(Ps. 19:10)

Prayer

Luke is the Gospel writer who particularly draws attention to the importance of Jesus' prayer life. There was an ongoing relationship with God as his heavenly Father. What he taught his disciples to do he did himself. Besides those quick prayers in moments of crisis (see John 12:28), Jesus spent long hours in prayer, especially at night or before daybreak, when he found peace from the crowds and the demands of his disciples (Luke 5:16). He also prayed, taking some of his close disciples with him.

Jesus prayed not merely to be an example to his followers, as some early Christians thought, but because he was a man dependent on God. It was 'in the days of his flesh' that he 'offered up prayers and supplications, with loud cries and tears' (Heb. 5:7). Though he was a sinless man and had no need to call on God for forgiveness, he still needed prayer and made every effort to keep those precious quiet times. His public life began with prayer when he was baptized by John in the Jordan and received the Spirit's anointing (Luke 3:21–22). There were also special occasions when he felt the need to be much in prayer. He spent a whole night in prayer before appointing the twelve apostles (Luke 6:12–13). It was during a time of prayer that he asked his disciples about himself and informed them about his death (Luke 9:18–22). The transfiguration took place in the context of prayer (Luke 9:28–29). When he entered the greatest test of his life, his hours of prayer in Gethsemane were very intense (Luke 22:39–46). Prior to that he had prayed for Peter (Luke 22:31–32) and all his followers (John 17), and while on the cross he prayed for his enemies (Luke 23:34). He died praying (Luke 23:46).

Spiritual graces

Jesus did not need saving faith, but all the spiritual graces seen in Christians were his to perfection, including the special three: faith, hope and love. There are psalms that speak of Messiah's trust and hope in God, especially when the enemies were doing their vilest (see Pss 54:4; 55:23; 56:3–4, 9–11). Jesus 'entrusted himself to him who judges justly' (1 Pet. 2:23), and patiently endured great hostility from sinners because his hope was in God (Heb. 12:2–3). He loved the Lord; he loved the world of lost sinners and yearned that his own race would be saved (Matt. 23:37); and he loved his own followers 'to the end' (John 13:1).

Christ's awareness of his person and mission

In attempting to understand how Jesus came to view himself and his mission does not mean we are attempting to study the psychology of Jesus. Those who attempt to psychoanalyse people who are no longer living usually end up telling us more about themselves than their subjects. Using the Gospel accounts we can study what our Lord thought about himself and his calling.[82]

Through the learning process common to all, Jesus not only uttered his first *abba* in reference to Joseph, but applied it quite naturally to Israel's God. We have no information as to when and how Mary and Joseph told Jesus about the angelic messages, the honour given to Jesus by the shepherds and the Magi, and the prophetic words of Simeon and Anna. With the passage of time and with nothing unusual happening, the initial excitement might well have worn off, especially if, as is commonly thought, her husband died before Jesus began his public work. If John the Baptist needed assurance of Jesus' calling and mission after only a few months of languishing in prison, what must Mary have thought after thirty years? We know that his mother and family found it difficult to appreciate his preaching ministry.

It is very probable that Jesus had no direct word from heaven until he was thirty. Prior to this he had been dependant on whatever his parents had told him and his meditation on the Scriptures and

---

82. See N. T. Wright, *Jesus and the Victory of God* (London: SPCK, 1996), pp. 479–481.

the Spirit's illumination. By the time he was twelve, however, Jesus was aware of his unique relationship to God and of his mission, and the impression given suggests that this was not a recent development. Perhaps the reason for Luke giving the account of Jesus' experience in the temple and of his response to his parents' concerns is to indicate that this was a crucial moment when son and parents first became acutely aware of the tension his person and calling would bring. Luke draws our attention to the contrast between Mary's concerned words 'your father and I' and Jesus' reference to God as 'my Father' (Luke 2:48–49). This gave Mary further food for thought (Luke 2:51; see 2:19). Only when Jesus had completed his mission would greater clarity come to her puzzled mind.

His God and heavenly Father certainly confirmed Jesus' identity following his baptism by John. He had a direct word from heaven: 'You are my beloved Son; with you I am well pleased' (Mark 1:11). A similar word of assurance came from his heavenly Father on the Mount of Transfiguration for the benefit of Peter, James and John (Mark 9:7). John records a further voice from heaven for the benefit of the crowd (John 12:28–30). At his baptism the Spirit anointed him for his life's work (Luke 4:18–21; John 1:32–33). As Owen helpfully shows, Jesus carried out every function of his office as Messiah in the power of the Spirit.[83] He was full of the Spirit as he left the Jordan, was led by the Spirit in the wilderness and returned in the power of the Spirit to begin his ministry (Luke 4:1, 14).

Jesus was aware of a divine necessity associated with his mission. All the Gospels suggest this none more so than Luke. No fewer than ten times the Greek word *dei* (it is necessary) is used with reference to our Lord. We first hear it from his lips when he was twelve (Luke 2:49). Jesus was fulfilling a divine plan. This did not mean he was a fatalist, but it did mean that at every period of his life he responded with willing obedience to the necessity laid upon him by his vocation (Luke 12:50).

Though he had, as Warfield observes, 'companions of his human heart: those to whom his affections turned in a purely

---

83. Owen, *Works of John Owen*, vol. 3, pp. 168–188.

human attachment',[84] he did not allow these to interfere with his mission. In his enjoyment of family and friends he never lost sight of his Father's purposes, where his friends are those who 'do what I command you' (John 15:14) and his family are those who do 'the will of my Father in heaven' (Matt. 12:50).

Conclusion – consider Jesus

Throughout the epistle to the Hebrews believers are directed to Jesus Christ. The reality of the humanity of Jesus is important to the author's argument concerning the salvation, comfort and encouragement of Christians. 'But we see him . . . namely Jesus' (Heb. 2:9). When the going is tough and the pressure to lose heart and give up is great, 'we have a great high priest . . . Jesus, the Son of God', one who is able 'to sympathise with our weaknesses', and 'one who in every respect has been tempted as we are, yet without sin' (Heb. 4:14–15). It is into the heavenly sanctuary that 'Jesus has gone as a forerunner on our behalf', and we have confidence to enter the heavenly holy place 'by the blood of Jesus' (Heb. 10:19). The call is, therefore, to 'consider Jesus' (Heb. 3:1; 12:3) and to look to Jesus (Heb. 12:2). For each succeeding generation 'Jesus Christ is the same yesterday and today and forever' (Heb. 13:8).

We have in the glory not only one who still bears the marks of his physical sufferings (John 20:20, 27; Rev. 5:6) but one who knows exactly what it is like to experience all the problems of human life in a fallen world. The emphasis in Hebrews on our Lord's human name stresses that our great high priest who is in the holy heavenly place has not divested himself of his human nature. His humanity for ever belongs to him. He is still Jesus. Having been a child himself, children can be assured that he is aware of their particular concerns. Adolescents can also find comfort in a mediator that knows all about the pressures of the teenage years. When the burdens of life grow greater in adult life, there is one who understands and cares. Young and old can rest in the

---

84. Warfield, *Person and Work of Christ*, p. 106.

confidence that Jesus our merciful and faithful high priest still remembers what it was like to be tempted and tested and that he still feels for his needy people and suffers with them. 'For because he himself has suffered when tempted, he is able to help those who are being tempted' (Heb. 2:18).

Many of the arguments over the impassability of God are somewhat academic in the light of the incarnation.[85] None other than Warfield penned the following:

> Men tell us that God is, by the very necessity of His nature, incapable of passion, incapable of being moved by inducements from without; that He dwells in holy calm and unchangeable blessedness, untouched by human sufferings or human sorrows for ever . . . Let us bless our God that it is not true.[86]

Within the Godhead there is real humanity with body, parts and passions. No-one can say that God does not feel and suffer what humans experience, whether on earth or in hell. In the person of the Son who is one with the Father and the Holy Spirit, God became incarnate. This is the one who in his human nature experienced the depths of human suffering and the heights of human joy. 'Before and apart from the incarnation, God knew such things by observation.' But even omniscient observation 'falls short of personal experience. That is what the incarnation made possible for God: real, personal experience of being human.'[87]

This heavenly man who is the world's representative and redeemer will also be the world's judge. No judge could be more

---

85. For recent treatments of this subject, see J. M. Frame, *The Doctrine of God* (Philadelphia: Presbyterian & Reformed, 2002), pp. 608–616; Grudem, *Systematic Theology*, pp. 165–166; Helm, *John Calvin's Ideas*, pp. 71–92; P. Helm, 'B. B. Warfield on Divine Passion', *Westminster Theological Journal* 69 (2007), pp. 95–104; Thomas G. Weinandy, *Does God Suffer?* (Edinburgh: T. & T. Clark, 1999).

86. B. B. Warfield, 'Imitating the Incarnation', in idem, *Person and Work of Christ*, p. 570.

87. Macleod, *Person of Christ*, p. 186.

understanding of human life in this world or of what the ultimate punishment or bliss will be like in the next.

Jesus is the perfect example to every believer of patient endurance. While the great cloud of witnesses from the Old Testament period is an enormous inspiration to faith, Jesus is an even better encouragement. We are to look to Jesus who is not only our greatest example of persevering faith but the one who can strengthen and help when our faith is weak.

But Jesus, of course, is not only the best believer there is who lived and died 'by faith'; he is 'the founder' of our salvation and 'the forerunner' who has gone on ahead to open up the way. Our Lord Jesus is the great shepherd of the sheep whose blood has established the new and everlasting covenant (Heb. 13:20).

In the final analysis, as we survey our Lord's inner, psychological life, we not only observe proofs of his real humanity, the perfect example of human life and one who can really empathize with humans in distress; we view a life lived in preparation for that crucial moment when he endured our curse and conquered the last enemy. He is still the man Christ Jesus, now at the right hand of the Majesty on high, who ever lives to be our saviour, our mediator and our helper.

3. THE CRY OF DERELICTION: THE BELOVED SON CURSED AND CONDEMNED

Paul Wells

> And at the ninth hour Jesus cried with a loud voice,
> 'Eloi, Eloi, lema sabachthani?' which means, 'My God,
> my God, why have you forsaken me?'
>
> (Mark 15:34)

No doubt the exegesis of this saying has suffered from well-meaning attempts to say too much, but it has also suffered from the tendency to say too little. It does not seem to me that there can be true progress in a worthy doctrine of the Atonement until we recognise in the saying the accents of desolation and then ask, in the light of the other sayings and wider indications of the thought of Jesus, what is implied. The implications are theological: the desolation is historic fact.[1]

On this note Vincent Taylor concluded a brief discussion of the word of dereliction over half a century ago. In spite of his vigorous rebuttal of penal substitution, with its 'revolting and unnecessary features', I formally agree with his evaluation. The

---

1. V. Taylor, *Jesus and His Sacrifice* (London: Macmillan, 1948), p. 163.

accents of dereliction demand an account corresponding to the mystery they portray, one that must surely be more satisfying than Taylor's psychological interpretation as a 'feeling of utter desolation, abandonment by the Father, an experience of defeat and despair'.[2] I agree that this can be achieved realistically only in the context of the seven words from the cross as a whole, an important insight that has tended to fall beyond the horizon of much scientific exegesis, even if there is a multitude of books on the subject in the field of popular piety.[3]

How then are we to approach the perplexing fourth utterance, so elliptical, so enigmatic and so seemingly final? (See below for a list of Jesus' seven utterances from the cross.) In the text, the *tone* escapes us. Would the hearers themselves have been able to get the meaning? What was expressed? Was it pathos, resignation, fear, despair, rage or bewilderment? I advance that perhaps it was none of these, but something more than all them together. Was *this* the way Jesus died or was the dereliction penultimate, a reef to be circumnavigated before the haven of victory was reached?

Fascinating questions these, ones for which we shall probably never find a satisfying answer. However does it necessarily follow that we are doomed to the kind of agnosticism that takes refuge in the following judgment? '[I]t is impossible to assess what this may have meant to Jesus. This is one of the most impenetrable mysteries of the entire Gospel narrative.'[4] In a sense I am bound to agree. The access certain commentators seem to have to Jesus' inner life is nigh on preternatural. However, we cannot, because of the unfathomable nature of the event, discount a priori the possibility of intelligence provided through the analogy of Scripture.

---

2. Ibid., p. 161.

3. Among the most recent, C. R. Seitz, *Seven Lasting Words* (Louisville: Westminster John Knox, 2001); and S. Hauerwas, *Cross-Shattered Christ: Meditations on the Seven Last Words* (London: Darton Longman & Todd, 2005).

4. D. A. Hagner, *Matthew 14–28*, Word Biblical Commentary 33B (Dallas: Word, 1995), p. 845.

The *Eloi* (or *Eli*), *Eloi lema sabachthani*, Aramaic transliterated
into Greek, followed by its translation in both Mark and Matthew,
quoting Psalm 22:1,[5] is not the kind of fish that can easily be
netted by exegetes and theologians, although many of our nets
may be as good as, or better than, Bultmann's! Was the abandonment caused by the bearing of sin? 'There is no specific reference
to this in the passage,'[6] which means of course that the fishing
season has started.

Because of the brevity of this word, hardly a word but a loud
cry,[7] and because of the absence of explanation by either of the
evangelists, presuppositions will play a more prominent role in
interpretation in this instance than might normally be the case.
There is less text to exert a control, at least if examination is
confined to the word itself and to its immediate context. To this
consideration we are bound to pay a little attention, in particular in
the light of how evangelicals, with their specific view of Scripture
as the inspired Word of God, might be expected to approach this
issue.

Some critical questions

Did Jesus really utter these words? It might appear that this could
be taken for granted owing to the solemnity of the moment, but

---

5. Matthew follows Mark rather closely and I shall refer primarily to Mark's
   Gospel. Matthew changes the Aramaic *Eloi* into the Hebrew *Eli*. R. E.
   Brown, *The Death of the Messiah*, 2 vols. (New York: Doubleday, 1994); vol. 2,
   pp. 1051–1058, gives a detailed linguistic analysis of the wording of the cry,
   including variants in the Codex Bezae and the apocryphal *Gospel of Peter*.

6. D. Guthrie, *New Testament Theology* (Leicester: IVP, 1981), p. 446.

7. The verbs *boan* and *anaboan* are used (cf. Luke 9:38 and Ps. 22:2a), and
   what proceeds from Jesus' mouth is termed as *phōnē megalē*. Brown suggests that the loud cry is 'an apocalyptic sign similar to the eschatological
   elements of darkness, rent sanctuary veil, earthquake and risen dead that
   accompany the death of Jesus in various gospels' (*Death of the Messiah*, vol.
   2, p. 1045).

not so. A good number of biblical scholars seem to opt for the approach that the seven words from the cross are of a theological, not a historical, nature.

Regarding the fourth word Raymond E. Brown takes three fundamental approaches in his detailed critical study of the death of the Messiah. Either these are *ipsissima verba* (precise words) of Jesus, or it was a 'wordless cry', or maybe Jesus said something else. Brown says that 'no one can say that the case for *ipsissima verba* is established', although the claim cannot be 'discounted'.[8] Xavier Léon-Dufour, a well-known Catholic biblical theologian, concludes, as do a number of scholars, that the cry expressed some 'basic words' of Jesus, who could well have said 'You are my God', which is found several times in the Psalms.[9] How such a conclusion can be reached at a distance of two thousand years against the evidence before us in the text leaves a sense of wonder.

For others, such as Jürgen Moltmann, the words are to be considered not as historical at all but theological.[10] The theological approach, it is claimed, reveals the significance of what happened, even though Jesus might never have said anything. The words can be authentic as a portrayal of the way Jesus died, without actually being historical. So Francine Bigaouette, in a voluminous study of the fourth word, affirms that whether Jesus said this or not is of little importance, as the 'truth of the witness of Matthew and Mark to the saving event' is not affected by it.[11] It is a confession of the identity of Jesus and not 'a narration of his dying act'.[12] Lessing's 'big ditch' and Ritschl's distinction between judgments of fact and value loom large under these interpretations.

Several factors seem to enter into these critical distinctions. The fact that the narrative in Mark records that Jesus cried again with a loud voice (15:37, reproduced by Matthew), is considered to be the

---

8. Ibid., pp. 1086, 1088.

9. X. Léon-Dufour, 'Le dernier cri de Jésus', *Etudes* 348 (1978), pp. 666–682.

10. J. Moltmann, *The Crucified God* (London: SCM, 1974), chs. 4–5.

11. F. Bigaouette, *Le cri de déréliction de Jésus* (Paris: Cerf, 2004), p. 22.

12. L. Caza, *Mon Dieu, mon Dieu, pourquoi m'as-tu abandonné?* (Paris: Cerf, 1989), p. 172.

real end of Jesus. The cry of dereliction is a doublet, inserted into the narrative for theological reasons. It is also argued on medical grounds that it is unlikely that a victim of death by crucifixion would be able to articulate words or maybe even a shriek because of suffocation. In addition, the fourth word is taken to be one of several signs of an apocalyptic nature, including the darkness (v. 33) and the rending of the veil in the temple (v. 38), all of which are interpretations of the climactic event in the light of expectations concerning the Day of the Lord.[13]

A further factor in this debate is the alleged impossibility of harmonizing the fourth word with the other words recorded by the evangelists. The danger is that in harmonizing it with the 'non-tragic' approach of Luke[14] the stark literal pessimism of Mark and Matthew is lost.[15] Jesus dies with an aura of confidence and hope rather than in tragic abandonment. There is good reason, we are informed, to think that Luke edited Mark, excising the desperate cry and choosing Psalm 31:5 rather than Psalm 22:1 as a description of the ultimate moment. The authenticity of the terrible reality of the death of Jesus is obscured.

The upshot of these critical approaches is that when the fourth word is separated from the other words, considered to be secondary theological interpretations, its isolation makes it malleable to various possible interpretations, whether it is considered to be historical or theological. Recent Roman Catholic scholarship in particular has expended a great amount of energy on the interpretation of the fourth word, very often in the interest of avoiding the excesses of its own tradition and of the penal substitutionary theory.[16]

---

13. Bigaouette, *Le cri*, p. 68.

14. Guthrie, *New Testament Theology*, p. 448, remarks that Luke makes no mention of the anointing at Bethany, the desertion of the disciples. Jesus commits himself to the Father in death and the word of abandon is absent. Luke alone records the prayer for his persecutors and the ministry of Jesus to others on the cross.

15. Brown, *Death of the Messiah*, vol. 2, pp. 1047–1048.

16. For a description of some Catholic excesses on penal substitution, see the classic study by J. Rivière, *Le dogme de la rédemption: Etude théologique*

The position proposed here, in contrast to these critical approaches, is that not only is the fourth word historical but it also has a theological character that is best understood in the context of the seven words as a whole.[17] Several reasons can be advanced to justify this position, one that is often foreign to 'scientific' exegesis. A prime consideration is the analogy of Scripture and the fact that Scripture must be given the freedom to provide its own attestation. A reading of the text provides no good reason for supposing that Jesus did not say any of these words from the cross. On the contrary, when it is argued that they are simply theological interpolations, many specious arguments are advanced as to what Jesus could or could not have said or done, and what could have happened. Finally, even the most competent exegetes know nothing of what Jesus felt, or what happened, other than what they find in the text, as Raymond Brown concedes.[18] The paradox is that the text itself is used to decompose the texts and invent new meanings. Divide and rule!

Further to these purely formal considerations, why should it be doubted that these are the words of Jesus as he pronounced them? This is the Master speaking. Which of the witnesses would presume to invent words to express such an unfathomable mystery on his behalf? It is almost ludicrous to think this could be

---

Footnote 16 (cont.)

(Paris: Gabalda, 1931), pp. 230–240. Recent Catholic works that seek to compensate include M. Winter, *The Atonement* (London: Geoffrey Chapman, 1995); P. Benoît, *Passion et Résurrection du Seigneur* (Paris: Cerf, 1966), pp. 220ff.; B. Carra de Vaux Saint Cyr, 'L'abandon de Christ en Croix', in H. Bouësse and J.-J. Latour, *Problèmes actuels de Christologie* (Paris: Desclée de Brouwer, 1965), pp. 295–316; Ch. Duquoc, *Christologie*, vol. 2 (Paris: Cerf, 1974), pp. 39ff.; B. Sesboüé, *Jésus Christ l'unique médiateur*, 2 vols. (Paris: Desclée, 1988), ch. 11. H. Urs von Balthasar, to name a rather rare exception, goes against the trend in his *Mysterium Paschale* (Edinburgh: T. & T. Clark, 1990).

17. The argument is developed in some detail in my *Entre ciel et terre: Les sept dernières paroles du Christ* (Lausanne: Ed. Contrastes, 1990).

18. Brown, *Death of the Messiah*, vol. 2, pp. 1047ff.

the case. In fact, considering the question from an inner textual point of view, to put these words in Jesus' mouth after the taunts about self-deliverance (Matt. 27:38–43; Mark 15:27–32) would tend to demonstrate that Jesus was *not* the Son of God he claimed to be. That, of course, might suit some people, but hardly evangelicals.

In addition, this is not just any moment in his ministry, but the ultimate event. It is a sacred place and the onlookers are standing on hallowed ground, the sanctuary where the final sacrifice is enacted. At this moment who can speak but the Lord? He alone knew what was happening and he alone could be the supreme interpreter of his own experience and the work of salvation that depended on it. If this is the climax of the history of redemption, it beggars belief to think that the God who spoke 'at many times and in many ways' would not speak to us 'by his Son' (Heb. 1:1–2). God alone can interpret God, particularly at *this* time.

Furthermore, there are those to whom Jesus spoke (the Father, God, convicted criminals, his nearest and dearest and those he spoke about, including himself in his fifth utterance). Words at times such as this, to say nothing of the tragic and dramatic circumstances, rarely pass unheeded.

Finally, the fourth utterance fits in neatly with the other six, in such a way that we can see the dynamic progression of Jesus' actions, which we can only call a saving ministry, on the cross. Far from losing its 'literal import' of abandonment and diluting its force in the context of the final word of Luke, it is precisely in the overall context of the seven utterances that the reality of the situation described in the word of dereliction can be comprehended.

Nor are these critical questions without theological import, both in the realms of Christology and soteriology. Did Jesus himself have any insight into his plight and the work he was undertaking? Was not this part of his special calling for which he came into the world – not to do his own will but the will of the Father, particularly when the fatal hour arrived (Mark 14:41)?[19]

---

19. Balthasar, *Mysterium Paschale*, ch. 3, sect. a.

From a soteriological perspective, did Jesus *die* with a *Why* on his lips? What difference does it make to say, as Moltmann does, that Jesus' end was one of profound anguish, despised and abandoned, God divided from God, the Son suffering the absence of the Father and the Father deprived of the Son, and that Jesus died victorious and confident of the perfect acceptability of his work? If the former is the case, then victory is postponed to the resurrection event, and we cannot speak about the triumph of the crucified in death, through death and over death. This means nothing less than that death still has its sting. There is something incomplete about the human experience of Christ as the second Adam if he dies a victim of death and not as the one who in his ultimate moment can draw himself up to the level of God and claim access to the divine presence as his own right.[20] If Jesus despairs of life, does he necessarily despair of victory?[21]

Seven last utterances

In the context of the seven utterances the word of dereliction is not the death word, but a word that describes Jesus' experience preceding death. There is no conclusive reason for thinking that Jesus could not have uttered two loud cries a little before and on the point of death, as both Mark and Matthew record, and that the final utterance they refer to is not the one mentioned in all four Gospels, albeit in a different register:

> [he] yielded up his spirit (Matt. 27:50)
> [he] breathed his last (Mark 15:37)
> 'Father, into your hands I commit my spirit!' And having said this he breathed his last. (Luke 23:46)
> and he bowed his head and gave up his spirit (John 19:30)

---

20. Moltmann, *Crucified God*, chs. 4–5; cf. Bigaouette, *Le cri*, pp. 48, 327.
21. Cf. R. H. Gundry, *Mark: A Commentary on His Apology for the Cross* (Grand Rapids: Eerdmans, 1993), pp. 966–967.

I conclude with Abraham Kuyper, as to the variation in form:

> If indeed in the four gospels words are put in Jesus' mouth with
> reference to the same occasion but *dis*similar in the form of their
> expression, Jesus naturally could not have used four different forms;
> but the Holy Spirit only aimed to bring about for the church an
> impression which completely corresponds to what came forth from
> Jesus.[22]

Should the elucidation in Luke be considered a purely theological affair? If it does provide theological meaning to Jesus' end, we
cannot conclude either that it is contrary to what has preceded or
even in opposition to what is recorded in the other Gospels. It is
not unnatural that the act of yielding or giving up the spirit and
breathing his last should also find verbal expression. Nor is there
any theological reason to suppose that Jesus would not have
spoken in this way at the end. The text must stand.

In the context of the seven utterances as a whole, the fourth is
not only numerically but also theologically central. Although the
order of the words is a subject of debate, the generally accepted
pattern easily discernable in modern synopses of the Gospels,
such as that edited by Kurt Aland, yields the following pattern:[23]

Seven utterances from the cross

1. Father, forgive them, for they know not what they do (Luke 23:34)
2. Today you will be with me in Paradise (Luke 23:43)
3. Woman, behold, your son . . . behold your mother (John 19:26, 27)
4. My God, my God, why have you forsaken me? (Matt. 27:46; Mark 15:34)
5. I thirst (John 19:28)

---

22. A. Kuyper, *Encyclopaedie*, vol. 2, p. 499, quoted by H. Bavinck, *Reformed Dogmatics*, vol. 1 (Grand Rapids: Baker Academic, 2003), p. 444.

23. With some questions in particular concerning the location of word 3. See K. Aland, *Synopsis of the Four Gospels* (Stuttgart: United Bible Societies, 1982), pp. 316–322. Cf. Brown for a discussion on the order and further references, *Death of the Messiah*, vol. 2, pp. 971 ff.

6. It is finished (John 19:30)

7. Father, into your hands I commit my spirit! (Luke 23:46).[24]

The seven utterances can be examined from several complementary perspectives: the locution itself (the nature of each word), the speaker and its meaning for him, the addressees and the performative function or the effect of the saying.[25]

An initial comment is appropriate: 'Crucifixions were marked by screams of rage and pain, wild curses and the shouts of indescribable despair by the unfortunate victim. The demeanour of Jesus during the death agony is not described by the evangelists.'[26] The seven utterances themselves are presented in each of the Gospel accounts with extreme sobriety and are surrounded by silence, no attempt being made to explain the mystery. They stand on their own in their stark factuality. Isolated from the others, each of the utterances would be at the mercy of our incomprehension, but taken together their order appears, with the help of the canonical context of the Old Testament and the apostolic interpretation of the New. Jesus acts in order to 'fulfil all righteousness' (Matt. 3:15) and the New Testament witness elucidates the nature of that fulfilment. The fourth utterance, like the others, must be interpreted in the light of the whole of biblical revelation.

1. In the first of the utterances, apparently spoken about the time when nails are being driven into his body, Jesus *prays* for his persecutors and for their forgiveness. The Son addresses the Father, and the Son's intercession is not simply a sign of strength of character or altruism in excruciating pain. This is surely the most abominable act of history and the worst sin man could perpetrate. Is it conceivable that sinners could lay hands on the

---

24. On the relation between the historical, literary and theological aspects of the seven utterances, see the appendix at the end of this chapter.

25. Cf. K. J. Vanhoozer on speech acts, *First Theology* (Downers Grove: IVP; Leicester: Apollos, 2002), pp. 154ff.

26. W. L. Lane, *The Gospel According to Mark* (Grand Rapids: Eerdmans, 1974), p. 572.

beloved Son and not suffer immediate divine vengeance?[27] Will not the story end right here unless an immediate plea is lodged and heeded? The prayer is a restraining act that holds back divine intervention in judgment. History continues as a history of sin on the basis of the general pardon obtained on the part of lost humanity by the Son. He alone could pray this prayer and he alone could obtain the remission of judgment. This is common grace that is the bedrock of the special grace that will follow.

2. That special grace is the subject of the second utterance. It is the dying Son who replies with *a promise* in answer to a despairing plea, the last and only hope left for the plaintiff. It is an immediate response, full of confidence ('Amen, today') that the one who speaks can fulfil his promise, proposing ultimate beatitude – to be with the Master himself. Paradise is present on the cross in Jesus' promise. But the dying thief will have to believe, as all sinners saved by grace will, that their Saviour is none other than the one who is crucified. It is not the suffering God who helps, to use Bonhoeffer's expression, but the dying Son. Jesus saves to the uttermost by becoming the 'prince of thieves', as Calvin said. The dying thief will enter paradise before the apostles and the martyrs.[28] This is particular, sovereign grace as Christ gives 'his admission tickets to paradise only with the stamp of the foreordination of God of them'.[29]

3. The third utterance can be termed a *requisition*. On the cross Christ is Lord of the church. The addressees are the mother of Jesus and the beloved disciple. Jesus restructures human relationships in the context of his people. In caring for his mother, he acts to heal the 'sword' piercing her soul (Luke 2:35) in an order full of compassion. Mary is not becoming mother of the church, as some Catholic

---

27. The vengeance of God upholds the divine honour and has a positive side, as it redresses wrong. It is a function of kingship and judgeship; cf.
E. Peels, *Shadow Sides: God in the Old Testament* (Carlisle: Paternoster, 2004), pp. 81ff., 113.

28. J. Calvin, *Commentaires sur l'Harmonie Evangélique* (Aix-en-Provence: Ed. Kerygma, 1995), pp. 202ff.

29. K. Schilder, *Christ Crucified* (Grand Rapids: Eerdmans, 1940), p. 320.

commentators would have us believe, but the mother of Jesus finds renewed hope in the new community.[30] Redemption does not cut against the grain of creation, but restores creation to its proper ends. Jesus' kingship over his new people is exercised from the cross.

In the first three utterances of the Messiah from the cross we behold the astonishing spectacle of Jesus acting to close down his earthly ministry. This he does in a sovereignly self-conscious way by acts of grace exercised in favour of humanity in a general, a special and a communal sense. Jesus' ministry toward humankind on this earth reaches its terminus here.

The final three utterances express a different orientation. They no longer have to do with human situations but concern the way Jesus looks forward to the end of his ministry. Beyond the suffering of the cross lies the Lordship that will be the fruit of his acceptance by the Father.

5. 'I thirst' has been the subject of some discussion; paradoxically, its meaning is less immediately obvious than that of the preceding words. Jesus addresses no-one, but gives voice to *his own condition*. Maybe it is a request, but not necessarily so. Should it be interpreted symbolically – as Christ's thirst for spiritual communion in the kingdom, eating and drinking afresh with his disciples (Luke 22:19), as the one who gives the water of life? (John 4) A rich vein of Johannine theology is there to be mined, and several evangelical commentators, following Augustine and Luther, have been prospectors.[31] More apropos, perhaps, is the interpretation of Klaas Schilder, who considers the context as being that of the thirst of physical suffering as in Psalm 22:15:

> my tongue sticks to my jaws;
> you lay me in the dust of death.

---

30. Cf. Benoit, *Passion et Résurrection du Seigneur*, p. 217; I. de la Potterie, *La passion de Jésus selon l'Évangile de Jean* (Paris: Cerf, 1986), p. 160: 'Mary symbolises the Church which is our Mother.'

31. See e.g. C. H. Spurgeon, *A Treasury of the New Testament*, vol. 2 (London: Marshall, Morgan & Scott, n.d.), pp. 665–666; and A. W. Pink, *The Seven Sayings of the Saviour on the Cross* (Grand Rapids: Baker, 1958), ch. 5.

Refusing the pain-killing beverage (Mark 15:23; Matt. 27:34), Jesus keeps himself fully conscious by taking the vinegar and water (Ps. 69:21, referred to in all the Gospels) and presenting himself to God through the perfect sacrifice of his humanity. He keeps himself on track to the bitter end in order to be prepared for death and to die fully aware of the work he is accomplishing.[32]

6. 'It is finished', *tetelestai*, can be related to the Messianic self-consciousness. It is a public *declaration*, made before both God and men. In its Godward reference it is a throw back to the opening words of the high priestly prayer in Gethsemane: 'having accomplished (*teleiōsas*) the work that you gave me to do' (John 17:4). The next stop is glory (vv. 3, 5; cf. 1 Pet. 1:10–12). Surely, Jesus is now certain of his success, of the fully acceptable nature of his work, of welcome by the Father? This is the stage beyond forsakeness: it is the road to life (Isa. 53:11; Ps. 16:11). Schilder can talk here of 'Christ in the justification', and Pink can affirm that the great purpose of God 'has been accomplished *de jure* as it will yet be *de facto*'.[33] In a historical perspective, what has been fulfilled are the promises of Scripture (Luke 24:27, 44–47). In Christ, all Scripture finds its resting point and the covenant reaches its proper conclusion. This word is broadcast in a strange and profound way, for both God and for humanity. It shows that the Father can be perfectly satisfied with the outcome of the cross, and that for this reason, sinners can know that salvation achieved by Christ is fully efficacious on their behalf.

7. In the light of this, the final saying is a *prayer* for acceptance. Once again, Jesus addresses the Father, as in the first utterance recorded by Luke.[34] It is, however, more than a simple prayer; it is a committal rooted in the sense of fulfilment. What action does this word perform? Christ swings open the door for his return home, taking with him the spoils of victory. The final word is the antechamber to kingdom power, the rule Christ will proclaim to

---

32. Schilder, *Christ Crucified*, ch. 18.

33. Ibid., ch. 19; Pink, *Seven Sayings*, p. 103.

34. Brown, *Death of the Messiah*, vol. 2, p. 1068.

his disciples in his resurrection appearance (Matt. 28:20). Hugh Martin's eloquence in respect to this is impressive:

> If he died a mere passive victim, He did not die a victor: and no subsequent glory can in that case redeem what was defeat. But he died a triumphant agent. He prevailed against death to live until He said, ''Tis finished', and then to die, not merely voluntarily, but by a positive priestly action, giving Himself to God. The cross itself is glorious; not from the subsequent resurrection and enthronement, but glorious from itself. It is itself a chariot of triumph. There is more agency and power in Christ's cross than in all His work as Creator of the universe. There is as much spiritual glory in the cross of Calvary, as in the throne of the Lamb in heaven.[35]

Christ dies confident that the arm of the Lord is not shortened and his hands can save. He quotes Psalm 31:5a with the confidence of 5b: 'you have redeemed me, O LORD, faithful God'.[36] By this act, Christ goes on, beyond death, into the presence of the Father, according to his power to 'lay down' his life and 'take it up again' (John 10:17–18).

I have tried in this section to illustrate the coherence of the seven utterances, a coherence that is not simply theological, but is based on the historical conclusion of our Lord's earthly ministry. What does the centrality of the utterance of dereliction (the fourth utterance) consist of? How is it one with the other six utterances, and is this unity expressed in such a way as to preserve the real abandonment of the fourth utterance?

Perhaps the best way of answering these questions is by considering the central utterance as the expression of the trials of the *Mediator*. The place of this utterance is appropriate to the role of the Mediator *between* men and God. If the first utterances refer to human situations and the final three utterances express a Godward

---

35. H. Martin, 'The Atonement: In Its Relations to the Covenant, the Priesthood, the Intercession of Our Lord', in A. A. Hodge and H. Martin, *The Atonement* (Cherry Hill, N. J.: Mack, n.d.), pp. 36–37.

36. The whole psalm is relevant. See vv. 10, 12–14 and 2–4, 6–7, 15–16.

movement on the part of the Son, 'My God, my God, why have you forsaken me?' sees Christ in solitary confinement, forsaken by men, abandoned by God. As go-between, Christ finds himself in his personal experience in a 'no man's land' with a view to doing a work that, by necessity, only he can do.[37]

The location of this utterance, significant as it is for the unique position of Christ in the order of redemption, far from being 'theology fiction' is wholly suited to the particular nature of the desertion to which Christ submits. As such it bespeaks the terrors of suffering and judgment that impress themselves so relentlessly on the messianic conscience. No utterance illustrates better Christ's commitment to the plan of salvation, embraced in the very recesses of his anointed self-understanding.

Contextual interpretation of the fourth utterance

The moment

At the ninth hour, Christ who has been crucified since the third hour of the day, speaks this climactic utterance. It is the finale to three hours spent since noon in preternatural and infernal darkness.[38]

At the sixth hour, the scene at Golgotha changes. Something is about to happen that breaks the pattern of events hitherto. From 9am until 12 noon there has been a great deal of agitation around the person of the crucified: the casting of lots for his garments and the mockery of the rabble and passers-by. As before Herod and Pilate, Jesus has uttered not a word in self-defence, a fulfilment of the prophecy of Isaiah 53:7:

He was oppressed, and he was afflicted,

---

37. Cf. Calvin's chapter on the Mediator in his *Institutes of the Christian Religion* 2.12. In spite of his dialectical theology, E. Brunner's *The Mediator* (London: Lutterworth, 1934) is one of the classics of twentieth-century theology.

38. Luke says that the sun is eclipsed (*ekleipein*, Luke 22:45).

yet he opened not his mouth;
like a lamb that is led to the slaughter,
and like a sheep that before its shearers is silent,
so he opened not his mouth.

During the first three hours, when Jesus does speak, as he does in the first three utterances, he intervenes unexpectedly and sovereignly with words of grace. In spite of acute suffering, his resolution is shaken neither by the baseness of his persecutors nor by the verbal violence of their insidious abuse.

However, at midday darkness falls. Matthew and Mark both speak of a total blackout in the land (Matt. 27:45; Mark 15:33). The mockery ceases and the soldiers' dice stop rolling; the crowd is cowed by the stifling effect of the supernatural obscurity. This is the first of the three apocalyptic signs – the hour of Jesus has come, when he is given over to the powers of darkness (Luke 22:53b). It is perhaps too much to say that 'God hides his son from the blasphemers' leering', but it is certainly true that a veil is drawn over the suffering of Jesus.[39] Christ is isolated in his suffering and 'God has hidden his face from his Son.'[40]

This is certainly not theological significance without historical rooting. The temporal references to the moment of crucifixion, darkness, abandonment and death together with specific topographical locations, Golgotha, Jerusalem and 'the land' – whether taken to mean Judah or the whole earth[41] – serve to establish that this is history interpreted theologically.[42] What does the darkness mean? The most obvious primary parallel is with the three days of darkness over the land of Egypt preceding the Passover and the exodus (Exod. 10:21–29). The symbolism seems to indicate, and

---

39. Gundry, *Mark*, p. 947.

40. C. A. Evans, *Mark 8.27–16.20*, Word Biblical Commentary 34B (Nashville: Nelson, 2001), p. 507; cf. Hagner, *Matthew 14–28*, p. 843, on Matthew, 'supernatural darkness followed by remarkable events'.

41. Cf. *Gospel of Peter* 5.15.

42. Surprisingly, Lorraine Caza denies the temporal references and affirms that they shift the events outside everyday experience! (*Mon Dieu*, p. 227.)

quite a few commentators take it this way, that this event marks the new exodus, the sacrifice of the Lamb and the judgment of God's enemies (cf. Rev. 11:8).[43] Schilder says that Christ, crucified outside the city wall, is the atonement scapegoat abandoned to the wilderness.[44] Certainly, this is imaginative, but it rings true to an old Jewish tradition in which the scapegoat was pushed over a cliff.[45] This idea of atoning judgment links up with another more prominent manifestation of darkness, relating to the judgment of the Day of the Lord.[46] If it is the case, the metaphor of darkness illustrates that the forces of opposition that mass against God are the object of his anger and retribution. Would not this then indicate that this is at last the great Day of the Lord, when Christ is visited with the wrath of God in the judgment? Perhaps it is the most cogent explanation of why God places Christ in darkness as the Son undergoes separation from God and from the rest of humanity.

Gethsemane to Golgotha

In Gethsemane, the passion begins as it will end, with prayer: 'My Father, if it be possible, let this cup pass from me; nevertheless, not as I will, but as you will . . . My Father, if this cannot pass unless I drink it, your will be done' (Matt. 26:39, 42). The cup is referred to in each of the Synoptics, and the significance of the moment is underlined in Mark by a unique use of 'Abba, Father' (14:36). In John, there are references to both the cup and the 'hour': 'And what shall I say? "Father, save me from this hour"? But for this purpose I have come to this hour' (12:27; 18:11). The hour and the cup go together as Jesus in the garden is already in darkness and alone, prefiguring the darkness of the three hours.

---

43. Bigaouette takes all this to be theological symbolism, but her section on its meaning is nevertheless an excellent analysis (*Le cri*, pp. 229–266). Cf. Brown, *Death of the Messiah*, vol. 2, pp. 1034–1044.

44. Schilder, *Christ Crucified*, ch. 16.

45. A. Edersheim, *The Temple: Its Ministry and Services at the Time of Jesus Christ* (New York: James Pott, n.d.), p. 279.

46. Cf. Jer. 15:9; Joel 2:2, 10, 31; Amos 8:9; Zeph. 1:15.

Already he is distressed and troubled and his soul is 'very sorrow-
ful, even to death' (Mark 14:34). This anguish is not apprehension:
'it is as though something unexpected and terrible assailed Jesus,
provoking a real shock'.[47] Jesus falls to the ground in such distress
that all strength seems to desert him and he is 'projected onto the
earth'.[48]

Such anguish can be understood only in the light of what the
'cup' (*potērion*) meant for the Son. In the cup sayings, Jesus is alone
and finds himself face to face with the Father, with work to do. If
the hour is the eschatological hour looming on the horizon, the
cup doubtless announces the coming judgment. According to
Brown, of the thirty times *potērion* is used in the Septuagint, seven-
teen times it is a symbol of divine judgment either against the
enemies of God or against the elect people as a result of their
infidelity.[49] The guilty drink the cup of divine anger as a result of
their sin (Isa. 51:17–20; Jer. 25:15–17; etc.). In Mark 10:38–40, the
disciples have been put to the test ('Are you able to drink the cup?')
but now they are asleep. Alone, the Master is faced with the
prospect of suffering death like an enemy of God or a sinner
under the covenant curse.[50] In the garden, the pressing has begun;
Jesus sweats blood in the way crushed olives yield oil (Luke 22:44).
He is prey to anguish and affliction in contemplating the coming
hour that has already begun. If he laments his situation, he finds
the strength to submit to the will of the Father (Mark 14:36) to the
point of being given over into the hands of sinners (14:41) in
order to accomplish to the uttermost his mission as the suffering
Son of Man (8:31; 9:31; 10:33–34, 45).

As in the case of the darkness, the hour and the cup are por-
tents of judgment, the wrath of God and death. This is vital to

---

47. A. Feuillet, *L'Agonie de Gethsemané* (Paris: Gabalda, 1977), p. 80.
    Ekthambestai (to be astonished, terrified) is used only by Mark in the New
    Testament.
48. Ibid., pp. 82–83; and Benoit, *Passion et Résurrection du Seigneur*, p. 19.
49. Brown, *Death of the Messiah*, vol. 1, pp. 168–170.
50. On the hour and the cup, see the competent discussion in Bigaouette,
    Le cri, pp. 154–163.

an understanding of the cry of dereliction. However, from Gethsemane to Golgotha is a progressive immersion in judgment. In Gethsemane, Jesus can still pray. Why does he not pray any longer in the final abandonment? What is the reason for his silence during the three hours, followed by the surprising outburst 'My God, my God, why . . .'?

Apocalyptic signs

The darkening of the sun, as we have already seen, is one of the three apocalyptic signs surrounding the fourth utterance. There is also the 'loud voice' (*phōnē megalē*) that describes the utterance of the cry and the rending of the veil of the temple. Brown asks, 'Does the violent description of Jesus' outcry suggest that in his death struggle with evil he feels himself on the brink of defeat so that he must ask why God is not helping him?'[51] A rhetorical question that has no answer . . . at least perhaps no answer other than the fact that Jesus asserts himself supremely in the combat against evil. He has undergone an experience perceived as unique, a catastrophic abandonment that can be attributed neither to his own dispositions nor to those of the Father.

The rending of the veil in the temple at the moment of Jesus' giving up his spirit (Mark 15:39) is obviously a consequence of the death of the Son, following on from the abandonment, not an omen.[52] Some interpreters go so far as to try to structure the whole series of events at Golgotha around the liturgical worship of the early church, on the basis of the fact that Jesus' expiring corresponded to the moment of the evening sacrifice. This seems rather fanciful and just another way of fleeing into theology to avoid history.[53] More suited to the situation is the common idea, supported by Hebrews (9:11–12) that Jesus, as the paschal lamb,

---

51. Brown, *Death of the Messiah*, vol. 2, p. 1045; cf. Caza, *Mon Dieu*, pp. 124–128.

52. Gundry, *Mark*, pp. 948–950. On the inner or outer veil, see Evans, *Mark 8.27–16.20*, p. 510. For a detailed discussion of the whole, Brown, *Death of the Messiah*, vol. 2, pp. 1098–1117.

53. See in particular Caza, *Mon Dieu*, pp. 227–228.

opens a new way into the presence of God. It is Jesus' own body that is rent in death, illustrating the fact that God is no longer present in the temple building but in the new temple, which is the body of the Lord itself, in his sacrifice for his people.[54] The confession of the centurion in this immediate context 'Truly this man was the Son of God!' serves to indicate that the cross becomes the new place of worship instead of the temple and the point from which a new people of God will be gathered to confess the Son. This idea might imply that the rending of the veil prophesies the final destruction of the temple, predicted by Jesus (13:2) and the first inkling of the fate that awaits Jesus' priestly persecutors (14:62–65).

These features taken together indicate that Golgotha is a place where God is present in judgment. The darkness, the cup and the hour, the loud cry of the forsaken one and the rending of the veil all add their own brush strokes to the overall picture. What was begun in Gethsemane has its culmination at Calvary and the theme of visitation in retribution is the common denominator linking the various elements. Before considering whether the cry of dereliction was an indication of the judgment undergone by Jesus himself, there is the question of the cry and its relation to Psalm 22.

Psalm 22 and the abandonment

When Jesus uttered these words, was he referring to the whole psalm or just to the opening verse? Each position has able defenders. Those who adopt the minimalist approach do so for the following reason – if Jesus had the whole psalm in mind, or if he were thought to be reciting it all, then the starkness of the dereliction would be nullified by the consideration of an inevitable positive outcome. The abandonment was not all that catastrophic after all, just a passing squall.[55] However, the idea that Jesus had in

---

54. Bigaouette, *Le cri*, pp. 212–214.

55. See D. J. Moo, *The Old Testament in the Gospel Passion Narratives* (Sheffield: Almond, 1983), pp. 264–283; L. Jacquet, *Les Psaumes et le coeur de l'homme* (Gembloux: Duculot, 1975), pp. 518–523; Bigaouette, *Le cri*, pp. 191–195;

mind the psalm as a whole and that the opening verse can be considered as an encapsulating title is not without its adherents, and they have good cause to adopt this interpretation.

In fact, when the dynamic of the crucifixion is analysed, it is striking that the incidents presented in linear fashion in Psalm 22 are experienced by Jesus in reverse order. Joel Marcus establishes an interesting parallel in his monograph *The Way of the Lord*:

Mark 15	*Topic*	*Psalm 22*
24	division of garments	18
29	mockery/head wagging	7
30–31	save yourself!	8
32	reviling	6
34	cry of dereliction	1[56]

It is as though the Father were leading the Son via the events of the passion backward through the psalm to its dramatic opening verse. Could Jesus, who had maybe recently sung this very psalm, fail to heed the warning lights? If he knew *his* psalms, and he must have done, if he was alert to the unfolding scene, as he must have been, if we take the text to be a faithful historical narrative of the events, and we do, then it is difficult to avoid the conclusion that when Jesus cried out the first verse of the psalm, he knew he had reached the *end* of the line. From this point there was no going back, no going forward, only going *out*, the catastrophic cutting off in judgment from the land of the living.

Jesus knows that the whole experience of the psalm concerns him. It is his own psalm, the one he inspired for himself to pray, but more than that, the Word incarnate, in his flesh and blood, *is* the psalm incarnate.[57] And, horror of horrors, he is the psalm

Caza, *Mon Dieu*, pp. 419–422; J. Marcus, *The Way of the Lord: Christological Exegesis of the Old Testament in the Gospel of Mark* (Edinburgh: T. & T. Clark, 1992), pp. 172–184.

56. Marcus, *Way of the Lord*, p. 175; cf. Evans, *Mark 8.27–16.20*, p. 498.

57. Schilder, *Christ Crucified*, p. 394, 'the poet *par excellence* is appearing on Golgotha'.

incarnate as the *curse* of the covenant (Gal. 3:13), the beloved cursed, that blessing might come. Jesus is God's psalm, enduring the curse to eradicate the curse.

These prolegomena, protracted though they might appear, are the sine qua non for an adequate understanding of the tensions let loose in the three hours of darkness that culminate in the final dereliction, the cornerstone that supports the edifice of the seven utterances.

The Mediator in the abandonment

Why do exegetes sometimes come up with the most hair-brained theological conclusions that are manifestly not justified by their exegesis? There is something mysterious about it, perverse even, but it cannot be discounted that there are scandalous meanings in Scripture that they find highly undesirable. The Catholic scholar from Québec, Lorraine Caza, has written a monumental piece on the fourth utterance. Throughout her argument she informs us repeatedly that

> The scene of Jesus' death is essentially a confession of the identity of Jesus and not a narration of his dying act . . . [the moment of the cry of dereliction is focused upon to reveal] the identity of Jesus, and perhaps more the identity of the God of Jesus . . . The dying word of Jesus is language about Jesus and language about God . . . language about powerlessness and language expressing perplexity and incomprehension concerning the meaning of what is happening.[58]

To put it in a nutshell, for Caza God makes himself known not as the great thaumaturge, but the one who heals by meeting man where man is abandoned by God.[59] Is there a more feasible explanation than that God identifies with human powerlessness in order to gain the victory over sin through it? Is not Jesus the

---

58. Caza, *Mon Dieu*, pp. 172, 227, 328, 334. Translation mine.
59. Ibid., p. 335.

forsaken one, and God the one who abandons him? Is this theological interpretation feasible in the light of the fourth utterance?

The fundamental idea developed in this section is that while the abandonment of Christ is progressive, *this* point is its zenith. The cry of dereliction is the Mediator's word. What we know of God in relation to the cross, we know only through his experience. Jesus gives voice to something he has experienced from the olive press to the Place of the Skull that climaxes in the three hours of darkness. When Jesus cried *Eloi*, he had *already* experienced the catastrophic judgment in the abandonment and despairs of life, knowing that sin-bearing leads to condemnation that issues in death.[60]

The enigma of abandonment

When human activity ceases, during the three hours, divine activity continues in a confrontation that involves the Father and the Son alone. Christ has suffered all that his human persecutors can serve up, down to the bitterness of seeing his own betray him and flee. He has tasted anticipatory anguish in the garden and the dregs of human injustice. There is little of human suffering, if any, Jesus did not experience either before the cross or on it. The words he utters now, once he has severed his ties with humanity, are not just a reaction to injustice and physical pain, nor the distress of a dying man. They may well be all that can be said about any death in extreme circumstances, but they are a lot more. The 'Why' conveys something that defies understanding. The Son is bewildered by the seeming absence of the Father, an absence that strikes him to the heart, as his whole human identity hitherto has been determined by his special relationship with the Father and their close communion.

The Son falls from the sphere of special grace to the level of common humanity, as the well-documented change of address

---

60. Cf. Gundry, *Mark*, pp. 966–967, on the progressive abandonment. The ideas that follow in this section are presented in popular form in my books *Entre ciel et terre* and *Cross Words: The Biblical Doctrine of the Atonement* (Fearn: Christian Focus, 2006), ch. 12.

from Father to 'My God' illustrates. This reflects a new situation, one that projects the Mediator back to the situation of the original garden and the God–man relationship that was fractured by human rebellion. Between God and the second Adam, there is a contract to be respected. Schilder says the confrontation is one between God and Jesus with the covenant of works on the table.[61] As is the case for each of Adam's descendents, the requirement is perfect obedience. Only this can merit the divine approval and blessing. In this light, there is something profoundly pathetic about the 'Why'. These reasons can be described as expressing a conflict between theology and experience, as Peter Craigie puts it in his commentary on Psalm 22:

> It is a mystery because it appears to be rooted in a contradiction, namely the apparent contradiction between theology and experience. Theology, based on the experience of the past, affirmed unambiguously that trust resulted in deliverance. Indeed it was of the essence of the covenant faith that those who trusted in the holy God would not be disappointed . . . but experience was altogether at odds with theology . . . the God of the covenant, who was believed not to have deserted his faithful people, appeared to have forsaken this worshiper who, in sickness, faced the doors of death.[62]

Jesus can identify with the sufferer of Psalm 22 for three reasons, at least.

First, Jesus is *the righteous Son of the covenant*, who from the inception of his ministry has been identified as the Son of God (Mark 1:11) and has known the approval of the transfiguration (9:2ff.) Throughout all his trials he has borne witness to his justice before the Father. Even when he foresees the desertion on the disciples' part, he can still say they 'will leave me alone. Yet I am not alone, for the Father is with me' (John 16:32). This confidence is rooted in the promise of Isaiah's first Servant Song:

---

61. Schilder, *Christ Crucified*, pp. 397–400.
62. P. C. Craigie, *Psalms 1–50*, Word Biblical Commentary 19 (Waco: Word, 1983), p. 199.

Behold my servant, whom I uphold,
  my chosen, in whom my soul delights . . .
  I will take you by the hand and keep you . . .
(Isa. 42:1, 6)

Jesus believes that only those who forsake God will be forsaken
(2 Chr. 12:5; 15:2; 24:20; Jer. 2; 12:5ff.; cf. Deut. 31:6–8). The dereliction Christ undergoes cannot be the result of a withdrawal of
divine approval, paternal love or grace and favour. Either that, or
Jesus reacted in revolt like Jeremiah, that God had 'deceived' him,
an impossible thought (cf. Jer. 20:7–18).

Second, even as he prays 'My God' Jesus recognizes *the proximity
of the Father*, and this heightens the awfulness of the abandonment.[63] All through his ministry Jesus' message has been the
nearness of God and his kingdom. The programme of his work
on earth is 'He who sent me is with me. He has not left me alone,
for I always do the things that are pleasing to him . . . Father, I
thank you that you have heard me. I knew that you always hear me'
(John 8:29; 11:41). The word of dereliction conveys that in this situation Jesus learns something that is against all his experience and
expectations. The abandonment creates profound tension with his
holiness and divine anointing, and Christ has to rise to the test and
'through the eternal Spirit offered himself without blemish to
God' (Heb. 9:14).

A third and final paradoxical element lies in the fact that Jesus'
obedience to the will of God was and is complete. It can hardly be imagined that he was unaware of his own impeccability and the fact
that he had, in practice, always done the will of the Father. Even
when assailed to the extremity, the righteous Son *knows* that this is
the way. He himself prophesied death as being necessary – the
dei – to fulfil the Scriptures and all righteousness (cf. Matt.
16:21–28; 17:22–23; 20:17–19, 28). Moreover, he made the pledge
to drink the cup to the end in order to do the divine will with a
solemn engagement: 'not as I will, but as you will' (Matt. 26:39).
He had acted with assurance as Saviour by snatching a thief from

---

63. Caza, *Mon Dieu*, pp. 328–330.

the jaws of hell even while hanging on the cross. In addition to all this, he had Psalm 22 on his side, a psalm that 'weds the motif of suffering to that of eschatological victory . . . and revelation of God's kingdom'.[64] Would he not also be delivered from the 'mouth of the lion' and the 'bulls of Bashan'? Is not the initial despair transcended by trust and expectation of deliverance expressed in the following way?

Psalm 22
- God reigns: 3, 28
- God is to be praised: 3, 22–23
- trust that God will deliver: 4–5, 8, 20–21, 31
- presence/empowering of God: 11, 19, 24, 26
- deliverance from enemies: 12, 13, 21
- proclamation: 22, 25, 30–31
- the nations: 27[65]

The enigma is that Jesus knows all this to be true, but falls prey to contrary experience. He had to come to the first verse of the psalm as a depiction of the reality that he has been, and is, abandoned.

Yet the amazing thing is that even under this intense pressure Jesus does not waver in his faith. He *feels* the opposite of what he *knows* and yet he continues to trust. This is surely the acme of human resistance: Jesus is strong as steel. Feeling as he does he continued to implore the Father, with the reinforced repetition of '*My* God', claiming the right to call God his own in spite of adverse evidence. God's silence and his enemies' taunts keep Jesus in the line of faith and stretch his will to believe to its limits: 'He trusts in God; let God deliver him now, if he desires him. For he said, "I am the Son of God"' (Matt. 27:43; cf. Ps. 22:8). Continuing steadfast, Jesus knew in reality what David had intuited in hyperbole.

---

64. Marcus, *Way of the Lord*, p. 181.
65. Ibid., adapted from Marcus, who claims that 2 Tim. 4:17–18 and Heb. 2:12–13 are also midrash of Ps. 22.

Because of the non-intervention of God, only one possibility remains for filial obedience – to keep on keeping on, to hope against hope in the word of God and its promises as the bulwark against the storm of suffering. Jesus is racked between his faithful obedience to the Father and God's silence, torn by the antinomy of 'My' God and apparent rejection. The abandonment of the Son in such circumstances seems impossible. Jesus has shown all the attributes of true faithfulness, and has no reward for his pain. No justification can be found for this paradox either in the person of the Son himself, or in his perfect humanity, or in the way in which he has accomplished his mission. However, here he hangs – the just for the condemned, the blessed for the cursed, the holy for the unrighteous, the elect in the place of the reprobate! Does he remember 'Yet I have loved Jacob but Esau I have hated' (Mal. 1:2–3)? So *why* should he be here?

The depths of abandonment

Note that Jesus does not ask God not to abandon him but why he has done it.[66] This is the reality of it: Jesus has been forsaken by *God*. 'His cry expresses the profound horror of separation from God' and the temptation to cushion the offence of the passionate outburst must be resisted.[67]

If, in a sense, the deepest meaning of the cry will always escape our understanding for the simple reason that only Jesus has undergone this experience, the reality of it should not be doubted. Utter misery, hopelessness, angst and terror characterize the horror of God separating himself from Christ. The word of dereliction 'contains the concentrated anguish of the world'.[68]

However, a coherent theological reason must be sought to elucidate the divine withdrawal from the Son. An analysis of the emotions of the Son will not do the trick. Neither depression, psychological anguish, despair, revolt against physical suffering,

---

66. *Sabachthani* in Aramaic is a perfect, indicating a completed action. Cf. Caza, *Mon Dieu*, p. 328.

67. Lane, *Gospel According to Mark*, pp. 572–573.

68. Spurgeon, *Treasury of the New Testament*, p. 671.

resentment at not being heard, nor even the old idea that the abandonment was felt and not real, begin to scratch the surface of the
human catastrophe of the cross.[69] It was felt because it was real and
it was real because it was felt. Jesus was not under any illusions.
Furthermore, to propose it was death 'in' God, the death 'of' God
or even that 'God is abandoned by God'[70] introduces a non-biblical
metaphysical question into a subject that, in any case, is inaccessible
to our comprehension. The consideration that the Son was abandoned *by* the Father keeps exegesis on a concrete tack.

What then is the reality of the abandonment in question? Some
commentators referring to the meaning of *sabachthani* as also being
'to forget', conclude that it is simply the absence of God that is felt
and not any negative judgment. This seems unsatisfactory to me.[71]
Because the abandonment concerns God and Jesus, there is something unfathomable about it, as there is concerning all the relations
between the different persons of the Trinity. It is as mysterious as the
eternal generation of the Son, his incarnation, or the procession of
the Holy Spirit. Such a consideration should make us lose our
appetite for speculation. Perhaps it is precisely for this reason that the
New Testament witnesses are so restrained and discrete. However, it
can be said that just as in all the external operations of the persons of
the Trinity there is no separation or division (*opera trinitatis ad extra
indivisa sunt*); even in the extremity of the cry of dereliction we cannot
suppose there is any division, separation or opposition in the *personal*
sense existing between the Father and his Son.[72]

---

69. Cf. G. Pella, 'Pourquoi tu m'as abandonné? Marc 15.33–39', *Hokhma* 39
    (1988), pp. 3–24.

70. As John R. W. Stott does, without much reference to Moltmann's *Crucified
    God*. See Stott's *The Cross of Christ* (Leicester: IVP, 1986), chs. 6, 13. Cf. the
    critique by D. Cobb, 'Les deux natures de Christ au Calvaire', *Hokhma* 67
    (1998), pp. 19–44.

71. On the precise wording of the cry, see Brown, *Death of the Messiah*, vol. 2,
    pp. 1051 ff., and particularly concerning the Codex Bezae, 'why have you
    reviled me', p. 1055.

72. See the recent article by B. McCormack, 'The Ontological
    Presuppositions of Barth's Doctrine of the Atonement', in C. E. Hill and

Hans Urs von Balthasar has discussed the idea of kenosis at different levels in the Father–Son relationship. At the highest transcendent level a hint of kenosis already exists in the fact that, in his position as Son, the Son is the object of eternal generation from the Father, which provides the deep rooting for the incarnation and finally for the ultimate kenosis of the abandonment (Phil. 2:8).[73] However, because kenotic distinctions are fraught with difficulties, perhaps the farthest we can go is to say that the position of the Son, in terms of trinitarian relations, is germane to incarnation and abandonment.

The best way to avoid freewheeling speculation is to think concretely of the position and function of Jesus in the covenant. The dereliction is certainly catastrophic; it corresponds to the covenant curse in which are joined the preterative aspects of withdrawal of communion, absence, favour and intimacy and the reprobative aspects of rejection and judgment.[74] Jesus on the cross is outside the gates of Jerusalem and outside the Father's sheepfold, rejected from the people of God and pushed away from fellowship with the Father. The covenant relation with its affection, blessing, mutual joy, the signs of fellowship, assurance of the love of God and salvation have all melted like dew in the sun. There is no table in this valley of the shadow of death. The paternal favours with which God surrounded his fragile and wayward people in the old covenant are cancelled, as Jesus is rejected from the covenant and the promises. Dereliction will issue in death: 'According to Scripture death is related to sin as its just reward. The Bible everywhere views human death not as a *natural* but as a *penal* event. It is an alien intrusion into God's good world . . .'[75]

F. A. James (eds.), *The Glory of the Atonement* (Leicester: Apollos, 2004), pp. 346–366, on the 'ontological significance of penal substitution' and the joint action of the Trinity, p. 364: 'The triune God pours his wrath out on himself in and through the human nature he has made his own.'

73. Balthasar, *Mysterium Paschale*, ch. 1.

74. Cf. Schilder, *Christ Crucified*, chs. 6–7.

75. Stott, *Cross of Christ*, pp. 64–65.

However, in the covenant, Christ acts officially as representative and Mediator for others. When he is abandoned on the cross, it is not his *person* that is abandoned, as if the anger of God were against him as Son. Christ in his *function* is the object of desertion, because of the role he assumes for others. God was never for an instant angry with Christ, the beloved Son, but was at odds with sin.[76] His retribution was not against the person of Christ in the way a person's anger can be directed at another or at an object. In the function of Mediator he assumed for others, Christ acted with and for God and took the anger of God on himself. Forgiveness is not wrung from a violent and grudging God. Instead, Christ is the subject and the object of his own acts. By taking the anger of God against sin on himself, and dying for it, he obtained forgiveness for sinners.[77]

So if it is wholly true that Jesus was really abandoned by God, and if he cruelly felt the absence of communion with the Father in dereliction, the catastrophe was not undergone as a rupture or separation from God. Its reality is more complex, more unfathomable. Christ lived through abandonment at one with the Father; what he lacked was the irradiation in his suffering person of the consolations of the Holy Spirit.

Considered in another light, the abandonment of Christ can be related to the law of the covenant. God's law cannot condemn Jesus. On the contrary, it must exonerate him as the just and righteous one. Sinners alone merit abandonment and judgment under the stipulations of the law. Thus, when Christ in his fourth utterance expresses the reality of his situation, he is not verbalizing his own personal problem with regard to divine law. Officially, he occupies the place of others, and does so as their representative and covenant head.

Dereliction is the real experience of Christ, since he has renounced his personal rights and privileges as the beloved Son in order to assume responsibility for his people. He acts, however,

---

76. Calvin, *Institutes* 2.16.11–12.
77. Cf. J. I. Packer, 'What Did the Cross Achieve? The Logic of Penal Substitution', *Tyndale Bulletin* 25 (1974), pp. 25 ff.

constantly and persistently as God's only begotten, believing in the promise of divine deliverance. *Eli, Eli* invokes God as 'my Powerful One', even if it is the lament of grief, because of the indissoluble 'Why' that hangs heavily in the air.

It is to the 'Why' that we now address our attention.

Theological interpretation of the word of dereliction

This is where the rubber hits the road. Because of the mystery that like the darkness shrouded Christ's suffering for three hours, theological interpretation of the word of dereliction will depend to some extent on the intuitive and creative discernment of the theologian. In the first instance, I propose to make some general observations relating to the abandonment and the main models of the atonement. Second, I shall present some specific questions: Was the abandonment a judgment, was it hell and what does it mean in terms of trinitarian doctrine?

The abandonment and models of the atonement

Models of the atonement are many and varied but can be reduced to three fundamental paradigms: those of *example*, of *victory* and of *substitution* (or the 'commercial' model) – often attached to the names of their chief exponents, Abelard, Origen and Anselm.[78] When the question as to the theological meaning of the word of dereliction is raised, one way of tackling the issue is to ask which theological model might be most compatible with it and what that would imply for salvation.

Theories that insist on the example of the cross can appeal to it as an example of endurance in suffering and sacrificial love, but

---

78. P. Wells, *Cross Words*, ch. 2. Cf. C. Gunton, *The Actuality of Atonement* (Edinburgh: T. & T. Clark, 1998), for a detailed discussion of models and metaphors in atonement theology. B. B. Warfield speaks about five theories of atonement and demonstrates that the model of penal substitution is as well attested in the Christian tradition as others. See his articles in *The Works of Benjamin B. Warfield*, vol. 9 (Grand Rapids: Baker, 1981).

the example remains on an illustrative level only, and there can be no exact repetitions. It has indirect significance and has to be transferred on to another level of meaning in order to function as an example.[79] Christ presents an exhortatory model of persever-ance, self-giving and oblation in love as an example for other situations in which abnegation is required. However, the example does not save from anything and depends on imitation for its effectiveness. This leads to the conclusion that the exemplary model cannot convey the unique sense of the fourth utterance and the role of Christ as Mediator between God and man. Since it actually accomplishes nothing for others, it is inadequate as an interpretation of the varieties of New Testament witnesses about the cross.

The victory model has achieved great popularity today but not because of its prominence in the apostolic witness, in spite of the claims made to this effect by Gustav Aulén in his epoch-making work *Christus Victor*.[80] It provides a safe haven for those seeking refuge from substitutionary atonement in one form or another and from what is considered to be a rationalistic and juridical logic of exchange that obscures the excessive love of God in salvation. Sometimes the popularity of this model is considered to be a litmus test of a shift from modernism to postmodernism.[81] In the

---

79. An interesting case of this procedure is the influential work of French anthropologist René Girard, although there are some elements of the victory motif in his thought. Girard has recently expressed his desire to reconsider the notion of sacrifice in Hebrews. Cf. P. Wells, 'Sacred Violence and the Cross: A Dialogue with René Girard', in D. van Keulen and M. Brinkman (eds.), *Christian Faith and Violence*, vol. 2 (Zoetermeer: Meinema, 2005), pp. 192–201.

80. G. Aulén, *Christus Victor* (London: SPCK, 1931). Contributing to this current trend are H. Boersma, J. B. Green, M. D. Baker, J. G. Stackhouse, J. Denny Weaver, W. Wink, M. Winter, N. T. Wright, an overwhelming majority of Roman Catholic biblical scholars and, on a popular level, S. Chalke.

81. Cf. e.g. K. J. Vanhoozer, 'The Atonement in Postmodernity: Guilt, Goats and Gifts', in Hill and James, *Glory of the Atonement*, pp. 367–404.

context of the fourth utterance it seems obvious that there is an incompatibility between abandonment and victory, unless one argues something like this – Christ won the victory because he resisted the temptation to give up or because in his dereliction he paradoxically overcame the devil. An appeal to the seven utterances as a whole is required, as the catastrophic aspects of abandonment already considered seem incompatible with any normal understanding of victory.[82]

The ingenuity of Roman Catholic scholars knows no bounds in this respect: many megabytes have been devoted to the task of reconciling dereliction and victory. In many cases an appeal is made to a dialectic between power and weakness, as Christ abandons all forms of power in order to become powerless. Francine Bigaouette's five-hundred-page book on the subject examines the themes of the judgment and the anger of God in relation to the fourth utterance; her remarkable conclusion is that it is a case of neither one nor the other:

> the objective abandonment of Jesus, that is the non-intervention of God to deliver him from his adversaries, is the occasion for a loss of consciousness of the presence of the Father; it constitutes the act by which God *judges the perversity of humans who reject the Son*. In this act of judgment, the divine anger is totally absorbed by a love that loses none of its power in victorious resistance over sin. Jesus is no more the object or the receptacle of divine anger than are human beings, although he accomplishes an act of destructive judgment on sin in total communion with the Father by giving himself over in love to the power of sinners.[83]

---

82. An excellent evaluation of the victory motif is H. Blocher, '*Agnus Victor*: The Atonement as Victory and Vicarious Punishment', in J. G. Stackhouse (ed.), *What Does it Mean to Be Saved?* (Grand Rapids: Baker, 2002), pp. 23–36.

83. Bigaouette, *Le cri*, p. 351. Translation and italics mine. The language of 'absorbing' anger is often a feature of victory theology. It is used by P. T. Forsyth, C. F. D. Moule, F. M. Young and P. S. Fiddes in their writings on the atonement, as well as in J. Goldingay (ed.), *Atonement Today* (London: SPCK, 1995). See H. Blocher's criticism in 'The Sacrifice of Jesus Christ:

From this point of view there is no wrath or anger of God in the word of dereliction, nor is Christ considered to be in our place. It is an invitation for us to participate with him in the victory of the love of God over perversity. The fourth utterance reveals the proximity of God and it is God's loving reply to our cries and weakness.[84]

There is a dual problem with this and other victory theories in general. On the one hand, as with the exemplary argument, it is difficult to tally the *dereliction* and victory without indulging in theological acrobatics. Is it a victory for God to abandon his own Son to this fate? Can the desertion be called an act of love? How can it absorb human perversity and defeat it? Do the power and weakness of God function in terms of a dialectical opposition that finds its synthesis in an unexpected victory? On the other hand, the victory model implies salvation through participation or identification. It can be made representational only by stretching the meaning of victory by saying something like 'Christ won the victory in our favour', which introduces a form of substitutionary language into the equation. As such, the victory theme falls short of what a theology of mediation or representative headship requires. For this reason it is difficult to link it with the application of salvation in justification and the imputation of righteousness. A victory can be imputed to another only in daring flights of imagination.[85]

The substitutionary model fares better and when combined with elements of truth in the first two models (because Christ *is* an

---

Footnote 83 (cont.)

    The Current Theological Situation', *European Journal of Theology* 8.1 (1999), pp. 23–36. Cf. Wells, *Cross Words*, pp. 141–144.

84. Ibid., pp. 468 ff. Bigaouette follows the lead of Caza, *Mon Dieu*, 419 ff., 507 ff. This trend in Roman scholarship stems from S. Lyonnet and L. Sabourin, *Sin, Redemption and Sacrifice: A Biblical and Patristic Study* (Rome: Biblical Institute Press, 1970).

85. This appears to explain why the victory theory and the so-called covenant nomism of the 'new perspective on Paul' tally; e.g. in the thought of N. T. Wright.

example and he *did* win a victory[86]), provides a more satisfactory context for understanding the cry of dereliction. It finds its most complete expression in vicarious punishment, or the penal aspect of substitution.[87] As the covenant representative, the Mediator stood in the place of his people to fulfil their obligations in full and complete righteousness and obedience, as well as taking on the consequences of their sin in judgment and death. 'In our place condemned he stood / sealed our pardon with his blood' is an apt portrayal of the role assumed by the Man of Sorrows.[88]

The notion of penal substitution dovetails with the biblical vocabulary concerning what occurred at the cross in the broadest perspective: sacrifice, ransom, redemption, expiation, propitiation, reconciliation, justification and imputation of justice. If Christ was actually in our place, the place of sinners, and in our humanity, it is no wonder that the abandonment was a real experience for him. The Father abandoned his beloved Son to the covenant curse, suffering and death. Can the exemplary or the victory motif provide a satisfactory answer to *why* this should be so? I think not. The dereliction was too much of a catastrophe for Christ himself for it to be interpreted in these terms.

Salvation comes through judgment. The apocalyptic signs of darkness, the loud cry and the rending of the temple veil, as we have already seen, all imply this. The acceptance of the cup by Christ and the fact that God 'did not spare his own Son but gave him up for us all' (Rom. 8:32; cf. John 3:16), language used in the Synoptics to describe the fate of Christ as the one who is sacrificed, confirm the impression that he died for sin (Mark 9:31; 10:33, 45; 14:41).

---

86. Wells, *Cross Words*, ch. 9.

87. Ibid., ch. 11. To say that Christ suffered 'on our behalf' (cf. J. McLeod Campbell, *The Nature of the Atonement* [Edinburgh: Hansel; Grand Rapids: Eerdmans, 1999], ch. 12, the theory of 'vicarious repentance') falls short of the biblical *hyper*, 'in our place' (Latin, *pro nobis*). See the recent article by A. T. B. McGowan, 'The Atonement as Penal Substitution', in A. T. B. McGowan (ed.), *Always Reforming* (Leicester: Apollos, 2006), pp. 183–210, for a useful overview on the subject.

88. Philip P. Bliss, 'Man of Sorrows' (nineteenth century).

Abandonment:

> God is the acting subject who because of his covenant and his justice
> gives up Israel to her enemies, to captivity (Lev 26.25, Dt 28.15ss).
> This act of God is in each instance an act of judgment, an act of
> divine anger. The one who is abandoned . . . is disposed of by God as
> his enemy.[89]

If Jesus is 'given over' by God, a passive expression, he is also
active in that he gives himself up in love (Mark 10:45; John
10:17–18; Rom. 3:25; Gal. 2:20; Eph. 5:2, 25; 1 John 4:10).

> None other than God was capable of *this* liquidation, certainly not a
> man, a sinner before God . . . only God could do it. Being incarnate in
> Christ he is in one person, 'subject and object' of judgment and of
> justification, standing beside men in order to defend for them the cause
> of God.[90]

Was the cry of dereliction an expression of judgment on Jesus,
did he experience hell, is propitiation in view here? Of course we
do not pretend it is possible to get pat answers to these questions
on the grounds of an exegesis of the fourth utterance alone.
However, in the light of the teaching of Jesus, the context of the
seven utterances as a whole and the apostolic witness of the New
Testament, the penal substitutionary theory is the most adequate
interpretation for the fourth utterance.

The meaning of the abandonment

The abandonment is not just a sign of a temporal judgment like
historical expectation of the Day of the Lord in the Old
Testament.[91] Nor is it only as in the case of the sufferer of Psalm
22, 'the terror of mortality in the absence of God and the presence

---

89. W. Popkes, *Christus Traditus* (Zurich: Zwingli, 1967), pp. 25, 41. Balthasar,
　　Mysterium Paschale, ch. 3, sect. d.
90. Balthasar, *Mysterium Paschale*, ch. 3, sect. f.
91. For the following section, see Wells, *Cross Words*, pp. 161–163.

of enemies . . . [and] God, in Jesus, entering into and participating in the terror of mortality'.[92] There was also something final about the cry of dereliction. The Son also tasted the supernatural reality of the judgment of hell. In the Old Testament, the absence of God is a descent into Sheol, the place of separation where there is no possible communion with God. No praise can rise from this place; the faithful earnestly desire deliverance from it and restoration to the land of the living:

> Therefore my heart is glad, and my whole being rejoices;
>   my flesh also dwells secure.
> For you will not abandon my soul to Sheol,
>   or let your holy one see corruption.
>
> You make known to me the path of life;
>   in your presence there is fullness of joy;
> at your right hand are pleasures forevermore.
>   (Ps. 16:10–11; cf. Pss 86:13; 103:2–4; 116:1–6)

The abandonment of Christ bears the mark of hell in three ways: in physical suffering, in spiritual affliction, and in divine judgment.

First, Jesus experienced judgment in his human nature during the three hours of darkness. The 'rights of man' have no place at the cross. All possibility of physical movement was removed from Jesus, neither could anything more be said – the Word incarnate was silent before his mockers. His lips were sealed (Isa. 53:7). The most terrible thing of all might well be that Christ was also deprived of freedom of thought, mentally bound and tormented as he was by the curse of the cross (Gal. 2:13). The incoherence of such suffering in the light of his spotless humanity was a great contradiction to bear. This judgment cannot have been merited and the thought must have preyed constantly on a holy mind. No aspect of his human constitution could have escaped the awareness that God had left him to unjust deserts.

---

92. Craigie, *Psalms 1–50*, p. 203.

Second, there was spiritual suffering implied in being excluded from the presence of God. The code of Sheol is the opposite of the law of God – it is the practice of hatred of others (Isa. 14:9–15). Jesus had already tasted it to the full and he would do so once again before he lamented his desertion. Furthermore, he would be mocked in his very God-forsakenness. 'Behold, he is calling Elijah . . . Wait, let us see whether Elijah will come to take him down' (Mark 15:35–36).[93] Concretely, on the cross Jesus was cut off from any communication with other human beings or with God and the consolation and support it could have afforded. It was spiritual quarantine on desolation row. The Son was truly 'despised and rejected by men, a man of sorrows . . . cut off out of the land of the living'. He 'was numbered with the transgressors; yet he bore the sin of many' (Isa. 53:3, 8, 12).

Third, when 'heaven hides, only hell remains'.[94] No-one can really know what this meant, as final, yet eternal, punishment in the lake of fire lies in the future (Rev. 20:15). The particular extremity of the suffering of Christ arose neither from human opposition, nor from physical pain.

> The punishment of desertion, suffered by Christ was not only a bodily but a spiritual and internal suffering. It arose not from any torment he could feel in his body, but from a most oppressive knowledge that God's wrath rests on him on account of sins . . . God suspending for a little while the favourable presence of grace and the influx of consolation and happiness that he might be able to suffer all the punishment due for sin.[95]

How agonizing it must have been for the Son of God to feel the pain of divine desertion because of his identity with sinners in

---

93. There is much speculation about the reference to Elijah. See Gundry, *Mark*, p. 967; Brown, *Death of the Messiah*, vol. 2, pp. 1043ff. Perhaps it is nothing more than the ranting of a demented crowd grasping at straws.

94. R. Stier, *The Words of the Lord Jesus*, vol. 7 (Edinburgh: T. & T. Clark, 1873), p. 484.

95. F. Turretin, *Institutes of Elenctic Theology*, vol. 2 (Phillipsburg: Presbyterian & Reformed, 1992), p. 354.

judgment! What meaning does reconciliation have if not precisely this – 'For our sake he [God] made him to be sin who knew no sin, so that in him we might become the righteousness of God' (2 Cor. 5:21)?

The abandonment of Christ corresponds to a descent into hell, as Christ knew full well that the Father rejects only the wicked. 'He was suffering the pains of hell. What the Father wanted to say to the Son was this: Have you desired to suffer the passion of hell? Then you must do so fully aware that you are doing so.'[96] He tasted the bitterest anguish because while he looked to God in faith, love and trust, he found that he was not accompanied in or saved from the ordeal. For three traumatic hours Christ knew the pangs of hell as if he were a sinner under the lash of divine judgment. 'This cry is like the lamentation of those who are abandoned for ever.'[97]

Was Golgotha more horrible than Christ had imagined it would be when he was in Gethsemane? For a moment, seeming to lose filial awareness, terror absorbed all his conscious faculties and the great cry rose from the depths of his being.[98] Tormented, bewildered, finding himself as it were in hell without belonging there, Christ strained for heaven but was transfixed, as it were, by the divine condemnation he was undergoing. Only he could have stood up to this soul-destroying paradox without total despair. On the cross he sank into man's hell of judgment to break its power. 'Dying on the cross, forsaken by his Father . . . it was damnation – and damnation taken lovingly.'[99]

The cry of dereliction was the conclusion to the unspeakable agony combining suffering and longing. Christ seems to have known torments comparable to those of hell: a giving-over to the absence of God and the death that ensues were to be the conclusion to this judgment. Every person dies for his or her own sin; the

---

96. Schilder, *Christ Crucified*, p. 373.

97. J. Flavel, *Works*, vol. 2 (Edinburgh: Banner of Truth, 1968), p. 409.

98. See D. Macleod's fine section on Jesus' emotions in *The Person of Christ* (Leicester: IVP, 1998), ch. 6.

99. Quoted by A. Moody Stuart, *The Life of John Duncan* (Edinburgh: Banner of Truth, 1991), p. 105.

'wages of sin is death' and 'it is appointed for man to die once, and after that comes judgment' (Rom. 6:23; Heb. 9:27). Christ who knew no sin could not die because of sin; his death was the result of his undergoing judgment for the sins of those for whom he died. It was his lot as Mediator to taste the punishments of hell before knowing death. This may well be the key to the profound loss expressed by the fourth utterance. God 'put forward' Jesus Christ 'as a propitiation by his blood': first, propitiation, and then blood, meaning death (Rom. 3:25).[100] 'It is a striking example of the wrath of God, that he did not spare his only Son, and was appeased by no other means than this as the price of expiation.'[101]

Finally, what was the meaning of the cry of dereliction for Jesus in respect to his incarnate complexity, two natures in one person? Jürgen Moltmann's position is well known:

> Here, in the relationship between the Father and the Son, a death was
> experienced which has been rightly described as 'eternal death', 'the
> death of God'. Here 'God' is forsaken by 'God'. If we take the
> relinquishment of the Father's name in Jesus' death cry seriously, then
> this is even the breakdown of the relationship that constitutes the very
> life of the Trinity: if the Father forsakes the Son, the Son does not
> merely lose his sonship. The Father loses his fatherhood as well.[102]

I must demur, challenging though Moltmann may be. Not only are we a long stop from exegesis, but also from the confessions of the Reformed churches that link the cry to the suffering of Jesus in his humanity.[103] Christ was on the cross, says Calvin, as

---

100. See the articles by D. A. Carson and R. Gaffin on the subject of propitia-
     tion and atonement in Pauline theology, in Hill and James, *Glory of the
     Atonement*, pp. 119–162; and G. Williams, 'The Cross and the
     Punishment of Sin', in D. Petersen (ed.), *Where Wrath and Mercy Meet*
     (Carlisle: Paternoster, 2001), pp. 68–98.
101. Calvin, *Commentaires sur l'Harmonie Évangélique*, p. 206.
102. J. Moltmann, *The Trinity and the Kingdom of God* (London: SCM, 1981), p. 80.
103. H. Blocher, *Le mal et la croix* (Méry-sur-Oise: Ed. Sator, 1990), pp. 99–105,
     points out the influence of Hegel on Moltmann's thought about

though God 'had withdrawn from him all hope of life . . . in *our person* he suffered the curse for our sin that separated us from God'.[104]

As a man, Jesus suffered with us and like us, but primarily for us. God 'by sending his own Son in the likeness of sinful flesh and for sin, he condemned sin in the flesh' (Rom. 8:3). But in and through this suffering the unity of the Trinity was unbroken and unbreakable:

> The mysterious unity of the Father and the Son rendered it possible for God at once to endure and to inflict penal suffering, and to do both under conditions which constitute the infliction and the endurance of the grandest moment in the moral history of God.[105]

The struggle endured at the cross does not speak of a rupture between the Father and the Son; rather, it lay in the ripping the Son experienced in his personal thoughts and in his own emotions. It was divine judgment working from the inside out. The answer to question 68 in the Geneva Catechism is instructive :

- Since he is God Himself, how could he be in such dread, as if He were forsaken by God?
- According to his human nature He was in that extremity; and that in order to allow this, His Deity held itself back a little, as if concealed, that is, did not show its power.[106]

---

suffering and opposition within God, while noting the toning down in his later works of the more pointed statements in Moltmann's *The Crucified God*.

104. J. Calvin, Sermon sur Matthieu 27.45–54, 'Sermons sur la Passion', in G. Baum, E. Cunitz and R. Reuss (eds.), *Calvini Opera* (Brunswick: Schwetchke, 1863–1900), vol. 46, p. 920 (my italics).

105. R. W. Dale, *The Atonement* (London 1902), p. 393, quoted by L. Morris in his *The Cross in the New Testament* (Grand Rapids: Eerdmans, 1965), p. 49, n. 97.

106. T. F. Torrance (ed.), *The School of Faith* (Edinburgh: James Clarke, 1959), p. 16. Cf. Heidelberg Catechism, qu. 17.

If the deity of Christ held back from his humanity in the dereliction, it must have done so not only out of horror over the curse of sin, but also because of the intimate approval of the course of divine justice and acquiescence to the work of divine wrath. If we cannot begin to take the measure of the inner tension Jesus experienced under judgment, we know it must have been unbearable.

What were the roles of divinity and humanity in the unique person of Christ? His humanity suffered and died, but without divinity a simple human nature could not have survived the weight of the divine anger.[107] 'It was requisite that the Mediator should be God, that he might sustain and keep the human nature from sinking under the infinite wrath of God and the power of death; give worth and efficacy to his sufferings . . .'[108]

During the three hours Jesus experienced the curse of God against sin, and at the climax he knew the reality of despair by being forsaken. Without the empowering of his divine nature, he would never have reached that point; but then a great wave of anguish suddenly swept over his lost human soul, swamping him under the weight of the wrath of God. What did his divine nature experience when he uttered the dreadful cry? How could we ever know what the divine Son experienced even in an instant? 'Tis mystery all – to encroach further on the unity of the incarnate Son is mere speculation.

Some implications for Christian experience

We can only feel a sense of awe when contemplating the architecture of the plan of salvation and the intricate way in which the unity and diversity of the actions of the trinitarian persons come to light in the cry of dereliction. As we reflect upon it, the anguish of the lament can only make us more aware of the depths of

---

107. Cf. the comments of Z. Ursinus, *Commentary on the Heidelberg Catechism* (Phillipsburg: Presbyterian & Reformed, n.d.), pp. 87–88.

108. 'Westminster Larger Catechism', qu. 38, in *The Confession of Faith* (Edinburgh: Free Presbyterian Church of Scotland, 1967), pp. 145–146.

misery to which our Lord descended and the multiple dimensions of his suffering. Never, in the whole course of human history, have words so solemn, so laden with consequences, been conceived in the human conscience and articulated in audible speech. We can never exhaust the wonder of this moment.

In his abandonment, Jesus stooped and stood alongside men to assume the fate of sinners. What a Saviour! His tragic lament reflects in the most poignant possible way, without any gainsaying, the miserable plight of 'normal' men and women. There is no way of salvation for fallen humanity by *natural* procedures. It must be a gracious act of condescension. The only thing that can open heaven is the *supernatural* abandonment of the Son. Theological universalism, religious syncretism, as well as every ideology of salvation by human betterment flounder and shatter on the rock of the fourth utterance.

The predicament of Jesus in the abandonment throws light on the sense of human responsibility to the Lord God. Even when under judgment Jesus *had to* continue to believe in and obey God. Sinful man, who neither knows the blessing of the divine presence nor believes, is none the less under the obligation to believe and to recognize the demands of God's law. Rebellion against God does not make a person less responsible to the Creator; rather, sin maximizes the importance of obedience, because every person is still bound by the conditions of the covenant of works. Perseverance in sin makes condemnation and judgment inevitable. In his role as covenant Mediator Jesus fulfilled both aspects of the demand of the covenant: perfect faith and obedience, and punishment and death. 'The cry has a ruthless authenticity which provides the assurance that the price of sin has been paid in full.'[109]

Jesus suffered under the divine accusation, but continued to believe in the Father. His faith was unshaken and his eyes searched the darkened heavens for a trace of the divine love. Instead of becoming a prisoner to suffering, Jesus held to the divine promise. 'In the days of his flesh, Jesus offered up prayers and supplications, with loud cries and tears, to him who was able to save him

---

109. Lane, *Gospel According to Mark*, p. 573.

from death, and he was heard because of his reverence' (Heb. 5:7).[110] When God left him to dereliction, he did not abandon God. Jesus was neither mentally separated from, nor opposed to, his God. Should he struggle to reconcile the conflicting tensions of perfect righteousness and judgment in his holy consciousness, he did not fall prey to spiritual schizophrenia. He fulfilled his mission with singularity of intention. When Christ died, he did so not deserted but victorious over sin and death and with complete assurance of his acceptance by the Father (vv. 8–9). This is no sleight of hand to whitewash the dereliction: he descended to the deepest depths to rise to the greatest heights. In the seventh utterance, he transferred himself to the level of the Father to place his spirit in his hands. 'Just as the seventh day was the day of rest and satisfaction, so the seventh utterance of the Saviour brings Him to the place of rest – the Father's hands.'[111] As an old maxim states, 'It was not death that approached Christ, but the opposite: Christ died without dying.'[112]

'The Saviour *continued trusting* though there was *no* deliverance, trusted though "forsaken" for a season.'[113] For the believer, union with Christ is unity with the one who acted thus. Christ is the 'founder and perfecter' of faith (Heb. 12:2), its guarantor, and because he has lived out trust fully in a situation of abandonment, Christians know that when united to this Saviour, they can never be forsaken. This is an encouragement to look to Christ in times of affliction, to persevere and to believe. Faith unites with a victorious Saviour. The way Christ acted on the cross is the living proof of his promise 'I give them eternal life, and they will never perish, and no one will snatch them out of my hand' (John 10:28; 6:39).

---

110. Most commentators refer to the cup of Gethsemane, but these words also apply to the cross and the word of dereliction, where Christ's priestly ministry reached its goal (cf. Calvin).

111. Pink, *Seven Sayings*, p. 123.

112. Attributed to Sedulius (ninth century), quoted by A. Edersheim, *The Life and Times of Jesus the Messiah*, vol. 2 (London: Longmans, Green, n.d.), p. 609. Cf. Martin, 'Atonement', pp. 36–43.

113. Pink, *Seven Sayings*, p. 76.

In like manner, when subjected to physical suffering and spiritual testing, faith continues to look to the Father for salvation, even should it be buffeted by unanswerable questions and situations that appear to be hopeless. Faith in Christ unites us to the One who lived through the ultimate abandonment; union with him is a calling to conformity to his image and an exhortation to live now with the same spirit he demonstrated then.[114] In a day where it is so easy to point the finger against all sorts of superficiality and brash claims to well-being, this reminds us that there is no biblical promise that we shall be delivered *from* suffering in this world, but the promise of a faith that saves *through* suffering. 'Christ's faith remained intact in extreme torment, in such a way that while lamenting his forsakenness he never ceased from availing himself of the timely assistance of God.'[115]

Finally, meditation on the word of dereliction stimulates praise and thankfulness because here believers contemplate their just deserts. The judgment Christ suffered in a moment is the fate of lost sinners for eternity. Every sin is deserving of death and hell. For believers the fact that judgment has already taken place in Christ means salvation. When God sent his Son into the world, he sent him to die. The Son came freely and voluntarily to death row and laid down his life for his friends. 'God shows his love for us in that while we were still sinners, Christ died for us' (Rom. 5:8). This is indeed infinite love and grace, to which Christ's people are eternally debtors!

Conclusion

The word of dereliction expresses the extreme anguish and torment, both of body and soul, of the condemnation Christ experienced as retribution for rebellion against God. In our place he accepted judgment for judgment, hell for hell and death for death.

---

114. Cf. R. Gaffin, 'Union with Christ', in McGowan, *Always Reforming*, pp. 271–288, on the broad perspectives and present aspects of the union.
115. Calvin, *Commentaires sur l'Harmonie Evangélique*, p. 208.

His cry translated on to the page of history the impression branded on a holy conscience by the trauma of separation and judgment. The one who is righteous and just finds himself in *this* position.[116] He bears the brunt of an awesome responsibility and drinks the cup to the dregs: 'my God, to what *end* have you forsaken me?'[117]

Christ *had* to be alone under the curse because isolation was the prerequisite of mediation. Only the righteous Son of God could say, from the sinner's place, *Eloi, Eloi, lema sabachthani?* He alone had that *right*, he alone was the God-man, the only Mediator between God and man, the man Christ Jesus (1 Tim. 2:5).

Appendix: A theological reconstruction of the seven utterances from the cross

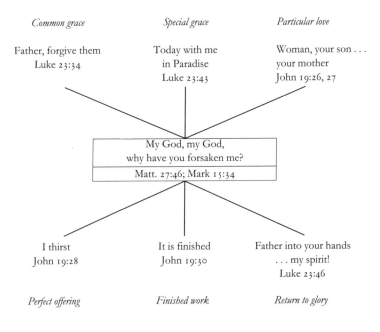

Common grace   *Special grace*   *Particular love*

Father, forgive them   Today with me   Woman, your son . . .
Luke 23:34   in Paradise   your mother
                         Luke 23:43   John 19:26, 27

My God, my God,
why have you forsaken me?
Matt. 27:46; Mark 15:34

I thirst   It is finished   Father into your hands
John 19:28   John 19:30   . . . my spirit!
                                                 Luke 23:46

Perfect offering   *Finished work*   *Return to glory*

---

116. Stier, *Words of the Lord Jesus*, p. 478.

117. So E. W. Hengstenberg, *Commentary on the Psalms*, vol. 1 (Cherry Hill, N. J.: Mack, n.d.), p. 369.

Explanation

1. Mediation is a specific action. It supposes something in common between the one who mediates and both sides for whom the action is undertaken, but also a distance from both sides. Mediation requires a distinction and an isolation from one and the other.

2. Jesus closes down his earthly ministry in the first three utterances and in the final three lays the foundation for his reception by the Father on the basis of his messianic understanding of salvation as a completed work. Mediation as isolation is totally germane to the location of the fourth utterance, which functions differently both from the first and the final triplet.

3. The reconstructed order of the seven utterances portrays the historical reality but also the meaning of mediation as isolation. There is a correspondence between the meaning of the events and the literary structure that highlights the capital and unique nature of the fourth utterance – Jesus on his own as the only Son abandoned, in the unique sacrifice for the one redemption, in an act that prefigures the final judgment.

4. Because Christ has undergone the judgment not only the right to resurrection is his, but also that of judgment of all flesh. There is progression *to* isolation and progression *from* isolation. As illustrated, each utterance has a specific function, but each utterance also has its foundation in the fourth utterance. As central, the fourth utterance justifies the existence of all the utterances from the cross and the teleological movement they express.

4. THE ASCENSION AND HEAVENLY MINISTRY OF CHRIST

Matthew Sleeman

Introduction: to bodily go where no man has gone before

Star Trek's famous split infinitive, thinly adjusted, makes a useful headline for introducing an examination of the heavenly Christ. To adopt one more slogan from *Star Trek*, Jesus' heavenly exist-ence during the period between his ascension and future return is 'life, but not as we know it', since the ascension decisively marks him out from all other humans as prophet, priest and king.[1] In practice, however, our Christologies too quickly blur or jump over Christ's heavenly life, marginalizing it as some-thing that cannot be known, or that does not have much bearing on our overall Christology. It becomes a misty valley between

---

1. Thomas F. Torrance, *Space, Time and Resurrection* (Edinburgh: Handsel, 1976), pp. 107–108, 112–122, proposes that Christ's ascension suggests an analytical order of king, priest and prophet for Christ's heavenly ministry. Cf. Gerrit Scott Dawson, *Jesus Ascended: The Meaning of Christ's Continued Incarnation* (London: T. & T. Clark, 2004), pp. 8–9.

the sunlit peaks of Christ's passion and his parousia. This chapter rejects such intimations, and proposes instead a more full-orbed understanding of what the Bible reveals concerning the heavenly Christ as necessary for our theology and integral to our discipleship.

Theological assumptions

This chapter assumes some fundamental theological premises. First, it is taken as a given, from the revelation of Scripture, that Christ rose bodily from the dead on the third day and that, having prepared a place for believers (John 14:3), he will return in glory to judge the living and the dead. Emphatically, at each turn, the Jesus of history *is* the Christ of faith.

Second, and obviously connected, it is axiomatic within all that follows that Jesus ascended – once again, bodily – into heaven.[2] His ascension has not disembodied him: it has not rendered him ubiquitous, far less has it reduced him simply to living 'in my heart'. Rather, Jesus has ascended as a man, has been received into heaven as a man, and will return to judge all people as a man, maintaining his incarnate humanity. At our resurrection, we shall meet him in resurrection bodies and he shall be no less or more corporeal than we shall be then.[3] Such is our heavenly citizenship: it is caught up with Christ, who is presently in heaven and cannot be divorced from the prospect of resurrection bodies (Phil. 3:20–21). Such is the upward call of God in Christ Jesus for all believers (Phil. 3:14), itself predicated upon God's prior exaltation of Jesus (Phil. 2:9).

Third, Christ's ascension into heaven is critical, public-sphere currency given that it confirms him as the Christ-Son of Psalm 2 who must be rightly acknowledged by all people. It sets priorities for the churches and judges the preoccupations of both church

---

2. This chapter also assumes that the New Testament presents a diverse but coherent concept of heaven. Cf. Ernest Best, *A Critical and Exegetical Commentary on Ephesians* (Edinburgh: T. & T. Clark, 1998), p. 115: 'The NT contains no unified concept of heaven.'

3. On this point, cf. Dawson, *Jesus Ascended*, pp. 3–9, 42–44, 51–52.

and world. All too often, as Geritt Scott Dawson expresses it, 'The World Is Too Much With Us'.[4] However, as Dawson declares, 'Recovering a proper and robust doctrine of the ascension can reconnect us to a sense of our true citizenship in heaven and the implications of that identity for life in the world.'[5] Properly attended to, the ascension provides a powerful antidote to crippling, chilling worldliness among the people of God. It forms a vital link within the glorious gospel metanarrative, which in turn provides a faithful plumb line for both involvement within, and separation from, the ways of the world. That the gospel is a Jesus-centred metanarrative cannot be denied,[6] and Jesus' ascension is a capstone within it. Its confession (cf. 1 Tim. 3:14–16) will eschew syncretism and consumer-oriented spirituality, and will fuel holistic Christian discipleship.

Hidden in embarrassment?

Yet the ascended Christ is hidden from us in at least two ways. The first is his obvious absence from our sight: Jesus is resolutely framed as having gone 'into heaven', the phrase being repeated four times within the only biblical description of the ascension event (Acts 1:10–11). This absence is signalled by the cloud of Acts 1:9, which remains impenetrable to mortal eyes despite four different expressions for 'seeing' being employed within Acts 1:9–11. This hiddenness is right and proper. The second dimension of the heavenly Christ's concealment is less obvious, but perhaps more profound for our Christological formulations, and – as this chapter will argue – this hiddenness should be challenged and reformed. This is the marginalization of the *heavenly* Christ, a concealment brought about by greater emphasis being placed upon Jesus' eternal pre-existence, his earthly ministry prior to his ascension, and his future return as ushering in the consummation of the

---

4. Ibid., pp. 13–27.

5. Ibid., p. 25.

6. D. A. Carson, *The Gagging of God: Christianity Confronts Pluralism* (Leicester: Apollos, 1996), esp. pp. 315–345. P. 434 makes explicit the heavenly dimension of the resultant Christian world view.

new heavens and new earth.[7] Clearly, such Christological topoi deserve our full attention but, as I shall argue, so too does the present (in time) but absent (in body) reality of the heavenly Christ.

The roots and risk of neglecting the heavenly Christ are clear within my own area of interest, Acts scholarship. There, a fixation with the physics (and metaphysics) of the ascension *event* has for too long clouded Luke's theology of Christ's ascended status. Thus, for example, it has been possible to write on 'the life of Jesus, after the ascension' (to quote the title of one published paper), but to make no mention of the ascension's impact within Acts beyond 1:11.[8] Where it has progressed further into Acts, reflection upon the ascended Christ within Acts rarely moves beyond isolated 'proof' texts such as 3:21.

Given my wider aims in this present discussion, the reasons for such preoccupation with the ascension event need only be sketched briefly. It has, at various turns, been fed by a narrowly materialist understanding of the ascension and an associated Enlightenment critique of such reductionism, compounded by the Enlightenment's own materialist reductionism. At a popular level, the presumptive confidence of such a dismissive world view was evident in April 1961 when Yuri Gagarin used part of his pioneering 89-minute orbit of the earth to radio back 'I don't see any God up here.' All too often, reduction of the ascension to a mere event has made the ascension somewhat embarrassing,[9] and has marginalized the heavenly Christ as an embarrassing skeleton located in an awkward cupboard.

---

7. This theological deflection – together with misunderstanding and uncertainty about the ascension as an event – is, I think, more significant in the ascension having become marginalized within Christian teaching than that the ascension is celebrated liturgically on a Thursday rather than a Sunday.

8. G. C. Fuller, 'The Life of Jesus, after the Ascension (Luke 24:50–53; Acts 1:9–11)', *Westminster Journal of Theology* 56 (1994), pp. 391–398.

9. Coming from a very different position, but resulting in similar reticence, 'There is no sense in trying to visualise the ascension as a literal event, like going up in a balloon. The achievements of Christian art in this field are among its worst perpetrations. But of course this is no reason why they should be used to make the whole thing ridiculous' (Karl Barth, *Church*

Hidden in heaven – but accessible from Earth

Within the orthodox creeds, however, there is no such embarrass-
ment because there is no such reduction – instead the creeds
present a more theological understanding of the heavenly Christ
that actually resists reduction simply to the event of the ascension,
but without rejecting the ascension as event. Rather than being
forced on to the back foot, therefore, Christian theology needs to
be robustly theological in its formulations of doctrine and in its
responses to those who are sceptical.[10] It is insufficient to accept,
and even to defend, sub-biblical rationalistic parameters for ascension discourse,[11] and it is wrong to reduce analysis of Scripture to
fit such a materialist agenda.[12]

Footnote 9 (cont.)

Dogmatics. Vol. 3: *The Doctrine of Creation Part 2,* ed. G. W. Bromiley and
T. F. Torrance, trans. G. W. Bromiley [Edinburgh: T. & T. Clark, 1960],
p. 453). Similarly, 'it was only Christian art which was not afraid to try to
depict it' (Karl Barth, *Church Dogmatics.* Vol. 4: *The Doctrine of Reconciliation
Part 2,* ed. G. W. Bromiley and T. F. Torrance, trans. G. W. Bromiley
[Edinburgh: T. & T. Clark, 1958], p. 153).

10. Cf. Bruce M. Metzger, 'The Meaning of Christ's Ascension', in J. M. Myers,
O. Reimherr and H. N. Bream (eds.), *Search the Scriptures: New Testament
Studies in Honor of Raymond T. Stamm* (Leiden: E. J. Brill, 1969), pp. 124–125,
concerning a schoolchild's literal-but-more understanding of moving to a
'higher' class; and Douglas Farrow, *Ascension and Ecclesia: On the Significance of
the Doctrine of the Ascension for Ecclesiology and Christian Cosmology* (Edinburgh:
T. & T. Clark, 1999), p. 39, recognizing that 'space travel was never in view',
even though there was *an* ascension. Cf. also C. S. Lewis, *Miracles: A
Preliminary Study* (London: Centenary, 1947), pp. 183–195; N. T. Wright, *The
Resurrection of the Son of God* (London: SPCK, 2003), pp. 654–655.

11. E.g. H. Latham, *The Risen Master: Sequel to Pastor Pastorum* (Cambridge:
Deighton Bell, 1926), pp. 380–382, who proposes that the cloud (Acts 1:9)
was low lying, so that as 'the visible body of our Lord rose to a great
height into the skies' (p. 381) the spectacle did not cause 'panic and wide-
spread commotion' (p. 381) among the citizens of Jerusalem.

12. Bultmann e.g. described Jesus as rising into the *kerygma* (gospel proclamation). In his 1941 essay 'New Testament and Mythology', Bultmann

In recent years, however, Christian theology has produced a resurgence of more nuanced thinking concerning the ascended Christ.[13] 'Heaven' is no longer an embarrassing destination: rather, 'Jesus ascended into heaven. He went to the "place" where God is . . . It is as simple and as difficult as that.'[14] In my own research I have drawn on the insights of contemporary geographical theory, which wrestles with similar questions concerning terrestrial space, drawing especially upon the work of Ed Soja. Like many geographers, Soja is seeking to understand the ways in which space shapes our reality. He wants to avoid reducing our understanding of space simply to material things or to ideas that exist separate from material things. His solution is a perspective on space he calls 'thirdspace', which, according to Soja, is 'simultaneously real [i.e. concerned with material things] and imagined [i.e. concerned with ideas about space] and more'.[15] Soja is not a Christian believer, and he does not apply his concept to heaven, but thirdspace seems to

---

judges that 'the stories of Christ's descent and ascent are finished' (Schubert M. Ogden [ed. and trans.], *Rudolph Bultmann: New Testament and Mythology and Other Basic Writings* [London: SCM, 1985 (1941)], p. 5). Clearly, however, Bultmann was not innovative in realizing the need to grapple with the nature of heaven (cf. e.g. Arthur J. Tait, *The Heavenly Session of our Lord: An Introduction to the History of the Doctrine* [London: Robert Scott Roxburghe House, 1912], pp. 212–223), and his reduction to *kerygma* is far from necessary. Dawson, *Jesus Ascended*, pp. 31–35, provides a brief but telling survey of such reductions across church history. See also Andrew Burgess, *The Ascension in Karl Barth* (Aldershot: Ashgate, 2004), pp. 162–187, engaging with Robert Jenson's understanding of Jesus' withdrawal into the church around the sacraments – a perspective Burgess, *Ascension in Karl Barth*, p. 198, rightly positions as neglecting Christ's ascension and heavenly session and as overplaying both church and the Supper.

13. This resurgence is evident in Torrance, *Space, Time and Resurrection*; Farrow, *Ascension and Ecclesia*; Burgess, *Ascension in Karl Barth*; and Dawson, *Jesus Ascended*.

14. Dawson, *Jesus Ascended*, pp. 39–42 (39).

15. Edward W. Soja, *Thirdspace* (Oxford: Blackwell, 1996), p. 11.

offer a fair summation of what is the biblical description of heaven and it provides a way into reading our 'places', which we occupy as earthly believers, in the light of heaven's influence. The 'and more' aspect comes through in Dawson's following description of heaven: 'Heaven is higher than we, not lower. It is beyond us, not beneath us. It is without, not within; more than our capacity to hold, not less. Heaven transcends us as a greater, truer, more splendid reality.'[16] The 'and more' dimension also appears in Andrew Burgess's conclusion: 'The ascension cannot be seen as simply absence – rather it creates the possibility of an altogether different form of presence.'[17]

T. F. Torrance has been foundational for this re-emergence of theological reflection concerning heaven and the ascension.[18] Torrance proposed that 'space and time are relational and variational concepts defined in accordance with the nature of the force that gives them their field of determination'.[19] Put simply, this means that space is always space *for* something, just as time is conceived as time for something. Thus, as a man, Jesus ascends into heaven, which is God's space, God's place, beyond all our notions of space and time. Understood as a relational place, heaven is thus 'where God has "room" for his divine life and activity in ever-deepening communion with humanity'[20] through the now-ascended Christ. As is evident in this explanation, 'statements regarding that ascension are *closed at man's end* (because bounded within the space-time limits of man's existence on earth) but are *infinitely open at God's end*, open to God's own eternal Being and the infinite room of his divine life'.[21] This relational view of space cannot be reduced to a

---

16. Dawson, *Jesus Ascended*, p. 41.

17. Burgess, *Ascension in Karl Barth*, p. 96.

18. Torrance, *Space, Time and Resurrection*, pp. 106–193. For an accessible summary of Torrance's thinking on this matter and of its connections with Calvin's thought and its consequences for conceiving of the ascension, see Dawson, *Jesus Ascended*, pp. 44–52.

19. Torrance, *Space, Time and Resurrection*, p. 130.

20. Dawson, *Jesus Ascended*, p. 49.

21. Torrance, *Space, Time and Resurrection*, pp. 131–132; italics original.

metaphor, however, since 'a body necessarily occupies space' – in short, 'There is a place where the human Jesus is.'[22] This is the positive aspect communicated by the 'Black Rubric' appended to the service of the Lord's Supper in *The Book of Common Prayer*: 'the natural Body and Blood of our Saviour Christ *are in Heaven*, and not here; it being against the truth of Christ's natural Body to be at one time in more places than one' (emphasis added).

Thus, even while Christ's flesh, his truly human flesh, remains and is glorified in heaven, the ascension establishes a gap between our present corruptible existence and the glorious heavenly reality of the ascended Christ. But this does not lead us into mysticism or metaphysical speculation. Instead, Jesus' absence draws us back to his historic presence among us, driving us to look back to his earthly incarnation, and demanding that we follow this Jesus exclusively. Syncretism is therefore excluded by the ascension's distancing effect: although Enoch and Elijah did not taste death, Jesus of Nazareth is supremely unique in that his entry into heaven confirms him as *the* mediator between God and humanity (cf. e.g. Acts 2:33–36). His ascension establishes the gospel concerning the canonically revealed Jesus as the one locus for us to access this bridging of mortal space and heavenly space: 'by withdrawing himself from our sight [Acts 1:9], Christ sends us back to the historical Jesus Christ as the *covenanted place* on earth and in time which God has appointed for meeting between man and himself'.[23] Saul's dependence upon Ananias in Acts 9, despite the Christophany he had received, is indicative of this movement back to the gospel concerning the historical Jesus.[24] There is no alternative or supplementary locus to which we may turn. Rather, 'The ascension thus means that to all eternity God insists on speaking to us through the historical Jesus.'[25] This is the opposite of all demythologizing.[26] Instead, his ascension into heaven means that

---

22. Dawson, *Jesus Ascended*, p. 49.
23. Torrance, *Space, Time and Resurrection*, p. 133; emphasis original.
24. Ibid., pp. 147–148.
25. Ibid., p. 133.
26. Ibid., p. 134.

'the historical Jesus does not belong to crumbling time, to time that fades away like all history into vanity and dust . . . [instead] within that history He is superior historical reality as actual and live happening in the continuous present'.[27]

Yet, vitally for us, at the same time:

> It is through the Spirit that things infinitely disconnected –
> disconnected by the 'distance' of the ascension – are nevertheless
> infinitely closely related. Through the Spirit Christ is nearer to us
> than we are to ourselves, and we who live and dwell on earth are yet
> made to sit with Christ 'in heavenly places', partaking of the divine
> nature in him.[28]

This the Spirit does through the word and the sacraments in the lives of those enjoying union with Christ.[29] Thus, as Dawson concludes, 'far from separating us from Jesus, the ascension makes the historical, yet living Jesus, the man in whose face the light of the glory of God shone (1 Corinthians 4:6), our perennial meeting place with God until he returns'.[30] As a result, the heavenly Jesus – although in body absent from the world – cannot be relegated to the distant past, nor cast as simply another object for human historical investigation. Rather, his withdrawal to heaven as priest-king and future judge allows the world time and space for repentance.[31]

Simultaneously, therefore, the Spirit presents both Christ and his church eschatologically, making 'a way across the boundary line that has been drawn through all things, even time itself, by Jesus-history

---

27. Thomas F. Torrance, *Royal Priesthood: A Theology of Ordained Ministry*, 2nd ed. (Edinburgh: T. & T. Clark, 1993), p. 57.

28. Torrance, *Space, Time and Resurrection*, p. 135.

29. Ibid., pp. 148–150. Concerning the believers' 'union with Christ', see Richard B. Gaffin, Jr., *By Faith, Not Sight: Paul and the Order of Salvation* (Milton Keynes: Paternoster, 2006), pp. 35–41, 58–68.

30. Dawson, *Jesus Ascended*, p. 51. The quotation is as given; the citation should read 2 Corinthians.

31. Torrance, *Royal Priesthood*, p. 60.

[and geography]'.[32] This boundary line, governed by Christ's heavenly location, concerns both the 'now but not yet' and the 'here but not here' of Christian eschatological tension. As Andrew Lincoln expresses it at the start of his monograph on the heavenly dimension within Pauline eschatology:

> [eschatological] language involves both vertical and horizontal referents, spatial and temporal categories. In other words eschatology involves heaven as well as the Last Day. All too often in treatments of eschatology the latter pole is given all the attention and the former is virtually ignored. Both sorts of language are to be given their full weight.[33]

Therefore, summarizing its crucial role for both our Christology and our pneumatology, the ascension is an anchor within the veil, 'an anchor that will not drag, no matter how fierce and terrible and devastating may be the storms that sweep over the earth and its history'.[34]

More recently, Torrance's thought has been picked up and developed by Douglas Farrow, with particular application to ecclesiology and cosmology.[35] Farrow's particular concern is that the church should struggle with Christ's absence, and not deny absence in the desire for a misconstrued Christological presence: 'The church that forgets the absence inevitably begins to misunderstand and misconstrue the presence.'[36] Thus the charge Farrow puts before us is that we are indeed rightly to be looking for his coming again with power and great glory (cf. Acts 17:30–31). In turn, Farrow's work has been popularized and applied to the life of

---

32. Farrow, *Ascension and Ecclesia*, p. 269, n. 53; square-bracketed comment added.

33. Andrew T. Lincoln, *Paradise Now and Not Yet: Studies in the Role of the Heavenly Dimension in Paul's Thought with Special Reference to His Eschatology* (Cambridge: Cambridge University Press, 1981), p. 5.

34. Torrance, *Space, Time and Resurrection*, p. 137.

35. Farrow, *Ascension and Ecclesia*.

36. Ibid., p. 272.

the local church by Dawson.[37] Also, Karl Barth's understanding of the ascension has recently been examined by Burgess, who engages with Farrow as one of his dialogue partners.[38] Burgess particularly critiques Farrow's clearly eucharistically driven understanding of church, rightly questioning Farrow's 'lack of interest in external proclamation of any kind'.[39]

My aim here, however, is not to adjudicate between debating theologians. Instead, having noted this resurgence in ascension scholarship, the main body of this present chapter turns to ask another question. In a recent *Churchman* article, David Wheaton asked 'What in Heaven Is Jesus Doing?'[40] In this present chapter, I shall review the biblical data relating to Christ's ascension with the intention of inverting Wheaton's question. Regarding the implications of Christ's ascension, I want to ask the question 'What on earth is the heavenly Jesus doing?'

The question is a telling one for churches. If we are Christ's people on earth, we cannot avoid this question and must instead embrace it. It is, nevertheless, a rarely asked one. I turn to answer it first from the Acts of the Apostles. As has already been noted, despite being the one New Testament writer who describes the ascension moment, Luke's writings are rarely the first port of call for those seeking to understand the earthly impact of the heavenly Christ. As I show below, however, they are a fruitful first reference for such a search.

---

37. Dawson, *Jesus Ascended*. Cf., from an ecumenical perspective, Peter Atkins, *Ascension Now: Implications of Christ's Ascension for Today's Church* (Collegeville, Minn.: Liturgical Press, 2001), esp. pp. 112–120.

38. Burgess, *Ascension in Karl Barth*.

39. Ibid., p. 139. Cf. ibid., pp. 136–140, 153–158. Burgess also considers that Farrow misunderstands Barth, since Barth distinguishes between church and world 'on the basis of the *Word*, not eucharist *per se*' (Burgess, *Ascension in Karl Barth*, p. 152; italics original). Cf. Torrance, *Space, Time and Resurrection*, p. 138 (emphasis original): 'So far as the Church in history and on earth is concerned . . . the great connecting link between world history and the heavenly session of Christ is to be found in *prayer and intercession*.'

40. David Wheaton, 'What in Heaven Is Jesus Doing?', *Churchman* 119.4 (2005), pp. 343–356.

Tracing the hidden Christ: biblical horizons

Acts

Elsewhere I have developed at length an examination of the impact of the heavenly Christ on the theology and direction of the Acts narrative.[41] Any such study has to contend with the power of 'absentee Christology',[42] an emphasis on Christ's earthly absence that very easily also stresses an assumed passivity on the part of the heavenly Jesus.[43] Its impact has been to reduce most appreciations of the heavenly Christ in Acts to the book's opening scene (1:1–11, at most) and occasional verses that provide some systematic impetus or controversy to the matter (e.g. 3:21). Those who have opposed the often taken-for-granted assumptions of 'absentee Christology' have been few and their writings occasional, but they deserve wider attention in formulating a Christology from Acts.[44]

---

41. Matthew T. Sleeman, '"Under Heaven": The Narrative-Geographical Implications of the Heavenly Christ for the Believers (and their Mission) within Acts 1:1–11:18' (PhD thesis, University of London, 2006). The present chapter assumes the importance of Christ being ascended for the content and practice of evangelism by the church within Acts, noting that 'the word is the real "hero" of Luke's narrative' (David Peterson, 'Luke's Theological Enterprise: Integration and Intent', in I. Howard Marshall and David Peterson [eds.], Witness to the Gospel: The Theology of Acts [Grand Rapids: Eerdmans, 1998], p. 541).

42. The phrase 'absentee Christology' was coined by C. F. D. Moule, 'The Christology of Acts', in Leander E. Keck and J. Louis Martyn (eds.), Studies in Luke-Acts: Essays Presented in Honor of Paul Schubert, Buckingham Professor of New Testament Criticism and Interpretation at Yale University (London: SPCK, 1966), pp. 179–180.

43. See Arie W. Zwiep, The Ascension of the Messiah in Lukan Christology (Leiden: E. J. Brill, 1997), p. 182.

44. See e.g. George MacRae, '"Whom Heaven Must Receive until the Time": Reflections on the Christology of Acts', Interpretation 27 (1973), pp. 151–165; Robert F. O'Toole, 'Activity of the Risen Christ in Luke-Acts', Biblica 62 (1981), pp. 471–498; Beverley Roberts Gaventa,

An unbiased reading of Acts as a whole uncovers indicators of the heavenly Christ at work across the narrative. Indeed, considering Luke-Acts as a whole, Luke's description of Jesus' journey towards Jerusalem as beginning '[w]hen the days drew near for him to be taken up' (Luke 9:51) strongly suggests a Lukan concern with Jesus' ascension that spans Luke and Acts as the two halves of Luke's literary canvas (cf. Luke 24:49; Acts 1:2, 22). In this sense, Jesus' ascension is well described as his 'triumphant exit',[45] mirroring and positioning his triumphal entry into Jerusalem (Luke 19:28–44) and pitching the 'journey' in Luke's Gospel as less a journey to Jerusalem and more as a journey *via Jerusalem* (and the cross and resurrection) *to heaven*. Indeed, Jesus' increasing proximity to Jerusalem (Luke 19:11) provokes the parable of the ten minas (19:12–27), which prepares Jesus' hearers for a time of isolation from their king but yet a time (and place) when they are still accountable to him for their actions and inactions in his absence. So, in this light, what can be said of the heavenly Jesus within Acts *after* his heavenly ascent in Acts 1:9?

First, Acts is structured by pivotal moments when Christ intervenes explicitly from heaven. Stephen's vision and declaration (7:55–56) and Saul's Damascus road experience (9:3–6) are obvious manifestations of this absent-but-active Christology that, within Acts, undermines any presumptive paralleling of 'absent' with 'passive'. In both instances, these Christological interventions from heaven are pivotal for the narrative flow of Acts and, when read within the narrative (as indeed they must be read), they assume greater importance than might initially appear to be the case. In the first instance, despite commentators' almost universal isolation of it from 7:2–51 without any defended or defensible reasoning, Stephen's vision and declaration in 7:55–56 forms the

---

Footnote 44 (cont.)

  'The Presence of the Absent Lord: The Characterization of Jesus in the Acts of the Apostles' (paper presented at the November 2003 Annual Meeting of the Society of Biblical Literature).

45. Mikeal C. Parsons, *The Departure of Jesus in Luke-Acts: The Ascension Narratives in Context* (Sheffield: JSOT Press, 1987), p. 112.

conclusion and climax to what is the longest speech in Acts. It also sparks Stephen's murder, which in turn launches the persecution that projects the church into its greatest diaspora (8:1b–3) and, with it, into its global mission (8:4; 11:19–26). Clearly, this vision of the heavenly Christ is no small moment within the Acts narrative!

The same can be said of Saul's conversion. The Christophany[46] that persuades Saul regarding Jesus as the Christ, the Son of God (9:3–6) is matched by Jesus appearing in a vision to Ananias (9:10–16). As well as initiating Saul/Paul's mission to Jews and Gentiles, this dual Christophanic communication also tells of a further such vision to Saul that will communicate Christ's mission to him (9:16). Furthermore, the threefold telling of Saul's conversion within Acts (in chs. 9, 22 and 26) communicates a richly layered and multifocused theological message that calls out for readers' ongoing reflection. The major constant throughout these retellings is Jesus' active and formative intervention. What develops, cumulatively, across the three tellings, is the theological impact of Jesus' intervention. Once again, therefore, the moment of active-but-absent Christology is powerfully formative for Acts as a whole and for the Christian movement within it.

Second, Acts demonstrates other active Christological moments beyond these pivotal interventions. Paul receives a Christological vision in the Jerusalem temple, a vision that not only confirms his Gentile mission (22:17–21) but that also, by being proclaimed at a later time to the mob outside the temple, provokes Paul's imprisonment and journey to Rome that fills Acts 21 – 28 (cf. 21:27 – 22:29). Such active Christology dominates Paul's life and mission, beginning with his conversion to Christ (9:3–6) and culminating in Paul's proclamation before King Agrippa (26:2–29). This defence fulfils Jesus' foundational projection of Paul's earthly ministry, which Jesus himself announced in Acts 9:15–16, 'he is a chosen instrument of mine to carry my name before the Gentiles and

---

46. For the present discussion, it is important to emphasize that this event was a Christophany, despite some commentators – without any warrant from the text – judging it to be a theophany.

kings and the people of Israel. For I will show him how much he must suffer for the sake of my name.' Standing before King Agrippa, having recounted his conversion to Jesus in what is his last major address in Acts,[47] Paul declares that he 'was not disobedient to the heavenly vision' (26:19) before concluding that 'the Christ must suffer and that, by being the first to rise from the dead, he would proclaim light both to our people and to the Gentiles' (26:23). This latter verse, where Jesus is the subject of the active verb, deconstructs an absent-and-passive Christology and casts a long retrospective shadow over the preceding narrative of Paul's ministry. From this retrospective marker, it becomes apparent that, throughout Paul's ministry, it has been *the heavenly Christ* throughout Acts proclaiming light to both Jew and Gentile.

How can this be? Here is a major challenge to the 'absentee Christology' that has dominated readings of Acts since Hans Conzelmann declared Acts to be the age of the church, not the age of Christ.[48] One way out of the conundrum would be to confine these reflections to Paul's ministry in some fashion that distances him from us, perhaps by means of Paul functioning in Acts as some sort of peculiar 'chosen instrument' (9:15) singled out for unique, non-normative Christological purposes. Without denying particularist dimensions to Paul's conversion and ministry, there are difficulties with adopting such a reading in Acts 26. It is noteworthy that, in the context of Acts 26, when Agrippa senses an evangelistic intent within Paul's words (26:28), Paul presents an expansive extension of his life as applicable for *all* his hearers (26:29).

Instead, let us search elsewhere in Acts for narrative moments where Jesus functions as the active subject of post-ascension activity. Such a search leads to the healing of Aeneas in 9:34, announced by Peter without explanation as occurring because 'Jesus Christ heals you' (9:34). Here, lacking any sense of mediation, Jesus is directly invoked by Peter in an explicit manner

---

47. This is the third time he has recounted his conversion in Acts, each account serving a particular narrative purpose. Cf. Acts 9 and Acts 22.

48. Hans Conzelmann, *The Theology of St. Luke* (London: Faber, 1960).

unparalleled elsewhere in Acts. Perhaps, as with Paul's declaration in 26:23, this functions as a retrospective verdict upon all such healings in Acts at Peter's hands as being due to the direct intervention of Jesus (e.g. 3:1–10; 5:12, 15).

Most significant for understanding 26:23 as a wider reference, however, is Jesus' role in sending the Spirit, announced by Peter on the day of Pentecost (Acts 2:33; cf. Luke 24:49): 'Being therefore exalted at the right hand of God, and having received from the Father the promise of the Holy Spirit, he [i.e. Jesus] has poured out this that you yourselves are seeing and hearing.' This verse precludes a simple 'replacement' theology within Acts, whereby the Spirit 'replaces' Jesus on earth.[49] Instead, the Spirit functions under the authority of the heavenly Jesus, who 'pours out' the Spirit from his central position of God-given honour and good fortune 'at the right hand of God'. The verb *anabainō*, used of ascending in 2:34, has both kingly and priestly connotations that attach to Jesus' ascended status as proclaimed within Acts 2.[50] Farrow rightly expounds Acts 1 – 2 as chronicling 'from below' what Daniel 7 'envisioned from above', in terms of Jesus as both priest and king.[51] Thus:

> In spite of the circumstances giving rise to Peter's address, it is not a sermon on the Holy Spirit we hear; nor is the focus on the resurrection. What we are offered is a sermon on the ascension of the risen Jesus to the throne, that is, to Israel's throne *and* the throne of the Presence from which the Spirit goes forth.[52]

Rather than simple replacement theology, it was necessary for Christ to be in heaven for the Spirit's expansive ministry on earth

---

49. On the contrary, 'Pentecost does not *resolve* the problem of the presence and the absence. It *creates* it, by adding a presence which discloses the absence' (Farrow, *Ascension and Ecclesia*, p. 271, n. 59; italics original).

50. Torrance, *Space, Time and Resurrection*, p. 108.

51. Farrow, *Ascension and Ecclesia*, pp. 24–26 (25).

52. Ibid., p. 25; italics original. Cf. similarly Torrance, *Space, Time and Resurrection*, pp. 136–137.

(Acts 3:20–21). The positive counterpoint is found in the emphatic assertion that Jesus did not see 'corruption' (2:27, 31; a point made even more emphatically in 13:34–37). The contrast is made with David: Jesus, unlike Solomon, is David's true son, enthroned and victorious, but '[b]y ascent rather than descent!'[53]

In short, every action performed by the Spirit's empowering within Acts reflects a Christological impulse. Thus 26:23, with its claim that Christ is still proclaiming light to Jews and Gentiles, is not to be understood as referring exclusively to Paul's ministry. Rather, 26:23 represents an extension to the Gentiles of what was made known in 5:31 (and 2:33) with more narrow reference to Israel. This conclusion is confirmed in a different way by both Paul *and* Barnabas assuming the mantle of the Isaianic Servant in Acts 13:46–47 (cf. 1:8). Taken together with the Christological dimensions of Acts already outlined above, this adds significant gravity to our understanding of Acts as Jesus' continuing words and deeds (cf. Acts 1:1, referring to Luke's Gospel as recounting 'all that Jesus *began* to do and teach'; my emphasis).

The cumulative effect of these reflections is that the heavenly Christ is a key character within the book of Acts. For sure, it remains true that Acts is unremittingly earthly in its focus. There is no speculation about heavenly journeys undertaken by Christ, and remarkably little concern with what Christ is doing in heaven. Christ is not extensively developed as a character within Acts, and he remains absent throughout the vast majority of the book, but his imprint remains formative throughout the narrative.

In consequence, it is insufficient to cast the bounds of Acts as simply 'to the end of the earth' (cf. 1:8). However expansive our global projections, the narrative map of Acts is incomplete without reference to heaven. Thus earthbound readings of Acts are insufficiently theological, and fail to come to terms with the

---

53. Peter Doble, ' "Something Greater Than Solomon": An Approach to Stephen's Speech', in Steve Moyise (ed.), *The Old Testament in the New Testament: Essays in Honour of J. L. North* (Sheffield: Sheffield University Press, 2000), p. 186, n. 16.

Christology being presented in Luke's second volume. Jesus being in heaven is the vital triangulating point of reference for all movement on earth (of which there is plenty within Acts). This renders insufficient any projection of the narrative as being simply outwards from Jerusalem, from Jerusalem to Rome, or even from Jerusalem 'to the end of the earth'. All places within Acts are cast as 'under heaven' and subject to its thrall (cf. 2:5), and heaven in Acts is to be understood Christologically. As such, all places within Acts, and the way these places order human activities, come under theological scrutiny and critique.

Under this reading, one of the key consequences of Jesus being in heaven that is communicated by Acts is a reshaping of earthly places. This reworking of space can be traced through the references to 'heaven' (*ouranos*) in Acts. Tellingly, these references are frequent in the early chapters (1:10–11; 2:2, 5, 34; 3:21; 4:12, 24; 7:49, 55–56; 9:3; 10:11–12, 16; 11:5–6, 9–10, 15) but then almost cease in later chapters.[54] The change comes once the believers' spaces have been ordered (within the narrative, at least) according to the priorities established by the now-heavenly Christ. Thus the Gentile household of Cornelius, brought under the gospel and accepted as such by the Jerusalem church, constitutes a climactic moment within the narrative development of Acts. Both the amount of narrative space given over to the account of this moment (10:1 – 11:18), and the subsequent narration concerning the Jew-Gentile church in Antioch (11:19–30), where believers were first called 'Christians' (11:26), highlight this climax in the way places are ordered within Acts according to the will of the heavenly Christ.

In my previous work I judged from these findings that Luke's second volume, as well as communicating salvation history, also presents salvation geography, geography being understood in its etymological sense as 'writing the earth'. Acts traces, within a narrative form, the impact of Jesus being in heaven for many and

---

54. The only two references, 14:15 and 17:24, serve a different function to the Christological dimension discussed here, but in each instance the assumptions created by the location in question coming under theological Christological critique.

various places on earth. Its trajectory is such that *any* place on earth can then be positioned within its scope.

Place is a complex category, and here I have time only to mark its Christological dimension.[55] Within Acts, all places, whether at the local scale of immediate surroundings or the macroscale of imperial structures, are subjected to a Christological critique. This occurs via the Christ himself being in, ruling from, a place other than an earthly place. That Jesus is in heaven engenders a critical edge to the claims and positioning of all other places within Acts. This critical geography then overspills into the world(s) of the reader. As we read Acts, especially as we read it as Scripture, its narrative presuppositions challenge to become our presuppositions as we view the places we occupy. Thus the heavenly Christ, as mediated to us through the Acts narrative, stirs our understanding, and our imagination, of the places we occupy. This Christological insight is rich and fruitful for our reading of Acts, and for our application of it to our lives and to the lives of those to whom we minister.

On this latter point, Acts provides an alternative, albeit complementary, narrative perspective concerning the heavenly Christ to that pursued in Hebrews.

Hebrews

Hebrews is the typical destination for those seeking an answer to Christ's present heavenly activity.[56] What, then, does this homiletic epistle add to our discussion of the ways in which a heavenly Christology influences earthly Christian discipleship? In short, Jesus' reception into the uncreated Holy of Holies 'spells out an altogether new existence for man [*sic*], and with him, for the whole creation'.[57] This answer can be expounded under three headings.

---

55. Regarding 'place', see Tim Cresswell, *Place: A Short Introduction* (Oxford: Blackwell, 2004), and http://pegasus.cc.ucf.edu/~janzb/place/.

56. Wheaton, 'What in Heaven?', is illustrative in this regard, Hebrews providing the backbone for his argument. He cites Heb. 1:3b [p. 344], 4:15–16 [p. 346], 2:18 [p. 347], 10:11–14 [p. 348], 7:25 [p. 351].

57. Farrow, *Ascension and Ecclesia*, p. 280.

The glorified Son who is the great high priest

Hebrews begins by expounding Jesus as the glorified Son. Two references illustrate that this status is ascended and heavenly: 1:3 declares that 'After making purification for sins, he sat down at the right hand of the Majesty on high', and 2:9 confirms that Jesus is 'crowned with glory and honour because of the suffering of death'. According to Hebrews, earthly believers are joined to these great truths concerning Jesus by our union with him, a union made possible through his 'bringing many sons to glory . . . through [his] death' (cf. 2:10–18).

Hebrews 4:14–16 picks up on this sonship, and develops it by linking it with Jesus' priestly ministry, proclaiming that 'we have a great high priest who has passed through the heavens, Jesus, the Son of God' (4:14).[58] This declaration leads to a hortatory injunction to maintain our confidence and hope. Whereas in the Old Testament such a call would have required repetitious coming to the tabernacle or temple in conscious, prayerful devotion, here in verse 16 the call to 'draw near', even 'to the throne of grace', is issued without the construction of any such special earthly places. Although Hebrews 12:18, 22 can describe the believer's conversion as 'drawing near' to God (perfect tense), the instruction in 4:16 (and 10:22) is to keep on drawing near to God, that is, to return again over the same gospel ground when realizing our sin, when praying, and when gathering together with other believers. This gospel ground is oriented heavenwards. Furthermore, we are to draw near with 'confidence' (4:16; 10:19) precisely because of Jesus' ascension into heaven as our sympathetic and sufficient high priest.

The heavenly Christ

All this rests upon *where* Christ has gone. Our hope extends to where Christ is – as Hebrews 6:19–20 expounds it, 'into the inner place behind the curtain, where Jesus has gone as a forerunner on our behalf, having become a high priest forever after the order of

---

58. The perfect tense indicates that this passing has left him in a new state or condition.

Melchizedek'. This he did 'by the power of an indestructible life' (7:16b), a reference to the heavenly exaltation of Christ.[59] The cross, resurrection and ascension need to be seen together as Jesus' cultic act of sacrificial offering, such that 'the sacrifice of the cross in its intrinsic nature was a heavenly act' in that '[i]t was a sacrifice performed with respect to the heavenly sanctuary' and consummated by Jesus' enthronement.[60]

This means not only that Jesus is exalted above the heavens (7:26), but also that it is his ascension which indicates and underpins the permanent nature of his high priesthood (7:23 – 8:2). Indeed, if he were on earth, he would not be a priest (8:4). Within heaven, however, 'he is able to save to the uttermost those who draw near to God through him, since he always lives to make intercession for them' (7:25; cf. Rom. 8:34,[61] Isa. 53:12; 1 John 2:1). The Greek word translated 'intercession' has a wider meaning than its English equivalent, and the present participle translated 'those who draw near' 'indicates those who are continually or habitually coming'.[62] This intercession *is* his person, fully human and fully God, his living[63] presence in heaven with God the Father. It is not

59. David Peterson, *Hebrews and Perfection: An Examination of the Concept of Perfection in the 'Epistle to the Hebrews'* (Cambridge: Cambridge University Press, 1982), pp. 110–111. (Cf. also Peterson's Appendix, pp. 191–195, 'When Did Jesus "Become" High Priest?')

60. Ibid., p. 192.

61. C. E. B. Cranfield, *A Critical and Exegetical Commentary on the Epistle to the Romans*. Vol. 1: *Introduction and Commentary on Romans I–VIII* (Edinburgh: T. & T. Clark, 1975), p. 439: 'Christ's high priestly intercession is accomplished as He continually shows and offers to His Father as our pledge that human nature which He assumed.' Clearly, this is the human nature in which Christ was crucified, raised and ascended.

62. Alan Stibbs, *The Finished Work of Christ* (London: Tyndale, 1954), p. 33. Heb. 8:3, as '[t]he only passage in the Epistle which could possibly lend itself to the idea of continual offering' (p. 31, n. 1), refers to *an act of offering* and this, contextually, is located within an emphatic and clear denial of continual offering (9:12; 10:10, 12, 14, 18).

63. Cf. 'by the power of an indestructible life' (Heb. 7:16b).

merely an external, legal transaction but is, rather, 'a reconciliation accomplished in his person and maintained by his person'.[64]

The three adjectives ascribed to Jesus as high priest in 7:26 explain the sufficiency of his person: he is 'holy, innocent, unstained'. This, together with his heavenly position ('separated from sinners, and exalted above the heavens'), means that his work requires no repetition or extension from him or from others (cf. 7:27–28). Rather, with the ascension, his priesthood and its intercession are now a heavenly ministry where he for ever presents 'Himself (and us *in Him* because of Himself *for us*) before the face of the Father'.[65]

Hebrews 10:11–18 makes this clear, dispelling any notion of a continuous liturgical action in heaven. Rather, Jesus is an enthroned (i.e. seated) priest-king who reigns.[66] His priestly work is complete and does not need to extend into eternity, as 9:24–25 confirms, but neither is his priestly ministry relegated to the past, and delimited by his act of atonement on the cross. In short, the present Lordship of Christ *is* a high-priestly office: his very presence there is enough to confirm its efficacy[67] and, as such, in this sense alone constitutes a perpetual offering.

Thus, with good reason Farrow judges that the rhetorical structure of Hebrews as a whole 'consciously mirrors Hebrews' central

---

64. Dawson, *Jesus Ascended*, pp. 128–130 (130). Cf. similarly Torrance, *Space, Time and Resurrection*, pp. 115–116.

65. Torrance, *Royal Priesthood*, p. 17.

66. Wheaton, 'What in Heaven?', pp. 351–353, is emphatic and helpfully expansive on this point. Cf. also Rev. 3:21 and Col. 3:1. The present participle 'seated' in Col. 3:1 describes an ongoing and constant 'state or condition' (Peter T. O'Brien, *Colossians, Philemon*, Word Biblical Commentary 44 [Waco: Word, 1982], p. 162).

67. On this point, see Peterson, *Hebrews and Perfection*, pp. 114–115. The Day of Atonement imagery that Hebrews draws upon confirms this connection between Calvary and heaven: once it is killed, the sacrifice must then be presented, *in the place designated for such a petition*. Concerning these connections with the Day of Atonement, see Dawson, *Jesus Ascended*, pp. 119–125.

focus on the significance of the ascension of Jesus'.[68] Farrow continues: 'The [epistolary] sermon is clearly moulded by a series of carefully balanced exhortations (following on an opening eulogy) to which is matched a series of messianic titles reflecting the ascension motives of cult and monarchy.'[69] Interspersed with warning passages, the structure – which Farrow rightly recognizes as being 'remarkably consistent' without being rigid – serves the overall theme of heavenly pilgrimage encapsulated within the phrase 'bringing many sons to glory' (Heb. 2:10).

Some earthly *implications*

Jesus has passed into God's space, God's place, that is, in 'the greater and more perfect tent (not made with hands, that is, not of this creation)' (Heb. 9:11). As well as signalling the eternal heavenly significance of Christ's sacrifice,[70] this heavenly locale critiques all earthly places and their claims to order space. This critical dimension to Christology is similar to that identified earlier in Acts. The adjective 'made with hands' (also in Heb. 9:24, which makes clear that heaven is here in view) also occurs in Acts 7:48 and 17:24, where, in differing settings, the heavenly Christ (cf. 7:55–56 and 17:30–31) also provokes a critical reassessment of places that would claim an authority over belief.[71] Instead, heaven – as the locale for the ascended Jesus – assumes such authority, and this will remain the case until he returns again to judge and to save (Heb. 9:24–28).

Alongside this critique of alternative claims made by earthly places and priests, Hebrews also pursues a positive agenda for how believers, instructed in these doctrines concerning the ascended Christ, are to live on earth. Hebrews 10:22–25 presents three present-tense hortatory injunctions that draw out the ongoing implications of Christ's heavenly session as the ruling and sufficient

---

68. Farrow, *Ascension and Ecclesia*, p. 279.
69. See the Appendix at the end of this chapter.
70. Peterson, *Hebrews and Perfection*, p. 192, sees this as being signalled in 9:11–14, 23–26; 10:12–14, 19ff.
71. Cf. also Mark 14:58.

Son-Priest for (respectively) the believers' faith, hope and love during this earthly life.

First, 10:22, 'let us draw near with a true heart in full assurance of faith, with our hearts sprinkled clean from an evil conscience and our bodies washed with pure water'. The perfect passive verbs translated 'sprinkled clean' and 'washed' indicate that the action of drawing near expresses an ongoing existing relationship with God.[72] Importantly, '[w]e offer ourselves to God not only based on what Jesus did in the past, but also *in him now*',[73] and, it can be added, in him *there*, that is, before the Father in heaven. Second, 10:23, 'Let us hold fast the confession of our hope without wavering, for he who promised is faithful.' Our hope runs ahead of us, in the shape of Jesus our forerunner, who has entered into heaven (cf. 2:10; 6:19–20); our salvation is, at present, not yet fully realized. Third, 10:24–25, 'And let us consider how to stir up one another to love and good works, not neglecting to meet together, as is the habit of some, but encouraging one another, and all the more as you see the Day drawing near.' There is a strong corporate dimension to the earthly implications of Christ being in heaven. Gathered worship is our earthly expression of how our heavenly minister (*leitourgos*) in the Holy Place (Heb. 8:2) is gathering up and presenting us to the Father (cf. 2:10–13).[74]

These same three themes are repeated in a different order in 10:32–35, with the clear imperative that the readers continue to endure within Hebrews' big-picture story that is presently marked by Jesus being in heaven. This imperative infuses the remaining chapters of the book. The same heavenly orientation links the diverse figures recited in Hebrews 11 (11:14–16, 39–40), and informs Hebrews 12, with its climactic presentation of Jesus as the pioneer and perfecter of faith, who continually reorders life for

---

72. Peterson, *Hebrews and Perfection*, p. 155.

73. Dawson, *Jesus Ascended*, p. 133; italics original.

74. This recognition is not to delimit believers' experience of being 'in God's presence' only to when they are gathered together, as Wheaton, 'What in Heaven?', pp. 345–347, makes clear. Neither, however, should it individualize what is clearly corporate.

believers on earth (12:1–4).[75] In sum, 'Jesus' *heavenly session* is related to the race of faith that he has already finished and his brothers must still run. Jesus has entered God's rest and believers are summoned to "guide their pilgrimage by looking to Jesus, considering both his earthly career and his celestial glory".'[76] The emphasis on looking for a heavenly reward (11:16, 26) returns in the final exhortations (13:13–14). This perspective enables believers to submit under discipline, as they are extolled to do in 12:5–11.[77]

As such, Hebrews matches the message of Acts. A new existence for believing humanity is heralded by Jesus' ascension, an existence governing earthly life. 'He "passes through" and is "exalted above the heavens" not only by becoming pre-eminent in honour, but by re-ordering the fundamental structures of created life around himself, making it presentable to God in and with himself.'[78] Full acknowledgment of this reality is anticipated in the believers' life on earth, and its anticipation functions as a critique of all other orderings of earthly space and places. Thus, what Acts presented in narrative form, Hebrews projects in the form of an extended hortatory sermon. We now turn to the book of Revelation, to see the same message concerning the ascended Christ, and the same earthly consequences, told in a still different literary form.

Revelation

Clearly, the book of Revelation concerns the heavenly Christ. Jesus book-ends Revelation, and it concerns him in his glorious ascended position. Yet, at the same time, it is also a book addressed to seven, local, earthly churches. Churches whom, from the evidence of the seven letters (2:1 – 3:22), Jesus knows

---

75. Concerning 12:1–4, see Peterson, *Hebrews and Perfection*, pp. 168–173.

76. Peterson, *Hebrews and Perfection*, p. 170, quoting David M. Hay, *Glory at the Right Hand: Psalm 110 in Early Christianity* (Nashville: Abingdon, 1973), p. 95; italics original to Peterson.

77. For further exposition of these verses, see Peterson, *Hebrews and Perfection*, pp. 173–174.

78. Farrow, *Ascension and Ecclesia*, p. 280.

intimately. He commends, commands and warns them with what is at times a frightening specificity. He is passionate that these local congregations conform to his will, in behaviour as well as belief. Here is a first marker put down by the book of Revelation: as seen in Acts, Jesus knows his churches and assumes active Lordship over them. The challenge for us and our churches is not hard to see. Far from passive, absentee Christology, the book of Revelation carries with it an implicit question for all its readers: what would the Jesus of Revelation say to your church?[79]

Second, the book of Revelation precludes any understanding of an isolated heavenly Jesus, or even Jesus and God the Father in some abstracted heavenly realm. Instead, John's vision pertains to a galaxy of divine glory, with enthroned elders, four living creatures and vast multitudes of believers oriented around the heavenly Jesus and the throne of God.

This portrayal of a life-world oriented around Christ far from exhausts the imagery of Revelation, but is enough to demonstrate that the implications of the heavenly Christ identified in Acts and Hebrews carry through within the different apocalyptic presentations portrayed in Revelation.[80] As was the case in Acts and Hebrews, Revelation is not intended to spark speculation regarding the heavenlies as much as to confirm and strengthen a heavenwards orientation among believers on earth. The behavioural implications of the opening letters are never far from the message of John's vision, all the way to its final consummation (e.g. 21:27; 22:11–16). Above all, Revelation, with its vision of the

---

79. See Dawson, *Jesus Ascended*, pp. 14–21, for one local church's confrontation with this searching question.

80. As within Acts and Hebrews, Revelation also communicates instruction about how believers are to understand and faithfully inhabit earthly places. Cf. Michael Gilbertson, *God and History in the Book of Revelation: New Testament Studies in Dialogue with Pannenberg and Moltmann* (Cambridge: Cambridge University Press, 2003), pp. 81–108, who explores 'The Spatial Dimension of the Book of Revelation', and how John uses space to make theological points about the relationship between God and history so as to encourage faithfulness to God in the here and now.

heavenly Christ, is a prophecy to be 'kept' in a moral and ethical sense (22:7).[81] The location, status and destiny of Christ in heaven is central to this exhortation to believers.

1 Corinthians 15

In different ways, other New Testament passages expound and develop these themes and implications arising from Christ's ascension. For example, in 1 Corinthians 15:25–27, the risen Christ[82] enjoys progressive increase in dominion over his enemies, culminating in subduing even death itself.

Such subjection of all things to Christ the heavenly man anticipates his representative nature, drawn out in verses 45–49. 'From heaven' (v. 47 English Standard Version, also New International Version) is better understood as concerned with Christ's qualitative post-ascension humanity rather than with his origins.[83] Thus, 'what characterizes the first man is that his life is of the present

---

81. Cf. the other occurrences of the same verb within Revelation, all with the same impetus for believers: 1:3; 2:26; 3:3, 8, 10; 12:17; 14:12; 16:15; 22:7, 9.

82. This requires seeing God as the intended (but unstated) subject of 'he has put' (v. 25), as suggested by the reference to Ps. 110:1. So C. K. Barrett, *A Commentary on the First Epistle to the Corinthians* (London: A. & C. Black, 1968), p. 358. For the alternative reading, whereby Jesus is the subject, thus following the grammatical sense of the verse, see Gordon Fee, *The First Epistle to the Corinthians*, New International Commentary on the New Testament (Grand Rapids: Eerdmans, 1987), pp. 755–756.

   Ben Witherington III, *Conflict and Community in Corinth: A Socio-Rhetorical Commentary on 1 and 2 Corinthians* (Grand Rapids: Eerdmans, 1995), pp. 304–305, reckons 1 Corinthians to be countering Roman imperial eschatology (cf. pp. 295–298). Whether or not this is Paul's intention, the consequences of Christ's heavenly session for such alternative earthly orderings of space and time can be clearly read out of this passage, providing theological critique for both original and contemporary hearers/readers.

83. Fee, *First Epistle to the Corinthians*, pp. 792–793, is persuasive on this point; Witherington, *Conflict and Community in Corinth*, p. 309, draws the same conclusion.

earth, earthly, whereas what characterizes the second man is that his life is "of heaven," that is, heavenly'.[84]

Thus verses 45–49 anticipate how believers in Christ will receive spiritual bodies and share in the life of the age to come. The issue in 1 Corinthians 15 is one of bodies (cf. vv. 20–21, 42–44, 50–55), bodies fit for the eschatological existence of 'those who are of heaven' (v. 48), bodies anticipated by the one man presently in heaven. He is the 'firstfruits' of what is to come (vv. 20, 23; cf. Col. 1:15, 18).[85] 'Glorified now, Jesus wears the flesh which is our inheritance. Though fully human still, and thus embodied, Jesus is yet fully God and able to communicate himself to the members of his body across all distance of realms, dimensions, hours or miles.'[86]

Although Christ's continuing humanity provides the pattern and guarantee of the glorified human that awaits us, and '[t]he Spirit links us now to this future as the guarantee of what we await',[87] our present Christian 'spirituality' is incomplete, awaiting this embodied finale. Earthbound believers are, in the present age, however, 'rising to the occasion'.[88] This is especially apparent if verse 49 originally maintained the hortatory reading 'let us also bear the image of the man of heaven'[89] rather than the future-oriented 'we shall also bear the image of the man of heaven'. As the harder

---

84. Fee, *First Epistle to the Corinthians*, p. 792. Also, p. 793: 'those are surely right who have seen the background as lying in his [Paul's] own encounter with the "heavenly Christ" on the Damascus Road, coupled with the theme of the restoration of Adam to heavenly existence found in Jewish apocalyptic literature'.

85. This horizon is cosmic: 'The whole of creation falls within the range of his Lordship' (Torrance, *Space, Time and Resurrection*, p. 155), given that he is the 'firstborn of all creation'. For further reflection on Christ as the first fruits of what we shall become, see Dawson, *Jesus Ascended*, pp. 108–114.

86. Ibid., p. 51.

87. Ibid., p. 47, going on to quote Rom. 5:5.

88. To adopt the heading given to 1 Cor. 15 by Witherington, *Conflict and Community in Corinth*, p. 291.

89. Given only as a footnoted alternative reading in both the New International Version and English Standard Version.

reading, and with the clearest manuscript support, the hortatory reading is to be preferred. This suggests that Paul is 'calling them to prepare now for the future that is to be'.[90] As verses 33–34 and 58 make clear, present behaviour is linked with eschatological belief. Both are to be guided by the character and behaviour of the 'man of heaven', while noting that we earthly believers have not yet gained the fullness of what is eschatologically bound up 'in Christ'. This fits with exhortation within Colossians and Ephesians that pursues a similar course of reasoning.

Colossians and Ephesians

If Christ is our representative and forerunner, and if we, by faith, are spiritually joined in union with him, then Christ's heavenly status and location impels us on a quest to ascend spiritually while serving him here on earth.[91] This is the challenge laid before us in Colossians 3. As Dawson observes:

> The study of the theology of the ascension is not an end in itself; its purpose is to lead us to 'gaze upon the beauty of the heavenly Christ in the Father's presence' so that we might be conformed more and more to be like him. Getting out of ourselves, we find the blessed life. Knowledge of what God has made known to use through the Spirit in the Word transforms our worship and prayer so that we experience reaching farther, getting closer, and more fully taking our place with Christ in the heavenly realms.[92]

In part this involves a paradoxical descent, whereby we allow the ascended Christ to critique our proud attempts to shape our places according to idolatrous orderings that deny all the glory due to Christ's present heavenly status. Such a critique applies both to the

---

90. Fee, *First Epistle to the Corinthians*, p. 795.

91. See Dawson, *Jesus Ascended*, pp. 172–179, 186–188, for more lengthy reflection upon this point than is possible here.

92. Ibid., p. 172, quoting Andrew Murray, *Holiest of All: An Exposition of the Epistle to the Hebrews* (London: James Nisbet, 1896), p. 65. Murray's original words lack 'the beauty of'.

interior attitudinal places of the heart and to the exterior places that reflect and create our social lives. Reflection upon Christ's heavenly glory drives such mortifying renunciation, a heavenly Christology fuelling discipleship and ecclesial identity, and the commitment to live out his death in our daily lives, bearing humility because of the hope of sharing his glory in the yet-to-be-completed narrative of Christology. Such is the impetus of Colossians 3:1–11.

At the same time, and in the same places, we are called also to respond positively to the heavenly Christ. Such is the charge within Colossians 3:12–17, which covers personal ethics, congregational relationships and practices, culminating in a life-sized commission for believers.

The ecclesial aspect of this charge laid upon believers in Colossians 3 echoes that already observed in Acts, Hebrews 10 and Revelation 1 – 3. Ephesians also builds its ecclesial vision (4:1b–16) on Christ's ascended status and its consequences (4:8–10; cf. 1:20–23).

I lack room here for a full discussion of Ephesians, but of particular note for our present discussion is 4:9. The Greek words translated 'of the earth' in the English Standard Version are typically read (as does the ESV) as a partitive genitive, that is, that Christ has descended to the lower parts *of the earth*, with the suggestion of a descent into Hades. An alternative and plausible option is that the genitive is appositional, rendering the meaning 'he descended into the lower parts [of the universe], that is, the earth'.[93] Under this reading, Christ's incarnation is in view or, perhaps, the descent occurs *after* the ascent, and indicates the descent of the Spirit on the day of Pentecost.[94] Under such a reading, the heavenly Christ

---

93. Daniel B. Wallace, *Greek Grammar Beyond the Basics: An Exegetical Syntax of the New Testament* (Grand Rapids: Zondervan, 1996), pp. 99–100. Appositional genitives are, by some writers, called epexegetical genitives.

94. W. Hall Harris, *The Descent of Christ: Ephesians 4:7–11 and Traditional Hebrew Imagery* (Grand Rapids: Baker, 1998). See esp. pp. 182–197 for a summary of Harris's argument and its implications. Harris recognizes that his argument 'cannot claim absolute certainty' (p. 197), but it offers suggestive consequences for our understanding of the heavenly Christ.

is even more important within the horizons of Ephesians (cf. e.g. 3:17; 5:18), and the argument of Ephesians correlates with the reading of Acts pursued earlier.

1 Peter

1 Peter 3:18–22 is a notoriously difficult passage for exegesis. It has been used to argue for Christ exercising a pre-incarnate ministry during the time of Noah, or for Christ experiencing a descent into Hades during the period between his death and resurrection. It is better understood however, as referring to his ascension, with these verses adopting a three-stage sequence in Christ's suffering and its consequences that is instructive concerning the heavenly Christ.[95] First, Christ has been put to death with respect to the flesh, and then he has been made alive with respect to the spirit (v. 18b). Here, 'flesh' and 'spirit' do not distinguish between material and immaterial parts of Christ's person (e.g. his 'body' and his 'soul') but, rather, they indicate two orders of being. The latter state is resurrection life beyond the sphere of mortal human limitations, of suffering, and of death, affecting the whole of Christ's person, not merely a part of him.[96] As always in the New Testament, this resurrection is bodily.

In this resurrection state, Christ has 'gone' (*poreutheis*, vv. 19, 22: in the latter instance, 'into heaven').[97] Indeed, verses 19–22 are concerned with Christ's ascension journey by virtue of which Christ exercises sovereignty over every power in the universe (v. 22). This is telling for our present discussion. Michaels goes as far as to judge Peter's intention in verses 19–22 as being to answer the

---

95. J. Ramsey Michaels, *1 Peter*, Word Biblical Commentary 49 (Waco: Word, 1988), pp. 198–201. In his discussion of these verses, Michaels draws extensively on W. J. Dalton, *Christ's Proclamation to the Spirit: A Study of 1 Peter 3:18–4:6*, Analecta biblica 23 (Rome: Pontifical Biblical Institute, 1965).

96. Michaels, *1 Peter*, pp. 204–205. The *men . . . de . . .* construction 'has the effect of subordinating the first to the second' (p. 205).

97. Clearly, this rejects any reading of Christ engaging in a post-passion, pre-resurrection activity, such as the medievalist notion of the 'harrowing of hell'.

question 'What did this heavenly journey in the Spirit entail, and what did it accomplish for Christian believers?'[98]

The earthly implications of Christ's journey and subsequent heavenly status are apparent within the surrounding context of 1 Peter. Believers are not to fear those who might persecute them (3:14) but are to endure such suffering (4:1–6), because baptism joins them with Christ and his victory, which is their salvation (cf. 3:21). Giving way to such pressure to return to a worldly way of life would not be the way of Noah, who resisted mockery and whose hope and obedience were instrumental in him and his family being saved from the flood. In this manner, Christ's heavenly journey serves the bigger picture of 1 Peter, that of elect exiles of the dispersion, born again to a living hope (1:1–5).

There is no need to read into 3:19 either the necessity of verbal proclamation, or that this proclamation has to be salvific. Rather, Christ's very act of going into heaven is declaratory, and it issues in the judicial declaration of the hearers' fate. In 3:19, Peter is 'dramatizing concretely the universality of Christ's lordship, which he will make explicit in v 22'.[99] This reading stands regardless of whether the recipients of Christ's preaching are those who perished in the flood or the 'sons of God' mentioned in Genesis 6:2. Given Jude 6 and 1 Enoch, the latter interpretation is more likely here, understood in the context of 1 Peter as representing the archetypal spirits and forces of evil. In this light, the heavenly Christ is in triumphal procession (cf. Eph. 3:10; 4:8–10). For the purposes of the present discussion, the readers of 1 Peter are in a situation analogous with that of the recipients of Ephesians 6, namely, that Christ has already won the victory, and they are to stand firm in him and on him. Although 1 Peter expresses this stance with respect to the heavenly Christ in more mythical language, the outcome is the same.

As elsewhere within early Christian literature, the ascension and heavenly session of Christ are joined with the resurrection, making one sequence of Christ's glorification. As verse 22 makes clear, it is

---

98. Michaels, *1 Peter*, p. 200.

99. Ibid., p. 206.

through baptism that Christians share in the victory of Christ, who presently rules over 'angels, authorities and powers' (cf. Eph. 1:20–22; Col. 1:16–18). Believers on earth are, though, within an eschatological tension, living within a 'here-but-not-here' as well as a 'now-but-not-yet' reality. The devil is still powerful (1 Pet. 5:8), even though the heavenly Christ – integrally within his ascension and session – has already established his victory and has proclaimed it over all the evil forces throughout the universe, 'to the most remote and unlikely audience imaginable'.[100] There is, however, confidence for the believer facing trials of a practical, even daily, nature, in the reassurance that if Christ can 'subdue' or 'tame' 'disobedient spirits', how much more can he deal with remaining trials, even if 'Peter's actual viewpoint is not that "the future is now," only that in Jesus Christ "the future is assured."'[101]

These inferences drawn for earthly believers are remarkably practical. What follows in 1 Peter 4 is, like Colossians 3, a catalogue of applied Christian living, covering attitudes and actions, all of which spring from a correct understanding of Christ's heavenly status. Here are the spiritual disciplines that will mark out on earth the lives of those whose faith and allegiance is oriented towards a heavenly Lord, whose lives are shaped by a heavenly audit that recognizes the fleeting – even if hostile – nature of visible earthly glory in comparison with the life begotten again from the imperishable seed through the living and abiding word of God (1 Pet. 1:22–25).

The challenge is also stark: either one is being built up into this heavenly living stone, or one stumbles on the offence of him (1 Pet. 2:4–8). It is relating with him, the heavenly Christ, that shapes a people (2:9–10; 5:10–11) and grants them on earth behaviourally distinctive status as sojourners and exiles (2:11–12). As 3:18–22 demonstrates, there is no neutrality, no space, that lies beyond the realm of this absent-but-involved and supreme Christ. Likewise,

---

100. Ibid. Noting, however, with ibid., p. 210, that 'The location of their strongholds, and hence the geography of Christ's mission to them, is not Peter's main concern.'

101. Ibid., p. 221.

there is no withdrawing from a hostile world but, rather, declarative involvement through word and deed (e.g. 3:1–2, 15–17). Instead, building on Christ occurs within the same places as does the stumbling caused by him. It is only with a robust sense of his heavenly status that such a tension can be preserved.

Attending to the hidden Christ: some biblical implications

The prevailing claim throughout this chapter, supported by the preceding survey across the New Testament, is that Jesus' heavenly session influences how believers view and inhabit earthly places and spaces. Given that human identity and human places form one another in a mutual manner, both these markers need to be properly oriented by the true man who is in heaven and, where necessary, need to be corrected by reference to him. The second part of the chapter now looks at some of the implications arising from Christ's ascended status for ecclesiology, our understanding of the sacraments, and the pursuit of theology within the public sphere.

Practical ecclesiology
A central premise of Torrance's work, outlined earlier, is that Christ's descent and ascent creates and controls the very existence of the church.[102] In terms of the church's mission, this understanding of the ascension both precludes timeless or spaceless ecclesiology and calls for open structures and a cultural relativism regarding expressions of church,[103] albeit within the horizons set up by Scripture's revelation concerning Christ.

---

102. Torrance, *Royal Priesthood.* Cf. Burgess, *Ascension in Karl Barth*, p. 19, commenting on Barth's theology, 'the ascension informs a dynamic of *presence* and *absence* – Jesus Christ's coincident presence and absence during "this time between", as church and individual Christians occupy the space created for them by the "unnatural" delay of the *eschaton*'.

103. Torrance, *Space, Time and Resurrection*, pp. 136–137.

Therefore, as we have seen, Christ's ascension engenders a corporate calling, and Christ's heavenly session challenges us as to
what expression this corporate calling takes on earth. The foundational implication for our ecclesiology is that our locus, our
catholicism, is found in heaven rather than on earth.[104] We are
supremely oriented not around any earthly structure, whether congregational or denominational, but around the heavenly Christ, to
whom we are continually 'drawing near'. Earthly structures are
rendered secondary and provisional by our reference towards the
heavenly Christ with whom we are joined, and to whom the Spirit
brings us during our earthly ecclesial gatherings, even if some such
structures are implicit within the charge not to neglect meeting
together (Heb. 10:25).

The result should be a light hold upon ecclesial structures, and a
disciplined desire that they – and we – be continually reforming.
Christ who is 'preparing a place' for us is also the Lord and well-
spring of our constructing of places within this present world. At
the same time, however, the searching territoriality of the heavenly
Christ ruling over our earthly spaces and his desire for his good
pleasure in his servants' lives (cf. Matt. 25:14–30) means we must
work hard at developing ecclesial practices and structures that seek
to conform Christ's earthly bride increasingly to his revealed will.
This balance reflects how a robust doctrine of the ascended Christ
renders us believers on earth –local assembled congregations – as
participants, rather than passive spectators, in a covenantal mutual
indwelling or *perichoresis* (from *chōra*, meaning 'space' or 'room')
with Christ in heaven. Thus Dawson, reflecting on Hebrews
2:10–18, says:

> Such a passage transforms our understanding of worship, filling us with
> new layers of imagination as we visualize the unseen reality around us.

104. This heavenly dimension to Christology and ecclesiology strongly sug-
     gests that we are to view ourselves as *heavenly* catholics, in the etymological
     sense of catholicity, meaning 'according to the whole'. Concerning such a
     heavenly locus of the church, see David Peterson, 'The Locus of the
     Church: Heaven or Earth?', *Churchman* 112.3 (1998), pp. 199–213.

The glorified, ascended, still incarnate Jesus is in the Holy Place, within the true tabernacle (Hebrews 8:2) of which every earthly house of worship is at best a shadow. Yet in the Holy Spirit he is not removed from us. The Spirit is the Spirit of Jesus, and brings his presence to us in worship, most especially in the preaching of the Word and the administration of the sacraments. And the Spirit lifts us up, spiritually, in our worship to the throne of God where Jesus serves as our advocate, priest, intercessor and worship leader. Through the Spirit, then, the ascended Jesus comes to be in our midst and through the same Spirit we are brought in Christ our High Priest into the Father's welcoming presence.[105]

For some, this kind of vision of ecclesial life is full of excitement; others are more cautious, wondering what this means in practice and how we assess the faithfulness and success of such projects. But these are exactly the kinds of challenges recovering an understanding of the absent-but-active heavenly Christ will present to us.

Sacraments

These ecclesial questions easily lead into issues relating to the sacraments. In the light of the discussion thus far, what are the implications of Christ being ascended for how we understand the sacraments?[106]

Most importantly, Christ's bodily ascension into heaven means that we cannot dissolve his humanity into either ubiquity or metaphor. He is truly ascended into heaven, and is truly human,

---

105. Dawson, *Jesus Ascended*, p. 136. Furthermore, in our everyday prayers individual believers are, by faith, participating in Jesus' continuing prayers. Conscious appropriation of this privileged position in our prayers will provide bold assurance, faithful direction, and Spirit-given unity to our prayers, as we are drawn to look away from ourselves and towards our heavenly brother and Lord. His prayers become ours, and our prayers become his.

106. The following discussion focuses on the Lord's Supper, but parallel comments can also be applied to baptism.

and this controls our understanding of the sacraments. As such, he is out of our control: this needs to be observed, lest we fall into Simony, as originally construed (Acts 8:18–24), even if no money changes hands. Christ and his benefaction are sovereignly beyond us. The Anglican 'Black Rubric' recognizes this: 'the natural Body and Blood of our Saviour Christ are in Heaven, *and not here*; it being against the truth of Christ's natural Body to be at one time in more places than one' (emphasis added).

Therefore, taken seriously, Christ's ascension precludes a variety of erroneous readings of his body. If Christ's body is 'abstracted from the absent Nazarene', then the pre-Reformation church's stance becomes possible, whereby Christ was placed 'fully in the church's possession' and 'the church . . . controlled the parousia. At the ringing of a bell the *Christus absens* became the *Christus praesens*.'[107] Such a misrepresentation required a completely absent Christ; indeed, it excluded him. The full perversion of this pre-Reformation belief, whereby '[s]eated comfortably with the Christ-child in its lap, the church soon became his regent rather than his servant',[108] is revealed for what it is by a proper doctrine of Christ's ascension. In its light, the bread and wine clearly do not contain Christ's body, which is exclusively in heaven, and so ecclesial possession and control of Christ's presence are precluded. Similarly, claims regarding the elevation of Mary, even the ascent of Mary,[109] are rendered inappropriate and hostile to a doctrine of Christ's ascension.

In contrast, the biblical portrait of Christ, outlined above, positions him clearly in heaven: such as, it propounds 'a thoroughly eschatological treatment of the problem of the presence and the absence'.[110] Thus, as an example of reformed liturgy, the prayer of

---

107. Farrow, *Ascension and Ecclesia*, pp. 156, 157.

108. Ibid., p. 157.

109. Another false dissolution of absence, by which the veneration of Mary becomes 'the Church's testimony to herself' (ibid., p. 157, quoting Otto Semmelroth, *Mary, Archetype of the Church*, trans. Maria von Eroes and John Devlin [Dublin: Gill, 1964], p. 174).

110. Farrow, *Ascension and Ecclesia*, p. 164.

consecration in the service of the Lord's Supper presented in the *Book of Common Prayer* begins with a declaration of the true relation of the sacrament to the sacrifice. This declaration emphasizes the sacrament's eschatological nature: *we* continue 'a perpetual memory of that his precious death and sacrifice until his coming again'.

Yet if the early reformers agreed that the crux of the Supper was not the church's offering but Christ's offering at Calvary, they still disagreed about the matter of Christ's possible presence at the Supper. As Farrow has shown, their understanding of the ascension played a part in these debates.

The Reformation's early progress and subsequent impasse in this matter can be traced with reference to Zwingli and Luther. Zwingli's solution rightly stressed Christ's bodily absence, and also emphasized that none should think themselves able to fetch him to hide under the consecrated elements. In contrast, and in a desire to avoid *confining* Christ to heaven, Luther's position resorted to ubiquity in an attempt to preserve sacramental realism, but this jeopardized the Chalcedonian axiom of 'without confusion' regarding Christ's human and divine natures. Ubiquity also risked the presence of Christ in the elements becoming 'a mere corollary of [his] massive cosmic presence'[111] rather than a unique and indispensable presence within the sacraments. As such, any significance for the Lord's Supper, and for the church's particularity established upon it, is diminished.

The theological outcome of Zwingli and Luther debating these issues at the Colloquy of Marburg in 1529 was stark. Luther considered Zwingli to be succumbing to Nestorianism, in that he judged Zwingli to be denying the unity of Christ in that the body did not have the properties of divine nature such as ubiquity, and that Zwingli concluded that Luther had collapsed the two natures into one, thereby committing a Eutychian error,[112] by holding that the body has the property of ubiquity.

---

111. Jaroslav Pelikan, *The Christian Tradition: A History of the Development of Doctrine*. Vol. 4: *Reformation of Church and Dogma, 1300–1700* (Chicago: University of Chicago Press, 1984), p. 202.

112. Calvin makes the same conclusion (*Institutes* 4.17.30). All quotations from Calvin's *Institutes* are from John T. McNeil (ed.), trans. Ford Lewis

Calvin's way through this impasse depended upon his understanding of Christ's ascension and subsequent session,[113] and his
formulations remain helpful for us as we piece together the implications of Christ's heavenly session. First, Calvin recognized that
ubiquity is not an option, given Christ's truly human nature.[114] This
first non-negotiable is matched by a second, namely, Christ's heavenly majesty.[115] As a consequence, various interpretations of the
Supper, both those of Rome and of Calvin's critics among his
fellow reformers, are dismissed as errors, in that they fail to take
seriously Christ's embodied and heavenly state.[116] In a move char-
acteristic of Calvin's wider theologizing, this is 'not a question
of what God could do, but what he has willed to do'.[117] Thus
'Flesh must . . . be flesh; spirit, spirit – each thing in the state and
condition wherein God created it. But such is the condition of
flesh that it must subsist in one definite place, with its own size and
form.'[118]

As such, Calvin and the Black Rubric are as one.[119] This is not
to in any way diminish God's power but is, rather, to praise it –
and to seek to do so within the bounds of Scripture as a whole

---

Footnote 112 (cont.)

    Battles, *Calvin: Institutes of the Christian Religion*, Library of Christian
    Classics, vols. 20–21 (Philadelphia: Westminster, 1960).

113. Cf. ibid. 2.16.14–16, regarding Christ's ascension as truly inaugurating
    his kingdom and signalling his rule of heaven and earth. From heaven,
    he shall return as judge of all people (ibid. 2.16.17).

114. Ibid. 4.17.19, 30.

115. Ibid. 4.17.19; cf. 4.17.32.

116. Ibid. 4.17.20–23.

117. Ibid. 4.17.24.

118. Ibid.

119. Clearly, Christ's embodied and heavenly state constitutes one funda-
    mental obstacle precluding optimism regarding attempts to gloss
    over substantive and fundamental doctrinal differences concerning
    the Supper. Cf. the *Joint Declaration on Doctrine of Justification* made
    by the Lutheran World Federation and the Roman Catholic Church
    in 1999.

without plunging into the 'abyss of God's omnipresence'.[120] As with Matthew 26:8–11 and Acts 3:21, Calvin asserts that Christ remains in heaven until the last day.[121] But what, then, of Matthew 28:20? Christ is certainly promising 'invincible help to his disciples', but this help is also *invisible*, since 'the context shows that Christ is speaking with no reference whatsoever to his flesh'.[122]

The solution Calvin posits is pneumatological[123] – it is the role of the Spirit that allows Calvin 'to reckon more bravely than the other reformers with the absence of Christ as genuine problem for the church'.[124] For, as the cloud of Acts 1:9 genuinely hides Christ from mortal sight,[125] Christ is, until the parousia, located in a genuinely heavenly *site*. As Luke 24:39 and other New Testament texts declare, Christ's resurrection body is not merely spiritual.[126] Calvin then deals with possible objections regarding Christ's resurrection body in the course of his pre-ascension appearances. More crucially for the present discussion, after the ascension into heaven, 'he wishes to be sought there alone'.[127] Therefore, in the Supper, 'the whole Christ is present, but not in his wholeness'.[128] Christ 'is spiritual to us, not because He has laid aside the body and been changed into a spirit, but because it is by the power of His Spirit that He regenerates and governs His own'.[129] In one pithy paragraph, Calvin posits that Christ is not brought down to us, but that we are lifted up to him.[130] Calvin is happy to leave this work of

---

120. Calvin, *Institutes* 4.17.24.

121. Ibid. 4.17.26.

122. Ibid. 4.17.30.

123. See esp. ibid. 4.17.12, 33.

124. Farrow, *Ascension and Ecclesia*, p. 175.

125. Calvin, *Institutes* 4.17.27.

126. Ibid. 4.17.29.

127. Ibid.

128. Ibid. 4.17.30.

129. John Calvin, *The Second Epistle of Paul the Apostle to the Corinthians and the Epistles to Timothy, Titus and Philemon*, trans. T. A. Smail (Grand Rapids: Eerdmans, 1964), p. 75, concerning 2 Cor. 5:16.

130. Calvin, *Institutes* 4.17.31.

the Spirit as 'a secret too lofty for either my mind to comprehend or my words to declare'.[131]

Calvin goes on to declare that this excludes adoration of the elements,[132] but the question remains – does Calvin *positively* develop his understanding of the believers' union with Christ through the Spirit? Certainly, Calvin manages to preserve Christ's particularity without sacrificing sacramental realism, and he does so by a relational, Christocentric concept of space. Although not everywhere present, the heavenly Christ is, by the Spirit, everywhere accessible.[133]

Yet Farrow discerns here a problem as a failure to think eschatologically:

> When absence is taken seriously and the missing third member – the parousia – is added to the descent and ascent scheme, the symmetry is broken, the suffocating circle is opened up. What emerges as of first importance is not a pattern but a particular, namely, 'this same Jesus,' who will come in like manner as he departed.[134]

Farrow's insight holds, and is helpful, even if his verdict cast on Calvin's limitations is somewhat stark.[135] Calvin does position the

---

131. Ibid. 4.17.32. This sentiment continues into the polemics of sect. 4.17.33. Cf. ibid. 4.17.10: 'What, then, our mind does not comprehend, let faith conceive: that the Spirit truly unites things separated in space.' Calvin himself appeals to an analogy of how 'the sun, shedding its beams upon earth, casts its substance in some measure upon it in order to beget, nourish, and give growth to its offspring' (ibid. 4.17.12).

132. Ibid. 4.17.35–37.

133. Farrow, *Ascension and Ecclesia*, pp. 177–178.

134. Ibid., p. 265. Similarly, Torrance, *Royal Priesthood*, p. 58.

135. Cf. e.g. Torrance, *Space, Time and Resurrection*, p. 132, who claims to speak 'with Calvin' on this matter. As Dawson, *Jesus Ascended*, p. 45, more charitably observes regarding this argument's advance on the world view predominant at the time of the Reformation, '[t]his stunning theological insight outstripped the science of the day, and only makes cosmological sense after the discoveries of modern physics.' Calvin was one reformer

supper as 'a heavenly act', whereby Christ remains in heaven but 'He imparts Himself to us . . . by the secret power of the Holy Spirit, a power which is able not only to bring together, but also to join together, things which are separated by distance, and by a great distance at that'.[136]

Public theology?

As king in the full sense of Psalm 2, the ascended Christ lays claim not simply to a narrow ecclesial sphere, but the claims of his territoriality extend to all spheres of life. British evangelicals are beginning to recover a vision for theology that addresses the public sphere of the marketplace and its associated cultural and political realms. A robust doctrine of the heavenly Christ will be an integral component of such a project, if it is not to descend or diminish into sub-Christian culs-de-sac of withdrawal from the world, attempting to build the kingdom of heaven on earth, or conformity to the world.

Farrow helpfully links these potential culs-de-sac for our nascent public theologies to inadequate and sub-biblical notions of the ascended Christ. For example, whatever its immediate causes, withdrawal from the world is prefaced with or legitimated

---

who came especially close to such a realization (see esp. *Institutes* 4.17.28), and Calvin's insights anticipate later cosmological advances. Dawson, *Jesus Ascended*, p. 49, concludes, 'Holding together the spiritual and the physical, Calvin leapt ahead of his contemporaries, and his thought could not actually be appreciated until a century ago when science began to see past the old dualisms.' This new understanding arising in physics was 'that the relations between things or persons constitute an essential part of what they truly are' (Dawson, *Jesus Ascended*, p. 49), rather than space as some kind of receptacle that necessarily contains or circumscribes Christ. For further on Torrance's engagement with modern science and its appreciations of space and time, see Torrance, *Space, Time and Resurrection*, pp. 130–131, 179–193.

136. John Calvin, *The First Epistle of Paul the Apostle to the Corinthians*, trans. John W. Fraser (Grand Rapids: Eerdmans, 1960), p. 247, concerning 1 Cor. 11:24.

by a downplaying of Jesus' continuing humanity and his cosmic reign, and is accompanied by a retreat into a spiritualized view of Christ and, consequently, of the Christian life. The result is an atomistic understanding of a church administering a privatized ministry of word and sacraments, matched with an intellectualizing tendency, and a foreshortened vision for mission and kingdom among the people and places of this world.[137] As a result, as Farrow expresses it well, 'some of the fizz disappears from the ecclesial winepress'![138] Clearly, withdrawal from the world can have a variety of causes, but an enfleshed, heavenly and returning Christ who oversees and directs the great commission of Matthew 28:18–20 is not one of them, and he is a great antidote against them. This is confirmed by the cosmic, new-creation aspects of his heavenly session as a real, human king enthroned in heaven and ruling over the whole world, destined to judge the living and the dead.

Another potential cul-de-sac, the pursuit of purely earthly visions of the kingdom of heaven with their associated denial of any eschatological distance, can also arise from a spiritualizing reduction of the ascended Christ. By contrast, a robust doctrine of the heavenly Christ, as laid out above, preserves the earthly church from mistaking itself as a valid substitute for what – and who – is in the heavenlies, and where the true eschatological locus lies. The same doctrine of the heavenly Christ who is genuinely other to our world order also controls tendencies towards the church becoming conformed to the world. If sinfully misplaced as a substitute for the heavenlies, our churches become cosy, constrictive entities and/or needs-hungry structures demanding

---

137. Dawson, *Jesus Ascended*, p. 55: 'A Spiritualized Jesus allows the kings of the world to run free without restraint from the church, and allows the church to run after the things of the world without the downdraft pressure of the return of the embodied Jesus.' For further reflections on what the triumph of the ascended reigning Jesus means for believers as 'citizens of a far country' and the implications of 'Christ in the Marketplace', see ibid., pp. 143–161, 198–200.

138. Farrow, *Ascension and Ecclesia*, p. 102, n. 62.

maintenance, which neuter the earthly mission of the heavenly Christ. Historical experience has tainted the very idea of Christendom for many, and this is a significant sticking point for recovering a genuinely public theology.[139] An ecclesial humility as well as ecclesial vision engendered by the human-and-divine Christ's heavenly session, however, is a path to reimagining new and empowering (but provisional, rather than ineluctable) Christendom potentialities that have within themselves internal checks against the domesticating and de-eschatologizing tendencies of earthly ecclesial power.

Leaving aside such culs-de-sac, what directions can be plotted for an ascension-driven public theology? Expressed positively, we need new godly architects for such public theologies; the ascended Christ will be a cornerstone for their labours (cf. Acts 4:11–12). Clearly, theologians have a part to play in this, but we also need other thinkers and strategists who will develop theological theories and practices in a host of public spheres. It is all too easy to leave analysis at the macrolevel, blaming television, individualism and relativism, and to call for mortification in the face of such things.[140] We also need exegetes of culture who can trace closely the contours of its sinful counter-ascensions and alternative ascensions and can critique them in the light of Christ's ascension, properly understood.[141] Such is the perpetual need for ground-clearing prior to the positive project of constructing Christian public theologies.

---

139. For historical glimpses of what happens when the churches forget the ascension, see ibid., pp. 114–117, 128–131, concerning the patristic and medieval periods.

140. Cf. Wheaton, 'What in Heaven?', pp. 353–354.

141. E.g. secular cultural geographers deconstruct the grand narratives of global capitalism in a manner that needs to be theologically governed. Comparing their analyses of images associated with marketing financial products (e.g. http://www.lclark.edu/~goldman/global/pagesintro/mapfive.html) with an the artwork inspired by Christ's ascension (e.g. http://biblia.com/jesusm/passion.htm#Ascension, putting aside any reservations about such religious art, raises critical questions concerning

This positive project can and should be theologically controlled. For example, Calvin's pneumatological insight regarding the heavenly Christ also casts light on how the word and Spirit can function together as an impetus and a control for ascension-based engagement with the public sphere. The doctrine of Christ's ascension, developed across this chapter, positions and provides a theological control for Soja's understanding of 'thirdspace', mentioned earlier. The Spirit's simultaneous compression and preservation of distance between the heavenly Christ and believers on earth communicates the 'and more' dimension of thirdspace as an understanding of space that is 'simultaneously real [i.e. material] and imagined [i.e. ideas-based] and more'.[142] For Soja, the 'and more' dimension, which is the vital critical potential of thirdspace, is generally benign and emancipatory. Soja lacks an appreciation of the fall, and of Christ's ascension. Theologically, any attempt to locate such formative thirdspace anywhere *other* than in the work of the Holy Spirit given by Christ comes under the Scriptures' sustained critique regarding idolatry and its consequent spiritual bondage and blindness.

Interestingly, contemporary cultural studies operate within a similar critique of idolatry when they criticize and reject what is disparagingly termed the 'god trick', namely, the notion that it is

---

Footnote 141 (cont.)

the misappropriation of *theological* ideas pertaining to Christ's ascension and heavenly session for the sustenance of frequently taken-for-granted economic norms that all too easily become idols. In past generations the salvation geography generated by Christ's heavenly session led to Christians not resisting the fall of Jerusalem in AD 70 and contributed to the Roman Empire acknowledging Christ centuries later. Where is such a Christocentric public imagination in our society, in our churches? Where are the theologically informed commentators of our day and places who can both tease out, critique and counterposition the productions of places and spaces in our world, to the glory of the ascended Lord? How can churches and other evangelical ministries instruct and support such work?

142. Soja, *Thirdspace*, p. 11.

possible to have 'vision from everywhere and nowhere equally'.[143] The proposed alternative is 'situated knowledge', 'views from somewhere', wherein '[o]nly the god-trick is forbidden'.[144] Within cultural studies this critique of the 'god trick' is usually executed within presuppositions that deny the existence of God and even is marshalled to preclude the Christian voice. Nevertheless, the critique itself is eminently redeemable within a biblical framework that presumes the existence of a sovereign God – and, indeed, the ascended Christ – enjoying such a perspective (and without any hint of trickery). Indeed, such acknowledgment of human potential to presume the divine viewpoint for itself is necessary given the ongoing propensity of sinful human hearts to imagine and engineer rhetorical moves that hide and protect the speaker's proposals, even within a discourse that claims to accept all that is being said here concerning the ascended Christ. Concerning both ecclesial forms and the ministry of the word and sacraments, a hermeneutic of suspicion is always and everywhere necessary, even as the ascended Christ calls upon the church to engage with the world. Even (especially?) the church can perform 'god tricks'. Linking back with earlier discussion of the ascension's impact on ecclesiology, the form of Christ's presence with his church 'challenges an overblown confidence in the church as human institution',[145] leaving it subject to Scripture as its external authority and the control for its continuing reformation. Such a church is better equipped to enter the public sphere.

Conclusion: life, as we are coming to know it

In the course of our exploration of the hidden Christ, we have come a long way, and covered a lot of ground. The compass of

---

143. Donna J. Haraway, *Simians, Cyborgs and Women: The Reinvention of Nature* (London: Free Association, 1991), p. 191; see, more generally, pp. 188–196.
144. Ibid., pp. 196, 195.
145. Burgess, *Ascension in Karl Barth*, p. 58.

Christ's ascension has covered the earthly and the heavenly, the cosmic and the local, matters pertaining to both personal and corporate dimensions of life, and the public and private spheres.

Jesus' absence from us in heaven, like that of Moses when he ascended Sinai, creates opportunities and challenges for the people of God here on earth (cf. Acts 7:40). A denial of space is not the solution; only a properly formed theology of space can suffice, and such a theology will have as its touchstone the heavenly Christ. We await God's own version of Pilate's declaration 'Behold the man!' (cf. Acts 17:30–31; Rev. 1:10–18; cf. 1:7).[146] As Farrow concludes, our task is 'to proclaim the absence clearly' in our discipleship and worship, since '[t]he church that forgets the absence inevitably begins to misunderstand and misconstrue the presence'.[147] In his final challenge, Farrow holds out martyrdom as the willing and healthy norm of a church living within the tension of Christological presence and absence, occupying 'the tear- and blood-besplattered junction between two histories and two worlds' where we face 'two competing projects in the making of man' – that of God's own hands, and that of alternative sinful human agendas.[148] Choosing 'to identify the ascended one as someone other than Jesus' leads to a path by which we will 'arrive at Damascus without incident'.[149] To choose such a path leads to our condemnation since it is to deny 'the most potent facts in the life of the human race'.[150]

The alternative is life lived 'under heaven', within the earthly spaces for believers already shaped and continually upheld by the heavenly Christ. These spaces are characterized by a committed exposure and submission to God's word read, heard, taught and applied in our lives. These are spaces undergoing continual reformation, where earthly structures are held lightly and provisionally.

---

146. Farrow, *Ascension and Ecclesia*, p. 271.

147. Ibid., p. 272.

148. Ibid., p. 273.

149. Ibid.

150. H. B. Swete, *The Ascended Christ: A Study in the Earliest Christian Teaching* (London: Macmillan, 1910), p. 13.

Where spaces submit to the Lordship of the heavenly Christ, their claims are relativized and subject to service in his name; where spaces reject his Lordship they are subject to his judgment, both present and to come. To locate them in a non-exhaustive fashion, these places are our homes, our churches, our places of work and leisure, even the seat on the commuter train . . .

The eschatological desire for the heavenly Christ precludes too close an embrace of earthly space even while it demands such earthly spaces. In such a life we are also fed spiritually by regular participation in both sacraments.[151] Reflection upon our heavenly Christ directs and increases our confidence in prayer and worship.[152] Our hearts are lifted heavenwards, but without any denial of creaturely life. The cumulative effect is that our manner of life in every dimension becomes conformed increasingly to the will of our absent Lord who is present with us by the Spirit. The here-but-not-here eschatological tension both grounds us and raises us upwards. We let go of fleeting earthly loyalties precisely because he has gone to prepare a place for us. But, at the same time and in the same places, even the apparently menial daily activities are performed with increasing consciousness that our words, deeds and attitudes are to be pleasing to our heavenly Lord and are for his sake. To redeem the old lie, such lives are heavenly minded *in order to be of earthly good.*

In all this, by linking the heavenly Christ not only to his earthly incarnation but also to his still-awaited return *as a man*,[153] 'absentee Christology' is properly understood and, when viewed pneumatologically and in the light of Christological interventions in Acts, is stripped of its connotations of passivity. Here, also, is God's triumph, 'the triumph of a particular man, and with him of a whole

---

151. Regular worship among Jesus' people will mean we shall routinely witness baptisms. Each time, this is a herald to recall our own baptism, and our resultant union with Christ. Cf. 1 Pet. 3:21–22.

152. Dawson, *Jesus Ascended*, pp. 134–141, develops these observations at greater length than is possible here.

153. At very least, apart from any other meanings it might convey, this is the impulse of Acts 1:11.

world of particulars as created by God'.[154] The 'scandal of particularity' that rightly associates itself with Christianity is intensely Christological and, in the present, inherently heavenly. It leads to nothing less than the vision of a new creation,[155] and is accessed by looking to the Spirit and the written word, not beyond Christ's humanity to his divinity or to some claim for ubiquity or for a domesticated and earthly Christ.

As such, the heavenly Christ is most certainly 'placed', but as such is not placed (at least, not positively) with respect to ourselves, to our space: 'he is not above us or ahead of us or alongside us or within us, even if each of these metaphors has something helpful to say about his actual relation to us'.[156] But neither is he something *other* than a human being. This portrait of a particular heavenly human (all three terms are here important) is highly disturbing, challenging 'our entire frame of reference, physical and metaphysical, . . . allowing one particular man to stand over against us, as a question mark against our very existence'.[157]

All that has been expounded regarding Christ's ascension is clearly and primarily for God's glory but, without detracting from that, Andrew Murray's words remind us, in closing, of our great benefits accrued from Jesus' heavenly state:

> We are so familiar with all the blessed meaning there is in the words *for us*, in reference to Christ on the cross. What He did there was all for us; by it and in it we live. No less is it true of Christ within the veil. It is all *for us*; all that He is and has there is for us; it is our present possession; by it and in it we live with Him and in Him . . . We have yet to learn all that is contained in this Melchizedek priesthood. But this will be its chief glory – that He is a Priest for ever, a Priest in the power of an endless life, a Priest who opens to us the state of life to which He Himself has

---

154. Farrow, *Ascension and Ecclesia*, p. 265. Concerning the triumph of Jesus, see Dawson, *Jesus Ascended*, pp. 53–72, for longer exposition than is possible here.

155. Farrow, *Ascension and Ecclesia*, pp. 265–266.

156. Ibid., p. 266.

157. Ibid., pp. 266–267.

entered in, and brings us there to live here on earth with the life of eternity in our bosom.

Christian reader! Knowest thou the power of this hope, entering into that which is within the veil, whither the Forerunner is for us entered. Jesus is in heaven *for thee*, to secure thee a life on earth in the power and joy of heaven, to maintain the kingdom of heaven within thee, by that Spirit, through whom God's will is done on earth as it is in heaven. All that Jesus is and has, is heavenly. All that he gives and does, is heavenly. As High Priest at God's right hand, He blesses with all heavenly blessings. Oh, prepare thyself, as the glory of His person and ministry in the heavenly places are now to be opened up to thee, to look upon it, and appropriate it all, as thy personal possession. And believe that His High Priesthood not only consists in His having secured certain heavenly blessings for thee, but in his fitting and enabling thee to enter into the full person experience and enjoyment of them.[158]

---

158. Murray, *Holiest of All*, pp. 225–226; emphasis original.

Appendix: Douglas Farrow's rhetorical structure of Hebrews[159]

Chapters 1–12
The homily

1:1-4	3:1	4:14-16	8:1-6	10:19-25	12:1-3	12:28-29
	hothen . . . therefore . . .	*oun* . . . then . . .	*kephalaion* . . . 'the main point'	*oun* . . . then . . .	*toigaroun* . . . therefore . . .	*dio* . . . therefore . . .

'he sat down at the right hand'

'we have a high priest who sat down at the right hand'

'draw near' (4:14-16) 'draw near' (10:19-25)

'sharers of a heavenly calling' concentrate on Jesus

'let us run . . . fixing our eyes on Jesus'

'let us be grateful'

1:1-4	3:1	4:14-16	8:1-6	10:19-25	12:1-3	12:28-29
Son	High Priest / Apostle	High Priest / Son	High Priest / *leitourgos*	High Priest / Priest / Son(29)	'author and perfector'	mediator (24)

Chapter 13
Epistolary exhortations
Benediction: 'that Great Shepherd'[160]

---

159. Farrow, *Ascension and Ecclesia*, p. 279.

160. The Latimer Trust and the Oak Hill College Bursary Fund funded the research that underpins this chapter. I extend my thanks to them for their generous support.

5. THE LAST ADAM, THE LIFE-GIVING SPIRIT

Richard B. Gaffin, Jr.

Introduction

The invitation to prepare this conference paper came with the following fairly extensive brief, stipulating in advance not only questions the paper should address but also points it ought to explore:

> Jesus is the last Adam. He rose from the dead and ascended into heaven in this capacity. The outpouring of the Holy Spirit on the Day of Pentecost was an act of the ascended Christ. Both John's Gospel and Acts relate the giving and outpouring of the Holy Spirit to the glorification of Jesus. This paper will consider these strands of biblical truth and how they relate to the teaching that the last Adam is a life giving spirit. The following questions and issues will also be addressed. What is the significance of the fact that the Spirit is given not simply by a divine person in the Godhead but by the God-*man*? What light does this teaching throw upon the nature of Adam in his state of probation and what he lost for himself *and* for the human race? Is a proper pneumatology impossible without a full-orbed Christology which takes

account of Christ as the last Adam as life giving Spirit? What is the relevance of this teaching for the individual believer's life of faith and for the church's internal life and for its mission and witness to the world?

I am unaware of the person (or persons) who produced this brief but have been helped by it considerably in clarifying the way I want to go about developing this chapter. Accordingly, while in what follows I am unable to address each of these issues and questions with equal depth, its shape, in large part, is determined by them.

The chapter's title, as many readers are no doubt aware, is taken directly from the latter part of 1 Corinthians 15:45, rendered here 'the last Adam became the life-giving Spirit'. This affirmation, I take it, refers (1) to Christ specifically as resurrected or, more broadly, as exalted, and (2) to the person of the Holy Spirit. On the way to showing that as its sense, particularly in the interests of seeing something of its full implications, it will be valuable for us first to appreciate the integral way this affirmation is embedded and functions within its immediate context.

The context

1. John Murray has written, 'In 1 Corinthians 15:22, 45–49 Paul provides us with what is one of the most striking and significant rubrics in all of Scripture'.[1] This sweeping claim is arresting, especially for those, like myself, who have living memories of Professor Murray. If there is anything that marked his theologizing, especially his handling of Scripture, it was judicious carefulness; he was not given to overstatement. Being somewhat less circumspect than Murray, I can be inclined on a given day to say these verses are the most remarkable in the entire Bible. Obviously, one should be wary of such an extravagant claim. But in truth it is fair to observe that nowhere in Scripture do we get a more all-encompassing outlook on the work of Christ than in

---

1. J. Murray, *The Imputation of Adam's Sin* (Grand Rapids: Eerdmans, 1959), p. 39.

verses 44b–49. In this respect they correlate in their sweep with the likes of Colossians 1:15–20 and, outside Paul, the prologue to John's Gospel and Hebrews 1:1–4. From the perspective of systematic theology not only do they bear on virtually every major locus but they do so in a fundamental way. As we shall have occasion to see, the biblical doctrines of creation, including man as God's image, of the fall and sin, Christology, soteriology and eschatology are all addressed decisively by these verses.

Expanding the context matrix for verse 45 slightly on the one side, at verse 42 Paul, characteristically for him, begins a deliberately balanced contrasting parallelism that extends to verse 49:[2]

> So is the resurrection of the dead. It is sown in corruption; it is raised in incorruptibility. It is sown in dishonor; it is raised in glory. It is sown in weakness; it is raised in power. It is sown a natural body; it is raised a spiritual body. If there is a natural body, there is also a spiritual body. Thus it is written, 'The first man Adam became a living being'; the last Adam became the life-giving Spirit. But it is not the spiritual that is first but the natural, then the spiritual. The first man was of the earth, earthly; the second man is of heaven. As was the earthly one, so also are those who are earthly, and as is the heavenly one, so also are those who are heavenly. And just as we have borne the image of the earthly one, we shall also bear the image of the heavenly one.

This passage (the antithetical parallelism is apparent) functions to answer, in part, the questions raised in verse 35, 'How are the dead raised? With what kind of body do they come?' – a two-part question that concerns the mode of the resurrection and the nature of the resurrection body. From the brusqueness of Paul's immediate response, 'Fool' (v. 36; softened in most English translations), this question was apparently posed derisively by the opposition that Paul is having to deal with at Corinth and that

---

2. Translations throughout, following the English Standard Version fairly closely unless otherwise noted, are mine. Here I have been somewhat more literal than necessary and also made certain exegetical decisions. Support for the latter will be given as our discussion unfolds.

comes into view already at verse 12.[3] At any rate, Paul takes the question seriously and it triggers, in large part, his argument to the end of the chapter, within the dominant concern of most of the chapter (vv. 12ff.), the resurrection hope of the church.[4]

Verses 42–43 contrast the dead ('sown') body and the resurrection body of the believer by noting three qualities of each, paired antithetically: in turn, the incorruptibility that marks the resurrection body answers to the corruption of the pre-resurrection body, glory to dishonor, power to weakness. Verse 44a, then, is best read as providing a summary description of the two bodies. All told, the pre-resurrection body is (utilizing for the meanwhile an approximate transliteration of the Greek *psychikon*) 'psychical'.[5] On the other side, the one-word label best describing the resurrection body is 'spiritual'. Its sense, crucial for a proper understanding of this passage and the nature of the resurrection body will concern us below.

Skipping over verse 44b for the present, at verse 45 the contrast undergoes a significant broadening. What to this point has been a contrast between two bodies is expanded to include whole persons: Adam on the one side, Christ as 'the last Adam' on the other. Correlatively, in verse 47 they are contrasted, respectively, as 'the first man' and 'the second man'. This Adam–Christ pairing

---

3. Clearly, this opposition centred in denying the resurrection of the body. Without entering here into the considerable scholarly discussion concerning the specific background of this denial, it would appear safe to say that controlling it is an outlook stemming from the prevalent pagan Hellenistic mindset of the day with its depreciation of things material, including the body; see e.g. the discussions of G. D. Fee, *The First Epistle to the Corinthians* (Grand Rapids: Eerdmans, 1987), pp. 715–717; and A. C. Thiselton, *The First Epistle to the Corinthians* (Grand Rapids: Eerdmans, 2000), pp. 1172–1176.

4. It is important to keep in mind that the resurrection of unbelievers, though affirmed by Paul elsewhere (Acts 24:15), is outside his purview throughout the whole of ch. 15 (as is also the case in 1 Thess. 4:13ff.).

5. The difficulty that confronts English translation of this adjective, as well as of the noun *psychē* in v. 45b, will be addressed below.

plainly links this passage closely with its occurrence elsewhere in Paul, both earlier in this chapter in verses 21–22 and in the latter half of Romans 5, beginning at verse 12.

A notable difference between Romans 5 and 1 Corinthians is that, on the one side of the contrast, the former is oriented to Christ's obedience and death, and the latter to his resurrection and consequent life. But, common to both passages, the contrast is not between Adam and Christ simply as random persons or isolated individuals. Plainly their actions are decisive and determinative for others. They are representatives, corporate persons, heads within a contemplated solidarity, respectively, for all who are 'in' them.

Keeping to 1 Corinthians 15:45–49, that solidarity and representative significance is intimated in verse 45. Whatever else is involved in this statement, Adam and Christ are in view as they exemplify and are instances, respectively, of the pre-resurrection bodies (of all human beings) and the resurrection bodies of believers. But at the same time the all-determining headship of each is unmistakable in the way they are contrasted in verses 47–49.

In verse 48, on the one side, Adam is both constitutive for and so representative of the 'earthly' order; he is 'the earthly one' (*ho choikos*) par excellence. Accordingly, he has associated with him the others of this order, all human beings as 'the earthly ones' (*hoi choikoi*). In contrast, Christ is both constitutive for and representative of the 'heavenly' order; he is, pre-eminently, 'the heavenly one' (*ho epouranios*) and as such has associated with him the others of this order, all believers as 'the heavenly ones' (*hoi epouranioi*). These contrasting solidarities, with their respective heads, are reinforced by the culminating statement in verse 49. As believers have borne the image (*eikōn*) of 'the earthly one', Adam, they will also bear, bodily, the image of 'the heavenly one', the now resurrected and ascended Christ (cf. Rom. 8:29; Phil. 3:20).[6]

---

6. For a clearly delineated understanding of these verses, it is important to see, as our subsequent discussion will bear out, that 'of' or 'from heaven' (*ex ouranou*), v. 47, almost certainly does not have in view Christ's incarnation or his coming out of a state of pre-existence at his birth. Rather, it

2. Given this Adam–Christ contrast, with its endemic representative and corporate aspects, we may go on to propose that it is also fairly seen as *covenantal* in its nature and scope. Exegetically, this is readily seen on the Christ side of the parallelism. For instance, in the Romans 5 passage 'the one act of righteousness' (v. 18), culminating in his death (cf. 'obedient unto death', Phil. 2:8) and central to the contrast there, Jesus calls 'the new covenant in my blood' (Luke 22:20; cf. Matt. 26:28; 14:24), as does Paul himself in 1 Corinthians 11:25. Again, in 2 Corinthians 3:3ff., as an apostle of Christ serving in the Spirit, Paul, all told, is a 'minister of the new covenant', where 'the Spirit gives life' (v. 6). The verbal link (*zōopoiei*) with the participial description of the last Adam in 1 Corinthians 15:45c (*zōopoioun*) is evident; the material connection will become clear below.

Elsewhere, in Hebrews the language of covenant comes to the fore concerning Christ and his high priestly work. In contrast to the Mosaic covenant and the Levitical priesthood, Christ is both 'guarantor' and 'mediator of a better covenant' (7:22; 8:6), and 'mediator of a new covenant' (9:15; 12:24). His sacrificial death is, specifically, 'the blood of the covenant' (10:29), 'the blood of the eternal covenant' (13:20). Elementally, from a prophetic perspective, the messianic servant in Isaiah is 'a covenant for [or 'to'] the people' (*librît 'ām*, 42:6; 49:8). The likely sense of the construct here is to the effect that through him, as the Lord's anointed, the covenant will realize its full and true embodiment.

The work of Christ taken as a whole, particularly his death, then, is covenantal. The covenant arrangement and bond, established by God, is its context. Further, this work is comprehensively covenantal, specifically in its corporate and representative dimensions. This points us to consider that, even though there is no

---

Footnote 6 (cont.)

and, correlatively, 'heavenly' in vv. 48–49 are best taken as predicates of Christ as exalted or, more specifically, as ascended. He is 'of heaven' in the sense that his place of residence is there now, for the present, until his return. Following most commentators and virtually all translations, the main verb in v. 49b is, almost certainly, future indicative, rather than the variant aorist subjunctive.

explicit mention of covenant in Romans 5 and 1 Corinthians 15, what takes place in Adam, having similar corporate and representative dimensions, is likewise covenantal in character.

The 'theological logic' here is as follows: (a) the parallel there is between Adam and Christ as heads and representatives; (b) as such, Christ's identity and significance is covenantal; therefore, (c) Adam's identity and significance are covenantal. If the 'in Christ' is covenantal, then the 'in Adam' is likewise covenantal (cf. 1 Cor. 15:22). This conclusion is reinforced by both the universal sweep of the Adam–Christ antithesis as well as the comprehensive scope of the covenant as applied to Christ. Though not shared universally and resisted by some, this conclusion, I take it, is of the first order or magnitude of importance and one that will have to stand unless something in Scripture that decisively contradicts it is brought to light.

3. Returning to 1 Corinthians 15:42ff. in the light of these reflections, we encounter a remarkable feature, one that takes us beyond the scope of verses 21–22 as well as Romans 5:12ff. and gives the Adam–Christ contrast an even broader sweep. On the one side of the contrast, in verse 45, Adam is brought into view as 'living soul' (*psychē zōsan*). This description of the person of Adam is given as a quotation of Genesis 2:7, that is, directly from the account of his creation. In other words, here Adam is introduced not as fallen, as a sinner, as he is in Romans 5 as well as earlier in this chapter in verses 21–22. Rather, he is in view as created, as he was before the fall, as unfallen creature made in God's image. In its full scope, then, the contrast in verse 45 is between Adam as he was by virtue creation and Christ as he is by virtue of resurrection.

In fact, and this touches briefly on Paul's use of the Old Testament, it appears that in Genesis 2:7, seen in its context (the creation narrative), Paul finds not only a reference to Adam's creation but as well the *contrast* between him and the last Adam, or at least he sees there a pointer to that contrast. Several mutually reinforcing observations support this construal. (a) Paul glosses the quotation, from the Greek Bible, with 'first' (*prōtos*) and 'Adam' (*Adam*).[7] This

---

7. The Septuagint of Gen. 2:7 reads, *egeneto ho anthrōpos eis psychē zōsan*. There is no good reason to think that Paul has not supplied the glosses.

implies that he takes the text as open to the last Adam or at least to another Adam. (b) Verse 45c ('the last Adam became the life-giving Spirit') is likely to be read as dependent syntactically on 'it is written' (*gegraptai*); that is, it is implicitly part of what Genesis 2:7 says. (c) Corroborating this reading, verse 45c is an ellipsis, in which 'became' (*egeneto*) from the Genesis 2:7 quote is to be supplied.

In summary, from our observations on the use of Genesis 2:7 in verse 45: (a) Adam is in view as created and unfallen and, as such, contrasted with Christ, the last Adam, as resurrected. (b) The Adam of Genesis 2:7, as the 'first' anticipates a 'last'. The original creation has in view a consummation. Put more formally, protology anticipates or has in prospect an eschatology.

4. This facet of the passage – the reference to Adam before the fall – clear from verse 45, comes out as it is intimated already in the latter part of verse 44, in a detail that has been virtually overlooked, so far as I have seen, in its exegesis.[8]

The Scripture citation in verse 45 is introduced by 'thus', 'so' or 'so also' (*houtōs kai*). This conjunction functions to link verse 45 to what has just been said in verse 44. Specifically, the Scripture cited in verse 45 serves to support what is asserted in the last half of verse 44, in fact the *argument* of verse 44b, 'if there is a natural body, there is also a spiritual (body)'.

The form of verse 44, in particular the movement that takes place within it, should not be missed. As noted above, to verse 43 Paul contrasts the pre-resurrection and resurrection bodies by means of three sets of pointed polarities. Verse 44a, then, serves to sum up the antithesis between the two bodies with their mutually opposed attributes. The pre-resurrection body is 'psychical' (*psychikon*). The sense of this word is discussed below. The resurrection body is 'spiritual', in the sense, as we shall see, that it is the body enlivened and transformed by the Holy Spirit. The two adjectives, as already noted, are comprehensive in their designation, one-word labels, respectively, for the two bodies. The introduction of *psychikon* is already an indication of the turn the discussion is to take.

---

8. I follow here the insight of Geerhardus Vos, *The Pauline Eschatology* (Grand Rapids: Baker, 1979 [1930]), pp. 169–170, n. 19.

In verse 44b the deliberate, cadenced antithetical parallelism maintained up to this point is unexpectedly modified, in fact softened, so that verse 44b, as noted, has an argumentative, 'if . . . , then . . .' form. Paul now argues *from* the pre-resurrection body *to* the resurrection body. He is no longer simply contrasting them. Moreover, the form or structure of this argument needs to be grasped. It is not an argument that fits or can be contained within the scope of the antithesis being developed up to this point. Paul is not reasoning here as he does, for instance, in Romans 5, from the sin of Adam to the grace and righteousness revealed in Christ. There, verses 15 and 17, for instance, have the form, 'if . . . , much more . . .', with an essentially contrasting, even antithetical force: Christ's righteousness despite Adam's sin. Similar in force is the paralleling argumentation, 'as (or 'not as') . . . , so . . .' (vv. 15a, 16, 18, 19; 1 Cor. 15:22). In verse 44b, however, Paul argues without any indication of disjunction. He reasons directly, in linear fashion, from (the existence of) the pre-resurrection to (the existence of) the resurrection body.

This argumentative form already suggests that on the one side in verse 44b the pre-resurrection body is not simply identical with the pre-resurrection body of 44a. Verse 44b provides a different perspective on the pre-resurrection body than 44a.[9] Why, further, should we conclude that? Because the pre-resurrection body of 44a is marked by perishability, dishonour and weakness (vv. 42–43) and, for man as God's image-bearer, these are predicates not given with his creation but brought about by the fall, a result of the curse brought upon the creation by human sin (e.g. Rom. 5:12ff.; 1 Cor. 15:21–22).

Given his biblical world view, Paul could not argue directly, in the simple, linear fashion he does in verse 44b, from that sin-cursed body to the resurrection body, with its opposite, antithetical qualities of imperishability, glory and power. As Vos puts it, for Paul the abnormal body of sin and the eschatological, resurrection body are not so logically correlated that the one can be inferred

---

9. Note in the New International Version the paragraph break within v. 44 at 44b, indicating a shift in thought.

from the other.[10] Pointedly, for Paul one cannot argue directly from death to life; one cannot simply infer life from death. These reflections bring us to conclude that the 'psychical' body of verse 44b is the pre-fall, pre-eschatological body, the body before the fall and by virtue of creation.

This conclusion, finding a distinction between the 'psychical' bodies of verse 44a and 44b, could appear to rest on a doubtful and overly subtle exegesis if we had only verse 44 to consider on its own terms, although we would still have to account for the shift in syntax, already noted, from 44a to 44b. But that conclusion is put on a firm basis by what Paul immediately goes on to say in verse 45, where, as we have already noted, he clearly introduces Adam before the fall, the pre-fall constitution of his person, and does so to support the *argument* of verse 44b.

Pertinent to this supporting function of verse 45 is a consideration difficult to avoid masking in English translations. The nouns in verse 45 and the adjectives in verse 44, respectively, are correlative and so qualify each other. On the one side of the contrast, *psychē* (being, person, soul) and *psychikon* (usually rendered 'natural'; literally, 'soulish') are cognates, as are, on the other side, *pneuma* (Spirit) and *pneumatikon* (spiritual). Given the flow of the argument, the nouns in verse 45 anchor and define the scope of their respective adjectives in verse 44.

What is notoriously difficult here is a satisfactory English translation of *psychikon*, facing the apparently insurmountable challenge of not obscuring the tie in the Greek text, just noted, with *psychē* in verse 45 ('soul', referring, as it does in Gen. 2:7, not to a constituent part but Adam as a whole, so 'being', 'person'). The usual proponents, 'natural' and 'physical', are deficient; the latter, in fact, is thoroughly misleading. 'Physical', because it is paired here antithetically with 'spiritual', leaves the seriously erroneous impression that the resurrection body, in contrast, is

---

10. At a first glance v. 21 ('For since by man came death, by man also came the resurrection of the dead') might seem to be contrary evidence. However, the force of this 'since . . . also' construction is not 'since death, also life', but 'since by man . . . also by man'.

non-physical or immaterial (so e.g. the New Revised Standard Version).

The problem with the translation 'natural' is that it is ambiguous. From the normative vantage point of the original creation, while the body of verse 44b is quite appropriately termed 'natural', the sin-ravaged and mortal body of 44a is decidedly abnormal or 'unnatural'. Only in terms of creation as now fallen is it 'natural' (so Paul's only other use of the adjective in 2:14). The body of 44a, then, is, as it could be put somewhat dialectically, combining these two points of reference, 'now-natural-but-unnatural'.[11] These observations about translating *psychikon* serve to highlight a fundamental dimension of verse 44 I am intent on bringing out here. Pointedly, *psychikon* in 44a is a function of death; in 44b it is a function of (pre-eschatological) life.[12]

---

11. Dr David Coffin in personal conversation.

12. In an important and helpful article ('Paul Confronts Paganism in the Church: A Case Study of First Corinthians 15:45', *Journal of the Evangelical Theological Society* 49.4 [December 2006], pp. 713–737), which appeared after this chapter was submitted as a paper for the Affinity Conference, Peter Jones considers finding this distinction on the one side in v. 44 between the body after (44a) and then before (44b) the fall (as I have argued in R. B. Gaffin, Jr., *Resurrection and Redemption: A Study in Paul's Soteriology* [Phillipsburg, N. J.: Presbyterian & Reformed, 1987 (1978)], p. 79) 'ingenuous, but hardly convincing' (p. 724, n. 58). In his view (pp. 722–727), throughout the passage the pre-resurrection body is the pre-fall body. This leaves him in the position of having to make the doubtful argument that the verb 'sow' in vv. 42–44 is not referring to burial but instead means 'create'. Much more questionable is his contending for 'the possibility' that in v. 42 'in corruption' (*en phthora*) describes the pre-fall body and 'could well mean "created corruptible," that is, created with the genuine possibility of being corrupted' (p. 726). But Paul is not speaking here merely of the possibility of corruption. Clearly, in the next, closely related, occurrence of the noun and usages of the cognate adjective in vv. 50–54, in view is the existing corruptedness of the pre-resurrection body. What is removed by the resurrection change that will take place is not a concreated potential but the actual mortality that

5. Drawing together the threads of my exegesis, why does Paul proceed as he does in this passage? Why on the one side of the Adam–Christ contrast does he broaden its sweep to the normal, creation body from the abnormal body, subject to the effects of the fall, and by introducing Adam not only as fallen but as he was created, as he was before the fall? The answer to these questions involves considerations fundamental to a biblical world view, considerations that have an important bearing on the doctrines of creation, man as image bearer, sin, Christ, salvation and eschatology.[13]

Paul is concerned to show that the plan of God is such that from the outset, already at creation, prior to and apart from the fall, a higher kind of body and personal existence was anticipated and provided for. This is expressed by the notion of 'image' in the culminating statement in verse 49, which in the immediate context corresponds most directly with 44b, 'And as we have borne the image of the earthly one, we shall also bear the image of the heavenly one.' The *imago Dei* in which Adam was created, what Adam

---

Footnote 12 (cont.)

results from sin. The verses elsewhere in Paul cited by Jones to support his view, Gal. 6:8 and Col. 2:22, in fact do not. In the former, 'sowing' in one's own 'flesh' will result in 'corruption' that is actual, not merely potential, because the 'flesh' is in fact already corrupted by sin. In the latter, the regulations in view are destined for 'corruption' not simply because they are human but because, given human fallenness, they are sinful. But most decisive here is Rom. 8:20–23 (a passage Jones does not consider). Bodily redemption-resurrection for believers will mean their being set free, along with the entire creation, from 'bondage to corruption'; i.e. correlatively (the allusion to Genesis 3 is unmistakable) from the 'futility' to which creation has been 'subjected' because of the fall. Exegesis of 1 Cor. 15:42–45, including the correct understanding of v. 44, is clearly bounded by this consideration: on the one side of the contrast, Paul moves from the mortal post-fall and sin-cursed body in v. 42 to the pre-fall, sin-free body in v. 45. Exegesis must therefore account for that movement and its implications.

13. See the comment of Murray on this passage above, n. 1.

and those in him are by virtue of creation, is eschatologically oriented. That image comes to its intended and full realization in the exalted Christ and those in union with him. As already noted above, this passage shows that protology anticipates eschatology, and, correlatively, in this sense eschatology is prior to soteriology.

But more is in view here than bodies or even personal existences. A living body is not an abstraction; it does not exist in a vacuum. It necessarily implies a context; it is an index of an environment or 'world'. This broadening is reflected in this passage by the way in which the central terms of the contrast in verses 44–46, 'soul' and 'Spirit' with their corresponding adjectives are replaced in verses 47–49 by explicitly cosmological terms, 'earth', 'earthly' and 'heaven', 'heavenly'.

In this regard, in the interests of sound exegesis, it needs to be recognized that in verse 46 the neuter singular substantive expressions *to psychikon* (the natural) and *to pneumatikon* (the spiritual) are best taken as generalizing expressions, after which it would be a mistake to read an implied 'body' (*sōma*), as do some translations and commentaries. To do so misses the environmental broadening that Paul has already clearly intimated in verse 45 and works out in verses 47–49. Whereas *to psychikon* is the 'natural' order, *to pneumatikon* is the 'spiritual' order.

Why verse 46 has the form it does ('not this, but that and then this'), breaking with the balanced, two-member contrasting parallelism of the preceding verses and returned to in those that follow, is most probably explained as Paul's countering and correcting the Hellenistic thought pattern of his opponents. According to that outlook the 'spiritual' in the sense of the ideal order is 'first', that is, the archetypal 'world' that is prior in the sense of lying in back of the phenomenal, material world. At any rate, he here clearly reveals the historical and eschatological direction of this thinking. Perfection, the 'ideal', is to be sought in the unfolding of history toward its consummation, not at the beginning of history or above and beyond history but at its end.

We must appreciate, then, the comprehensive perspective this passage opens up. The two-part question Paul is dealing with, the mode of resurrection and the nature of the resurrection body for believers (cf. v. 35), is certainly important in its own right, but it is apparently a rather specific and restricted question. His answer, at a first glance, can seem like an exercise in theological 'overkill'. For the perspective he establishes, the outlook he brings to bear, is nothing less than cosmic in scope, encompassing the whole of history. These verses yield *in nuce* a 'philosophy' of history and its meaning.

This appears especially from the way in which Adam and Christ are introduced and function in the argument. In the overview provided here, Adam is 'first' (*prōtos*, v. 45); there is no-one *before* him. Christ (in his Adamic identity) is 'second' (*deuteros*, v. 47); there is no-one *between* Adam and Christ. The magnitude of Paul's outlook is such that no-one else in covenant history comes into consideration. Here no-one else 'counts' but Adam and Christ – not Noah, not Abraham and the promise, not Moses and the law given at Sinai, not David as the Lord's anointed. Here, we may say, Israel's unfolding 'story', as important and integral as that undoubtedly is elsewhere in Paul's theology and for his reflections on redemptive history, is below the storyline. Here Israel's history, though certainly included implicitly, is eclipsed and remains below the horizon encompassing the whole of history, as Paul sketches that horizon here. Further, Christ as 'second' is also 'last' (*eschatos*, v. 45); there is none *after* him. He is, literally, *the* eschatological man.

Further, as we have seen, as both Adam and Christ are plainly representatives and heads (vv. 48–49), they bring into view orders of life or environments of existence, for which each, respectively, is determinative. The order of Adam is first and has become subject to corruption and death through human sin (Rom. 5:12ff.; 1 Cor. 15:21–22). The order of Christ is second and last; it is incorruptible and eschatological. In view, then, comprehensively considered, is creation and its consummation, creation and new creation, or (in terms of the two-aeon construct taken over by Jesus and Paul as well as other New Testament writers from second temple Judaism and rooted in the Old Testament) this age and the age to come, each beginning with an Adam of its own.

6. Two mutually related considerations emerge in this passage: (a) creation *as a whole* (not only the person of Adam) and (b) creation *as creation* (not merely as fallen) are oriented to consummation. Protology, as already noted, looks toward an eschatology. History as such, not only after the fall, moves toward consummation. The alpha of human history anticipates an omega. Addressing an issue debated in the church virtually since its beginning, this passage appears to be decisive that the end is not simply a return to the beginning, a restoration of primal and pristine conditions as they were before the fall. Rather, while involving a return to the beginning in the sense that the debilitating conditions resulting from the fall are removed, there is still more, the more of consummation, an 'overplus' (W. J. Dumbrell).[14] The end is not simply 'Paradise Regained' but 'Paradise Plus'.

To focus these considerations in terms of Christology, Adam was created with a view to an eschatological order for the creation. That order, forfeited by Adam by sinning, has in fact been brought about by Christ, the last Adam. Conversely, the work of Christ is not only in response to human sin (to Adam as sinner), but, as response to sin, that work realizes the goal for creation prior to sin (for Adam as created). In a sense different from Romans 5:14 but surely consonant with and underlying what Paul says there, even before the fall Adam is '*typos* of the one to come'. Already by virtue of creation, Adam, as 'type' or 'pattern', prefigures and points to what he was called to become and what, in view of his forfeiting fall, has in fact been realized in Christ.

Herman Bavinck, the Dutch Reformed theologian of the late nineteenth and early twentieth centuries, in a highly important and helpful discussion of these issues, one that has greatly influenced my comments here, says that from the beginning the entire creation, including man, is 'infralapsarian'.[15] That is, he intends to say, creation from the beginning is structured with the fall, and so with what takes place in redemption, in view. While that is certainly true in a sense in view of the all-controlling decree of God (for Paul, see esp. Eph. 1:3–11), I am uncomfortable with such language. It

---

14. I recall seeing this expression in his *Covenant and Creation: An Old Testament Covenantal Theology* (Exeter: Paternoster, 1984) but cannot now document the page number.

15. Herman Bavinck, *Reformed Dogmatics* (Grand Rapids: Baker, 2004), vol. 2, p. 564.

must be used with care. Of itself it overstates and is susceptible to the notion, in conflict with the 'everything . . . very good' of Genesis 1:31, that the original creation is inherently defective and even in need of some sort of redemption. It disposes as well toward the serious error of suggesting a necessity for the incarnation apart from the fall.[16] Akin to the free offer of the gospel to elect and non-elect alike, we may say, the original goodness of the creation, including man, implies a well-meant offer of eschatological beatitude to Adam.

It seems better, then, to say, on balance, that Christ (redemption) is the means de facto (since the fall but without implying any necessity inhering in the original make-up of the creation before the fall) by which the eschatology in view for the creation since the beginning is now being realized. This surely gives to the actual consummation a Christological colouration or complexion, because of the fall and ensuing redemption that it would not otherwise have had apart from the fall. At the same time, however, that Christological cast is not calculable or to be anticipated from the constitution of creation before the fall. The Lamb, as he is the lamp-light of the New Jerusalem and on its throne (Rev. 21:23; 22:3, 5), is certainly purposed and secure as such in the counsels of eternity, but that reality cannot be inferred from or read out of the structure of creation before the fall. The 'overplus' as it is brought by Christ at the end cannot be anticipated from what is revealed at the beginning.

The glory Christ brings to the new creation involves a splendour simply unimaginable on the basis of the original creation. The 'superabundance' of grace in Christ that counters the abundance of sin originating with Adam and compounded by the entrance of the law (Rom. 5:20) does not in any way violate what was given with the original creation, but neither is it calculable from it. That grace, not only with reference to sin but also, in the light of 1 Corinthians 15:44b–49, with reference to the original creation, is 'an immeasurable excess' (New English Bible; *hypereperisseuō*). Involved relative to the pre-fall creation (beyond what

---

16. Certainly, Bavinck intends neither of these aberrant views.

may be in view in the immediate context of 1 Corinthians 2:9 but consonant with Paul's broader outlook) is 'what no eye has seen, nor ear heard, nor the heart of man imagined, what God has prepared for those who love him'.

Nevertheless, with this caveat kept in view concerning the incalculability of the Christological stamp on the consummation, a large-scale conclusion, according to 1 Corinthians 15:44b–49, is that Christ corresponds to Adam as he was already before the fall. The work of Christ cannot be comprehended, at least fully and with proper balance, apart from God's original purposes for Adam at creation. Those pre-fall purposes in Adam set the agenda, at least in part, for the work of Christ, the last Adam.

7. The way Paul introduces Adam before the fall into the discourse in 1 Corinthians 15:45–49 (implicitly, as we have seen, already in the argument of v. 44b) has a substantive bearing on a couple of perennial and interrelated issues that continue to be debated at present, particularly in Reformed theology. Here I can do little more than point out that bearing, as I see it, without being able to develop it much.

First, earlier we noted that as Christ's work, the Christ side of the Adam–Christ parallel in Romans 5 and 1 Corinthians 15, is comprehensively covenantal, so what occurred in Adam, the Adam side of the parallel, is no less covenantal in its dimensions. Paul's argumentation in 1 Corinthians 15:44b–49 not only reinforces this inference but also both explicitly extends its scope to the pre-fall order and also provides some indication of the nature of that pre-fall arrangement with Adam. A central thread of the argument is that what has in fact been realized in Christ's (death and) resurrection, his (humiliation and) exaltation, is conditioned on what was established in Adam before the fall (the argumentative form of v. 44b and the sustained parallel of vv. 45, 47–49).

Given that central thread, it seems fair to posit the following as Paul's understanding of the creation narrative in Genesis. In verse 45, as we noted earlier, he sees the account of Adam's creation in Genesis 2:7 as intimating or open to the role that, because of the fall, has been assumed by Christ as the last Adam. So, similarly, it would appear that he sees the commands of 2:16–17 not simply as stipulating the demands of an indefinitely extended or permanently contingent state of affairs, but rather as providing for a test of limited duration. In this probation, not only is Adam's disobedience sanctioned with (eschatological) death, but also, by implication, what he did not yet possess (eschatological life, a state of confirmed and permanent beatitude) was held out to him in consequence of his sustaining this probation by his trusting obedience.

The protology that plainly involved the mutable blessedness of humanity in Adam ('able and not able to sin and die' – the formulation going back at least as far as Augustine) was calculated to eventuate in an eschatology of undeniably immutable blessing ('not able to sin and die'). That eschatology, forfeited for humanity in Adam by his disobedience, has been secured for the new humanity in Christ, the last Adam, by his obedience. This construal rests solidly on Paul's argumentation in 1 Corinthians 15:44b–49.

All this is to say, in other terms, that the doctrine of the covenant of works as it has emerged in Reformed theology arises, at least in its main lines, from the fundamental structures of Paul's theology.[17] I am unable here to go into detail in establishing that in Paul's overall understanding of the law, at its moral core ('the Torah within the Torah', as it has been put[18]), it is expressive of God's enduring will and reflects concerns essential to his person incumbent on his image-bearing creatures from the time of creation. That seems an especially clear implication of his argument for the universality of human sin in Romans 1:18 – 3:20. These abiding concerns antedate, as well as endure beyond, the function of the law that Paul stresses (e.g. Rom. 5:20; 7:6–13; Gal. 3:19–25) – its negative, sin-highlighting and sin-exacerbating redemptive-historical function as given to Israel at Sinai until Christ. Given that understanding of God's law in

---

17. Whether 'works' is the best description of this original covenant arrangement may be left an open question here. In my view, that designation, though not mandatory, is certainly appropriate, with the factor also kept in view that God's all-embracing gratuity and condescending kindness ('grace', 'graciousness' in that sense) is present in the original, pre-fall covenant bond with Adam.

18. Ed. J. van den Berg, *De thora in de thora* (Aalten: de Graafschap, n.d.), vol. 1, p. 5.

Paul, the following insights of Bavinck capture controlling concerns
of his theology.

> As the probationary command relates to the moral law, so the covenant
> of works relates to man's creation in God's image. The moral law in its
> entirety stands or falls with the probationary command, and the image
> of God in mankind in its entirety stands or falls with the covenant of
> works. The covenant of works is the path to heavenly blessedness for
> man created in God's image and not yet fallen . . .
>
> Against the Lutherans and Remonstrants they [the Reformed]
> defended the thesis that, aside from the probationary command, Adam
> was also thoroughly bound to the moral law. He was not 'law-less' (*exlex*,
> bound by no law), even though he fulfilled it without any coercion,
> willingly and out of love.
>
> Adam knew the moral law by nature. Hence, it did not, like the
> probationary command, have to be revealed to him in a special way. It
> is essentially the same as the Ten Commandments but different in form,
> for the law given on Sinai presupposes sins and therefore almost always
> speaks in the negative ('Thou shalt not . . .'), while the moral law before
> the fall was much more positive. But precisely because in the pre-fall life
> of Adam the moral law in the nature of the case was entirely positive, it
> did not make clear to Adam's consciousness the possibility of sin.
> Hence, in addition to the *pre*scriptions there had to come a *pro*scription,
> and in addition to the moral law a positive law. In addition to the
> commandments, whose naturalness and reasonableness were obvious
> to Adam, this command was in a sense arbitrary and fortuitous. In the
> probationary command the entire moral law was put to Adam in a single
> throw, presenting him with this dilemma: either God or man, God's
> authority or his own insight, unconditional obedience or self-sufficient
> investigation, faith or skepticism. It was an awesome test that opened the
> way either to eternal blessedness or eternal destruction.[19]

Second, closely related to the preceding and consonant with the
covenant of works notion, Paul's understanding of the pre-fall

---

19. Bavinck, *Reformed Dogmatics*, vol. 2, pp. 572, 574, slightly modified in the
    light of the Dutch original.

arrangement with Adam, along with his understanding of the relationship of that arrangement to the work of Christ, supports the notion of Christ's obedience as an integral component of the righteousness imputed to believers in justification. For Paul, Christ's obedience culminating in the cross (Phil. 2:8) remedies human sin and its consequences, rooted in Adam's disobedience. His death is an atoning and propitiating sacrifice for sin, and that remediation of all sin, past, present and future, is surely where the primary and preponderant accent falls (e.g. Rom. 4:25; 1 Cor. 15:3–4; 2 Cor. 5:14–15). But from the perspective of 1 Corinthians 15:44b–49, the work of Christ, in his identity as the last Adam, is seen to be more than remedial. The original, pre-fall covenantal arrangement sets the agenda for the work of Christ. Christ succeeds where Adam failed. As head and substitute for those in him, Christ meets what, because of Adam's sin, is the resulting *double* demand of the *broken* pre-fall covenant, namely, obedience tested over time, probation (active obedience), as the way to eschatological life, and satisfaction/propitiation for sin (passive obedience) as deliverance from eschatological death.

To say no more to this large issue here than the following, the active–passive distinction, it should be recognized, does not describe two different sectors of Christ's work but two basic dimensions of the single, entire obedience that begins, publicly, at the Jordan and culminates on the cross. That whole obedience, in both its active and passive dimensions, constitutes the righteousness imputed in justification, securing both the forgiveness of sins and eschatological life. But that finished righteousness, the righteousness of Christ, who is now present with the church and indwells believers as the life-giving Spirit, also provides the model for sanctification, as ongoing Spirit-worked conformity to his image.

As a generalization, subject to further elaboration as well as qualification in view of his deity, it is fair to say that *everything* about Christ's obedience, active and passive, during his earthly ministry (his state of humiliation) involves a unique, non-exemplary, substitutionary aspect, imputed in justification, and *everything* about that obedience also has a paradigmatic, exemplary aspect that functions in sanctification. The climactic evidence and instance of this generalization is Christ's death. As the New Testament makes clear, the cross is both the atonement for my sin and the pattern for my life. For Paul, the latter, exemplary aspect is particularly clear in Philippians 3:10–11, 'being conformed to his death'.

The life-giving Spirit

In the light of the preceding reflections on its immediate context, we turn to focus directly on the last clause in verse 45 and the description there of Christ as 'the life-giving Spirit'.[20] Posing two questions will facilitate our discussion. First, what is the reference of the noun *pneuma*? And, secondly, since life-giving *pneuma* is what the last Adam 'became', when did that happen? What is the time-point of that becoming?

1. A couple of interlocking, mutually reinforcing considerations show, decisively it seems to me, that the noun in verse 45c refers to the person of the Holy Spirit.

First, *pneuma* in verse 45 and *pneumatikon*, twice in verse 44 and twice in verse 46 are, as we noted earlier, linked semantically. As cognate noun and adjective they qualify and explain each other (as do the noun *psychē* and the adjective *psychikon* on the other side of the contrast). Further, in verses 44 and 46 the respective adjectives are paired antithetically. That contrast occurs in only one other place in Paul (or, for that matter, the New Testament), earlier in 2:14–15. There, as most interpreters recognize, the activity of the Holy Spirit is plainly in view – his sovereign, exclusive work in mediating God's revealed wisdom. On the one side of the antithesis, in 2:15, 'the spiritual person' (*ho pneumatikos*) is the believer (cf. vv. 4–5), specifically as enlightened and transformed by the Spirit.[21]

---

20. This section utilizes material from R. B. Gaffin, Jr., '"Life-Giving Spirit": Probing the Center of Paul's Pneumatology', *Journal of the Evangelical Theological Society* 41.4 (December 1998), pp. 577–589.

21. I take it that the long-standing effort to enlist this passage in support of an anthropological trichotomy (with *pneumatikos* here referring to the human *pneuma* come to its revived ascendancy) is not successful and ought

Since nothing even suggests anything to the contrary in chapter 15, there, too, *pneumatikon*, on the one side of the contrast, refers to the activity of the Spirit. This conclusion is also consistent with Paul's use of that adjective elsewhere (e.g. Rom. 1:11; Eph. 1:3; Col. 1:9).[22] To amplify this point just a bit, the resurrection body of 15:44 is 'spiritual' neither in the sense of being adapted to the human 'spirit' nor because of its composition or immaterial substance, to mention persisting misconceptions, but because it embodies (!) the fullest outworking, the ultimate outcome, of the work of the Holy Spirit in the believer, along with the renewal to be experienced by the entire creation.[23] That eschatological body is the believer's hope of total (psycho-)physical transformation, and in that sense our bodies, too, enlivened and renovated by the Spirit. To conclude, as the adjective *pneumatikon* in verses 44 and 46 plainly refers to the activity of the Holy Spirit, so its correlative noun *pneuma* in verse 45 refers to the person of the Holy Spirit.

Second, this conclusion is reinforced by the participial modifier Paul uses. The last Adam did not simply become 'Spirit' but '*life-giving* (or 'life-producing') Spirit' (*pneuma zōopoioun*). The *pneuma* in view is not merely an existing entity but an acting subject.[24] Paul's

---

Footnote 21 (cont.)

    to be abandoned; see e.g. J. Murray, *Collected Writings of John Murray*,
    (Edinburgh: Banner of Truth Trust, 1977), vol. 2, pp. 23–33, esp. 23–29.

22. Eph. 6:12 ('the spiritual forces of evil', *ta pneumatika tēs ponērias*) appears to be the only exception.

23. Recall my observation above that the neuter singular substantives in v. 46 (*to psychikon, to pneumatikon*) are most probably generalizing expressions, referring to environments or orders of existence, after which it would be a mistake to read an elided *sōma*. To do so misses the broadening already given to the contrast in v. 45 and made explicit in the immediately following verses (pp. 47–49), where the basic contrast of the passage is continued in explicitly cosmological terms ('heaven'/'earth'). Elsewhere in Paul, Rom. 8:20–22, especially, point to this cosmic dimension of future eschatological renewal.

24. That is an important difference between this description of Christ and the generalization of John 3:6a, 'What is born of the Spirit is spirit'.

use of this verb elsewhere proves decisive here, especially his sweeping assertion about the new covenant in 2 Corinthians 3:6, 'the Spirit gives life'. In the contrasting parallelism that stamps this passage too, few, if any, will dispute that 'the Spirit' (*to pneuma*) in verse 6 is 'the Spirit of the living God' just mentioned in verse 3, in other words, the Holy Spirit. Further, Romans 8:11 attributes the 'life-giving' activity of resurrection to the person of the Spirit (cf. John 6:63).

For these reasons, *pneuma* in 1 Corinthians 15:45 is definite and refers to the person of the Holy Spirit.[25]

2. 'The life-giving Spirit', it should not be missed, is not a timeless description of Christ. Rather, he 'became' such: *egeneto*. There is little room for doubt about the time point of this 'becoming'. It is, as has already come to light in the first part of this chapter, his resurrection or, more broadly, together with the ascension, his exaltation. The flow of reasoning in chapter 15 makes that virtually

---

25. The absence of the article before *pneuma* has little weight as a counterargument (contra G. D. Fee, 'Christology and Pneumatology in Romans 8:9–11 – and Elsewhere: Some Reflections on Paul as a Trinitarian', in J. B. Green and M. Turner [eds.], *Jesus of Nazareth: Lord and Christ* [Grand Rapids: Eerdmans, 1994], p. 321, n. 38), if for no other reason in view of the koine tendency to omit the article before nouns designating persons, when, as here, a preposition precedes; see A. Blass, A. Debrunner and R. W. Funk, *A Grammar of the Greek New Testament* (Chicago: University of Chicago Press, 1961), pp. 133–134 (sects. 254, 255, 257). Elsewhere (*God's Empowering Presence: The Holy Spirit in the Letters of Paul* [Peabody, Mass.: Hendrickson, 1994], p. 24), Fee himself concludes that his own (extensive) analysis 'should help to put an end to speculation about the presence or absence of the article as determining whether Paul meant to refer to the Holy Spirit or not. The evidence confirms that Paul knows no such thing as "a spirit" or "a holy spirit" when using *pneuma* to refer to divine activity. He only and always means the Spirit of the living God, the Holy Spirit himself' (though his conclusion, earlier in his analysis [p. 16, n. 13], that *pneuma* in 1 Cor. 15:45 'does not easily fit any category' and 'does not refer to the Holy Spirit' seems to be at odds with or at least to weaken the overall conclusion just cited). I shall return to Fee's view of v. 45c below.

certain. The controlling thesis of the argumentation beginning at
verse 12, as much as any, is found in his use of the term 'first fruits'
(*aparchē*) applied to Christ as resurrected in verses 20 and 23. There
is a unity, an unbreakable bond, between his and believers' future
bodily resurrection because, to extend the metaphor as Paul obviously intends, his is the 'first fruits' (beginning of the resurrection)
'harvest' that will include theirs at his return.[26] His resurrection is
not merely an event, however stupendous, isolated in the past. In
its past historicity, it initiates the harvest of resurrection belonging
at the end of history that has already entered history.

This bond or solidarity in resurrection underlies the hypothetic-
al pattern of argument in verses 12–19 and gives it its cogency.
That solidarity is such, the two so much of one piece, that they are
better taken together as episodes of one event rather than two
separate events. Consequently, Paul can argue in both directions,
not only from the resurrection of Christ to the resurrection of
believers (v. 12), but also, conversely, that to deny their resurrection is to deny his (vv. 13, 15–16).

It would make no sense, then, for Paul to argue for the resurrection of believers as he does, staking everything on the inseparable
harvest bond between Christ's resurrection and theirs, if Christ
were 'life giving' by virtue, say, of his pre-existence or incarnation,
or any consideration other than his resurrection. This is not to
suggest that his pre-existence and incarnation are unimportant or
non-essential for Paul, but they lie outside his purview here.
Expressed aphoristically in key terms of the chapter itself, as 'first
fruits' of the resurrection harvest Christ is 'the life-giving Spirit'
(v. 45); conversely, as 'the life-giving Spirit' he is 'the first fruits'.

According to verse 47, the last Adam, as 'the second man', is
now, by virtue of ascension, 'from heaven'.[27] He is 'the heavenly

---

26. As noted earlier, it should be kept in mind that the resurrection of un-
    believers is not within Paul's purview in this chapter; see above, n. 4.

27. What was noted earlier bears repeating here. In view of the immediate
    context, this prepositional phrase is almost certainly an exaltation predi-
    cate ('heaven' is where Christ now belongs), not a description of origin,
    say, out of pre-existence at the incarnation.

one' (v. 48), whose image, by virtue of his own resurrection, believers will bear fully, at the time of their bodily resurrection (v. 49; cf. Phil. 3:20–21). All told, then, the last Adam, as he has become 'the life-giving Spirit', is specifically the *exalted* Christ.

3. Certainly, in the immediate context this 'life-giving' contemplates Christ's future action, when he will resurrect the mortal bodies of believers (cf. v. 22). It seems difficult to deny, however, that his *present* activity is implicitly in view as well. That the resurrected Christ, as life-giver, currently exists in a suspended state of inactivity would be a strange notion indeed to attribute to Paul. And in fact, as he explicitly teaches elsewhere, believers have already been raised with Christ. The resurrection life of the believer, in union with Christ, is not only future but present (e.g. Rom. 6:2–6; Gal. 2:20; Eph. 2:5–6; Col. 3:1–4). Christ, as resurrected and ascended, is already active in the church in the life-giving, resurrection power of the Spirit. And that activity is rooted in who *he* has become and now is, 'the life-giving Spirit'. The Christian's own resurrection has an already / not yet structure, rooted in the activity of Christ, 'the first fruits', as 'the life-giving Spirit'.

4. On the face of this passage is Paul's inherently eschatological conception of the Spirit's activity. The sustained link here between the Spirit and resurrection, the primal eschatological event, is hardly merely incidental. The eschatological aeon, the resurrection order, is, by way of eminence, 'spiritual'. That is the virtual sense in verse 46 of the generalizing expression, 'the spiritual'.[28] Elsewhere, the instrumentality of the Spirit in the resurrection is explicit in

---

28. Vos observes, 'Coming back to Paul we may adopt for guidance the twofold aspect in which the eschatological function of the Spirit appears in his teaching. On the one hand the Spirit is the resurrection-source, on the other He appears as the substratum of the resurrection-life, the element, as it were, in which, as in its circumambient atmosphere the life of the coming aeon shall be lived. He produces the event and in continuance underlies the state which is the result of it. He is the Creator and sustainer at once, the *Creator Spiritus* and the Sustainer of the supernatural state of the future life in one' (*Pauline Eschatology*, p. 163; cf. pp. 59, 165, 169).

Romans 8:11 (cf. 1:4) and implied in 1 Corinthians 6:14 ('through his [God's] power') and in Romans 6:4 ('through the Father's glory').[29]

That this eschatological aspect is inalienable, not waiting to be assumed by the Spirit only in the future at Christ's return, is especially clear from two of the metaphors Paul uses to describe the present work of the Spirit in the church and within believers. He is 'the first fruits' of their full adoption to be realized in 'the redemption [the resurrection] of the body' (Rom. 8:23). Similarly, he is 'the deposit' toward the resurrection body (2 Cor. 5:5). Again, in his sealing activity as 'the Spirit of promise', he is the 'deposit' on the church's 'inheritance' (Eph. 1:14), an unambiguously eschatological reality (cf. 4:30).

Note how effectively both of these metaphors capture the already / not yet structure of Paul's eschatology, the partial yet nonetheless consummate quality of the Spirit's work in the believer. That present experience is of a piece with the full experience of the Spirit's activity at Christ's return and therefore anticipates that future activity. Most broadly, within the terms of our passage, in contrast to the Adam of the original creation, Christ, as he has become the life-giving Spirit, is Lord of the eschatological new creation. Even now, as resurrected and ascended (Eph. 1:20), he is already 'head over everything for the church' (v. 22), a universal, eschatological Lordship that will be openly revealed and acknowledged at his return (Rom. 14:11; Phil. 2:10–11).

5. Turning now to the modern and contemporary understanding of verse 45c, a curiously mixed state of affairs presents itself. On the one hand, it seems fair to say, across a broad front a substantial majority of commentators and other interpreters who address the issue, recognize a reference to the Holy Spirit in verse 45.[30] That may be seen, for instance, in various articles in the *Dictionary of Paul*

---

29. Divine glory and power are consistently presented in Paul as the activity of the Spirit. So, in our passage the body as raised 'in glory' and 'in power' (v. 43) is, accordingly, the 'spiritual' body.

30. Often, though, in preoccupation with the Adam–Christ contrast, the issue is not even raised.

and His Letters.[31] At the same time, however, giving rise to a certain
overall dissonance or at least ambiguity, virtually all the standard
English translations, for whatever reasons, continue to render
'spirit' in verse 45 with a lower case 's'. Notable exceptions are the
Living Bible (and now the New Living Translation), the Good
News Translation (formerly Today's English Version) and, most
recently (1999), the Holman Christian Standard Bible. They, correctly I believe, capitalize 'Spirit'.[32]

From the viewpoint of contemporary evangelical and historic
Christian orthodoxy, the apparent resistance to this translation and
the supporting exegetical sketch given above is surely to be appreciated. To find here a reference to the person of the Holy Spirit
seems clearly to put Paul at odds, even in conflict, with later
church trinitarian and Christological doctrine. It would appear to
make him, as the historical-critical tradition has long and typically
argued, an advocate of a so-called 'functional' Christology that has
no place for a personal distinction in deity between Christ and the
Spirit.

This objection needs to be considered and alleviated. But then,
too, we must ask, what *exegetical* arguments are there against a reference to the Holy Spirit in verse 45? I cite two here, the principal
objections raised by Gordon Fee in his valuable critiques of the
functional Spirit-Christology that James Dunn and others find in
Paul.[33] First, Fee maintains, Paul's interest in the context is soteriological (Christ's own resurrection as the basis of our future, bodily
resurrection), not Christological and/or pneumatological. Second,
Fee proposes that the expression 'life-giving *pneuma*' was coined by

---

31. Eds. G. F. Hawthorne and R. P. Martin (Downers Grove: IVP, 1993); e.g.,
    sects. 12a and 263b (L. J. Kreitzer), 107b, 108a, 112a (B. Witherington III),
    349a (R. B. Gaffin, Jr.), 407b (T. Paige), 435a (G. M. Burge), 554 (J. J. Scott).

32. Although the translation of *egeneto* by 'is' (GNT, NLT) or 'was' (LB) misses or
    perhaps even distorts the timed and dynamic reference in view. Of the
    translations above, only the GNT has the definite article.

33. See Fee, 'Christology and Pneumatology in Romans 8:9–11', pp. 319–322;
    and idem, *God's Empowering Presence*, pp. 264–267, 831ff., and the refer-
    ences to Dunn and others cited there.

Paul in his effort to find an appropriate contrasting parallel to the description of Adam as 'living *psychē*' in Genesis 2:7, which he has just cited; Paul is probably alluding to the 'breath [*rûaḥ*] of life' just mentioned in the same Genesis text and so intends a looser, less exact expression.

Assuming that these arguments have been fairly represented here, at least in their basic contours, are they satisfying exegetically? I respond to them briefly in reverse order.[34] To deny a reference to the Holy Spirit in verse 45 at the very least undercuts a reference to his activity in the cognate adjective 'spiritual' in verse 44 and ends up giving it a more indefinite sense of something like 'supernatural'.[35] That easily tends toward the persisting misconception that it describes the (immaterial) composition of the resurrection body (though that is not Fee's own view). Along the same line, it has to be asked, within the first-century thought world of Paul and his readers, what is a 'life-giving spirit' with a lower case 's'? What would that probably communicate, at least without further qualification such as is lacking here, other than the notion of an angel or some other essentially immaterial being or apparition? But *pneuma* in that sense is exactly what Jesus, as resurrected, denies himself to be in Luke 24:37–39.

Furthermore, to say that in this passage Paul 'is intent on one thing', that his 'whole point is soteriological-eschatological',[36] surely overstates (or, given the nothing less than cosmic sweep of immediate context, understates!). Paul's *main* point (the believer's hope of bodily resurrection) is certainly soteriological and eschatological, but that does not exclude, just in the interests of making

---

34. A view similar to Fee's and along similar lines is taken by Jones, 'Paul Confronts Paganism', pp. 716–717 (he rejects the view that *pneuma zōopoioun* refers to the person of the Spirit and proposes translating it as 'a heavenly, life-giving mode of existence'). The comments that follow here may serve as a partial response to his view as well.

35. As does Fee, 'Christology and Pneumatology', p. 320 (n. 34); *God's Empowering Presence*, p. 263.

36. 'Christology and Pneumatology', p. 320; cf. the somewhat more qualified statement in *God's Empowering Presence*, p. 264.

that point, that verse 45 also says something about Christ and, as I have tried to show, the Holy Spirit. Present in this passage as well are Christological and pneumatological dimensions – profoundly so.

Are we left, then, with the conclusion that verse 45 teaches something like Dunn's functional Spirit-Christology? Hardly. Such a Christology is not only absent here but is foreign to Paul's theology as a whole. Both Dunn and many who oppose his view, it seems to me, share a mistaken assumption, namely that to see a reference to the Holy Spirit in verse 45 necessitates the functional Christology argued by him and others.

The way out of this impasse is first to recognize Paul's clearly trinitarian understanding of God. And here we are indebted to no one more than Fee himself for so convincingly demonstrating that understanding in his *God's Empowering Presence*.[37] As far as I can see, this treatment is without a peer in recent literature on Paul's theology and ought to settle the matter for anyone with doubts. At any rate, I assume its basic conclusions here. Paul's trinitarian conception of God is not at issue but is properly made an assumption in the interpretation of 1 Corinthians 15:45.

It is quite gratuitous, then, to find here a functional Christology that denies the personal distinction between Christ and the Spirit and so would be irreconcilable with later church formulation of trinitarian doctrine. Instead, the scope of Paul's argument, in particular its limits and its salvation-historical focus, need to be kept in view. Essential-eternal, ontological-trinitarian relationships are simply outside his purview here. As we have already noted, he is concerned here not with who Christ is timelessly, eternally, in his pre-existence, but with what he 'became', with what has happened to him in history, specifically in his resurrection.

Moreover, his interest in Christ here is not in terms of his true deity but of his genuine humanity. Paul could hardly have been

---

37. Pp. 825–845; esp. 839–842. The personal, parallel distinction between God (the Father), Christ as Lord, and the (Holy) Spirit – underlying subsequent doctrinal formulation – is clear enough in e.g. 1 Cor. 12:4–6; 2 Cor. 13:13; Eph. 4:4–6.

more emphatic on that. Christ is in view in this passage specifically in his identity as 'the last *Adam*', 'the second *man*'. When Dunn, for one, largely on the basis of this passage, concludes epigrammatically (and in italics), 'as the Spirit was the "divinity" of Jesus (. . .), so Jesus became the personality of the Spirit', the apostle's focus is blurred and the limits it entails are totally missed.[38]

6. It is one thing to show that 1 Corinthians 15:45 is not a source of trinitarian confusion but still another to honour the terms in which Paul expresses himself here. In view is the momentous, epochal significance of the resurrection/exaltation for Christ personally. Paul means to affirm what has not always been adequately recognized in the church's Christology. In his resurrection, something really *happened* to Jesus. By that experience he was and remains a 'changed man', in the truest and deepest, in fact an eschatological, sense. As Paul puts it elsewhere, by the declarative energy of the Holy Spirit in his resurrection, God's Son became what he was not before, 'the Son of God with power' (Rom. 1:4).[39] Relatively speaking, according to 2 Corinthians 13:4, while Christ was crucified in (a state of) 'weakness', he now 'lives by God's power'. His is now, by virtue of the resurrection and ascension, what he did not previously possess, a *glorified* humanity.

Focused here, moreover, more pointedly than anywhere else in Paul, is the meaning of his resurrection (and ascension) for the relationship between Christ and the Spirit. In context two closely related aspects are in view. (a) Christ's own climactic transformation *by* the Spirit. He is the first to receive a 'spiritual body'. (b) Along with that transformation, is his unique and unprecedented

---

38. J. D. G. Dunn, *Jesus and the Spirit* (Philadelphia: Westminster, 1975), p. 325. Subsequently, Dunn has qualified the reasoning that led to this sort of formulation and has modified his views on Spirit-Christology; see e.g. his 'Rediscovering the Spirit (2)', *Expository Times* 94 (October 1982), pp. 9–18. (I thank D. Y. Park for calling this development to my attention.)

39. Most likely *en dynamei* should be construed adjectively with *huiou theou* ('Son of God in power', 'powerful Son of God') and expresses the new and climactic phase of his sonship entered into at and by the resurrection (cf. 2 Cor. 13:4); see Gaffin, *Resurrection and Redemption*, p. 110, n. 100.

reception *of* the Spirit. The result is an intimacy, a bond between them that surpasses what previously existed. The result, in fact, is a new and permanent equation or oneness, appropriately captured by saying, as Paul does, that Christ has 'become' the Spirit.

It should be noted, further, that the relationship between Christ and the Spirit before the resurrection is also outside Paul's purview here. Certainly, elsewhere he does not deny such a relationship. 1 Corinthians 10:3–4, however we settle its further exegesis, appears to have in view the conjoint activity of the Spirit and the preincarnate Christ already under the old covenant.[40] His point, rather, is that now, based on his death and dating from his resurrection and ascension, that joint action is given its stable and consummate basis in the history of redemption. Now, at last, such action is the crowning consequence of the work of the incarnate Christ actually accomplished, once for all, in history.

From the viewpoint of an overall theology of the New Testament, 1 Corinthians 15:45c is fairly and helpfully seen as a one-sentence commentary on the significance of Pentecost, along with the resurrection and ascension. Paul here telescopes what Peter delineates in his Pentecost sermon in Acts 2:32–33, 'God has raised this Jesus to life, and we are all witnesses of the fact. Exalted therefore to the right hand of God, he has received from the Father the promised Holy Spirit and has poured out what you now see and hear.' As 'the life-giving Spirit' (the resurrected and ascended) Christ is the one who baptizes with the Spirit (cf. Luke 3:16 and parallels).

It bears emphasizing again that this oneness or unity, though certainly sweeping, is at the same time circumscribed in a specific respect. It concerns the conjoint *activity* of Christ and the Spirit in giving and ministering life – resurrection, eschatological life. In *this* sense, then, the equation in view may be dubbed 'functional', or perhaps 'eschatological', or, to use an older theological category, 'economic' (rather than 'ontological'), without in any way obliterating the distinction between the second and third persons of the triune God.

---

40. Note, outside Paul, 1 Pet. 1:10–11: the Spirit comprehensively at work in the Old Testament prophets is, specifically, 'the Spirit of Christ'.

7. Subsequently, Paul writes to the Corinthians, 'the Lord is the Spirit' (2 Cor. 3:17). Currently, something of a scholarly consensus seems to be emerging that here, contrary to the majority view throughout most of the twentieth century,[41] 'the Lord' (*ho kyrios*) is not a reference to Christ but applies Exodus 34:34, just cited in verse 16, to the Spirit.[42]

This view has exegetical weight and may well prove to be correct, although the Christological view is not so implausible or so easily dismissed as many who argue for a reference to the Spirit seem to think.[43] What is particularly doubtful, however, at least in some, if I read them correctly, is the tendency, perhaps as overreaction against the Christological understanding, virtually to evacuate the subsequent occurrences of *kyrios* in verses 17 and 18, as well as the verses as a whole, of anything more than the most tenuous and indirect reference to Christ.[44] To say that this is 'a pneumatological passage, not a Christological one'[45] poses a risky disjunction indeed for any passage in Paul, where, as here, the Spirit's activity subsequent to Christ's resurrection is in view.

---

41. See e.g. the literature cited in J. D. G. Dunn, '2 Corinthians III. 17 – "The Lord Is the Spirit"', *Journal of Theological Studies* NS 31.2 (October 1970), p. 309, n. 1.

42. In addition to those cited above in n. 41, Dunn, '2 Corinthians III. 17', pp. 309–320; and R. B. Hays, *Echoes of Scripture in the Letters of Paul* (New Haven: Yale University Press, 1989), pp. 143–144.

43. See the apposite comment in this regard of M. Silva in *Westminster Theological Journal* 59.1 (October 1997), pp. 124–125, in review of S. J. Hafemann, *Paul, Moses, and the History of Israel* (Tübingen: J. C. B. Mohr, 1995).

44. E.g. L. L. Belleville, *Reflections of Glory* (Sheffield: JSOT Press, 1991), pp. 256ff.; *2 Corinthians* (Downers Grove: IVP, 1996), pp. 109–110; N. T. Wright, *The Climax of the Covenant* (Edinburgh: T. & T. Clark, 1991), pp. 183–184. To a lesser degree, Fee, 'Christology and Pneumatology', pp. 319–320; *God's Empowering Presence*, pp. 311–314; and Hafemann, *Paul, Moses*, pp. 396–400.

45. As does Fee, 'Christology and Pneumatology', p. 319; cf. *God's Empowering Presence*, p. 312.

Verse 17b ('the Spirit of the Lord') already distinguishes between 'the Spirit' and 'the Lord', so that the latter probably refers to Christ, particularly in the light of what immediately follows in verse 18. There, 'the glory of the Lord' is surely not the Spirit's glory in distinction from Christ, but Christ's glory. In beholding/reflecting that glory, Paul continues, believers are being transformed into 'the same image', and that image can only be the glory image of the exalted Christ. In the verses that follow, 4:4 ('the light of the gospel of the glory of Christ, who is the image of God'), especially, points to that conclusion (note as well Rom. 8:29, 'conformed to the image of his Son', and, in our passage, 1 Cor. 15:49, 'the image of the heavenly one'). Paul knows of no other transforming glory that believers behold 'with unveiled faces' than 'the glory of God in the [gospel-]face of Christ' (4:6), mediated, to be sure, to them and within them by the Spirit.[46]

In Paul, whether in this passage or elsewhere, Christ never retreats into the background before the Spirit. Nor does the Spirit in any way supplant Christ. Paul is faithful to the outlook of Jesus expressed in John 14 – 16 that in going to the Father in his glorification-ascension (14:12; cf. 20:17), he would ask the Father to send the Spirit, and that in coming as Helper-Advocate (v. 16), the Spirit would be the 'vicar' of Christ, not the reverse. As 'the Spirit of truth' he has no agenda of his own. His role in the church is basically self-effacing and Christ-enhancing (16:13–14 especially point to that). So much is that so that his presence in the church is the presence of the ascended and bodily departed Jesus. For the Spirit to come is for Christ to make good on his promise to the church 'I will not leave you as orphans; I will come to you' (14:18). 1 Corinthians 15:45c, for one, encapsulates and elaborates the fulfilment of that promise.

---

46. Wright's (as he recognizes, innovative) proposal that in v. 18 the 'mirror' that believers behold is *one another* (his italics) and, correlatively, that 'the same image' is 'the same image as each other', as believers reflect the glory of the Spirit (*Climax of the Covenant*, pp. 185, 188), seems a particularly strained and unlikely elimination of any Christological reference from v. 18.

It is difficult to imagine, then, that Paul would not expect
2 Corinthians 3:17–18 to be read in the light of what he wrote
earlier in 1 Corinthians 15:45. The transforming reality in view in
2 Corinthians 3 roots in the truth of 1 Corinthians 15. However we
settle the exegesis of 2 Corinthians 3:17a ('the Lord is the Spirit'),
the 'is' (*estin*) there is based on the 'became' of 1 Corinthians 15:45b.

In 2 Corinthians 3:17a, too, we should be clear, essential, trinitarian identities and relationships are not being denied or blurred,
but are quite outside Paul's purview. His focus is the conjoint
activity of the Spirit and Christ as *glorified*. The exaltation experienced by the incarnate Christ results in a (working) relationship
with the Holy Spirit of new and unprecedented intimacy. Here
they are one, specifically, in giving (eschatological) 'freedom'
(3:17b), the close correlative of the resurrection life in view in
1 Corinthians 15. That correlation is particularly unmistakable in
the phrasing of Romans 8:2, 'the *Spirit* of *life* in *Christ Jesus* has set
me *free*'.

8. The truth of 1 Corinthians 15:45c is not only central to Paul's
Christology and pneumatology but is his most pivotal pronounce-
ment on the relationship between the exalted Christ and the Spirit.
Because of that it is also the cornerstone of his entire teaching on
the Holy Spirit and the Christian life. Life in the Spirit has its
specific eschatological quality because it is the shared life of the
resurrected Christ, in union with him. There is no activity of the
Spirit within the believer that is not also the activity of Christ.
Christ at work in the church is the Spirit at work. Romans 8:9–10
is particularly instructive here. There, in short compass, 'you . . .
in the Spirit' (9a), 'the Spirit . . . in you' (9b), 'belonging to Christ'
(9d, equivalent, I would judge, to the frequent 'in Christ'), and
'Christ in you' (10a) are virtually interchangeable. These four
phrases hardly describe different realities or states of affairs, distinct from each other and to be experienced sequentially or in a
certain order, but the same reality in its full, rich dimensions. The
presence of the Spirit is the presence of Christ; there is no relationship with Christ that is not also fellowship with the Spirit. To
belong to Christ is to be possessed by the Spirit. Elsewhere, within
the comprehensive sweep of the prayer at the close of Ephesians
3, for 'you to be strengthened by [the] Spirit inwardly' is nothing

other than for 'Christ to dwell in your hearts through faith' (vv. 16–17).

This truth about the believer's experience, it bears stressing, is true not because of some more or less arbitrary divine arrangement, but pre-eminently because of what is true *prior* to our experience, in the experience of Christ, because of, in virtue of his death and resurrection, who the Spirit now is, 'the Spirit of Christ' (Rom. 8:9c), and who Christ has become, 'the life-giving Spirit'. It is perhaps worth noting that in these passages, too, Paul is not denying the eternal, hypostatic distinction between the Son of God and the Spirit of God. Nor does he intend, not even in view of the preceding paragraph, an absolute identity in their activity between Christ and the Spirit, not even after the resurrection. That is clear, for instance, later on in Romans 8. The intercession of the ascended Christ, there, at God's right hand (v. 34), is distinguished from the Spirit's complementary interceding, here, within the believer (vv. 26–27). But, in the light of verses 9 and 10, in that inner prayer of the Spirit, Christ, too, is present. It is, we may say, his prayer also.

The life-giving Spirit and the church today

1. If we turn now to relate the preceding reflections on Paul's theology more explicitly to the life of the church today, the following state of affairs confronts us. The Holy Spirit and eschatology, simply inseparable for Paul and at the very heart of his gospel, remain largely unrelated in traditional Christian doctrine and evangelical piety. What has sometimes been captured fleetingly, say, in the hymnody of the church, has been too often lacking in its teaching and practical outlook. There has been an undeniable and persistent tendency to isolate the work of the Spirit and eschatological realities from each other. This has happened as part of a larger tendency to divorce the present life of the church from its future. Typically, the work of the Spirit has been viewed individualistically, as a matter of what God is doing in 'my' life, in the inner life of the believer, without any particular reference or connection to God's eschatological purposes.

Surely, the Spirit's work in the believer is intensely personal. But it is not therefore private. How many believers today recognize that the present activity of the Spirit within the church and in their lives is of one piece with God's great work of restoring the entire creation, begun in sending his Son 'in the fullness of time' (Gal. 4:4) and to be consummated at his return (Rom. 8:18–25)? How many Christians grasp that in union with Christ, the life-giving Spirit, the Christian life in its entirety, is essentially and necessarily resurrection life? How many comprehend that, at the core of their being ('the inner self', 2 Cor. 4:16), believers will never be more resurrected than they already are? Such probing questions open up a broad horizon of issues and concerns as to the dimensions, more precisely, of this present resurrection experience, as to the magnitude, more concretely, of the Spirit's eschatological activity in the church. Here I am able to touch only briefly on two matters, as pertinent as any, it seems.

2. First, an observation on the resurgent Pentecostal spirituality of recent decades, one that I offer in the hope that charismatics and non-charismatics alike could agree, without having to settle their remaining differences. It is widely maintained that Pentecostal denominations and the broader charismatic movement evidence, as it has been claimed, 'the specifically eschatological dimension of the doctrines of Pneumatology and the kingdom of God'.[47] The perception is commonplace that spiritual gifts, especially miraculous gifts like prophecy, tongues and healing, belong to realized eschatology.[48]

---

47. J. Ruthven, *On the Cessation of the Charismata* (Sheffield: Academic Press, 1993), p. 196 (original italics and caps removed); cf. pp. 115–123.

48. E.g. D. A. Carson, *Showing the Spirit: A Theological Exposition of 1 Corinthians 12–14* (Grand Rapids: Baker, 1987), p. 151 (expressed more cautiously than some others); J. Deere, *Surprised by the Power of the Spirit* (Grand Rapids: Zondervan, 1993), pp. 225–226, 285, n. 6; Fee, *God's Empowering Presence*, p. 893; W. Grudem, *Systematic Theology: An Introduction to Biblical Doctrine* (Grand Rapids: Zondervan, 1994), pp. 1019, 1063–1064; M. Turner, 'Spiritual Gifts Then and Now', *Vox Evangelica* 15 (1985), pp. 61–62, n. 175.

Paul's teaching, however, moves in a different, even opposite, direction. For instance, 1 Corinthians 13:8–13 has as a primary concern to point out that prophecy and tongues are temporary in the life of the church.[49] Whether or not before the parousia, Paul is clear, they will cease. That, in effect, is to say they have a less than eschatological significance. No, the response will come, that conclusion misses the point. By the language of cessation Paul intends to show that these gifts belong to the 'already' of eschatology, but not to the 'not yet'.[50]

But does that rejoinder really suffice? It has to be asked, can realities of realized *eschatology* really be said, as Paul does, to 'cease' and 'pass away' (v. 8)?! Can that possibly be said of what is *eschatological*? Such realities, by their very nature, *endure*. In terms of Paul's metaphors for the Spirit, the arrival of the rest of the harvest does not involve the removal of the 'first fruits'. The payment of the balance hardly results in subtracting the 'down payment' or 'deposit'. Or, going to what is surely the heart of the Spirit's activity, the resurrection of the body, of 'the outer self' (2 Cor. 4:16), at Christ's return will certainly not mean the undoing of the resurrection, already experienced, of the inner self.

Contemporary discussion of this passage (on all sides, I would observe) too frequently obscures or even misses Paul's primary concern. For the present, until Jesus returns, it is not our knowledge, along with the word gifts that may contribute to that knowledge, but our faith, hope and love that have abiding, that is, eschatological significance. In contrast to the partial, obscured, dimly mirrored quality of the believer's present knowledge brought

---

49. Note that here I am *not* raising the much-debated issue of *how long* Paul says they are to continue, whether or not, here or elsewhere, he teaches that they will continue to the parousia. I address this question in R. Gaffin, Jr., *Perspectives on Pentecost: New Testament Teaching on the Gifts of the Holy Spirit* (Phillipsburg, N. J.: Presbyterian & Reformed, 1979), pp. 89–116; and R. Gaffin, Jr., 'A Cessationist View', in W. Grudem (ed.), *Are Miraculous Gifts for Today? Four Views* (Grand Rapids: Zondervan, 1996), pp. 25–64, 149–155, 284–297, 334–340.

50. E.g. Fee and Grudem as cited in n. 48 above.

by such gifts, faith in hoping and especially loving (cf. Gal. 5:6) has what we might call an eschatological 'reach' or 'grasp' (vv. 12–13).

This reading of the passage helps with the perennial problem exegesis has wrestled with in verse 13 – how it is that faith and hope can be said to continue after the parousia, in the light, say, of 2 Corinthians 5:7: for the present, in contrast to our resurrection future, 'we walk by faith, not by sight', and Romans 8:24, 'hope that is seen is not hope'. That question misses the point. The 'abiding' in view does not take place beyond the parousia, but concerns the present, eschatological worth of faith and hope (as well as love), in the midst of the non-enduring, sub-eschatological quality of our present knowledge, including whatever word gifts bring that knowledge. Phenomena like prophecy and tongues, when they may occur, are but provisional, less-than-eschatological epiphenomena or manifestations of the Spirit's work.

All told, Paul would not have us miss the categorical distinction between the gift (singular) and the gifts (plural) of the Spirit, between the eschatological gift, Christ, the indwelling, life-giving Spirit himself, in whom all believers share, and those sub-eschatological giftings, none of which, by divine design, is intended for or received by every believer (1 Cor. 12:28–30, for one, makes that clear enough).

The truly enduring work of the Spirit is the resurrection renewal already experienced by every believer. And that renewal manifests itself in what Paul calls 'fruit', like faith, hope and love, joy and peace (to mention just some, Gal. 5:22–23), with, we should note, the virtually unlimited potential for their concrete expression, both in the corporate witness as well as the personal lives of the people of God. This fruit, pre-eminently love, not the gifts, embodies the eschatological 'first fruits' and 'deposit' of the Spirit. However imperfectly manifested for the present through and by the outer self, such fruit is eschatological at its core. Not in particular gifts, however important such gifts undoubtedly are for the health of the church, but in these fruit we experience the eschatological 'touch of the Spirit' in our lives today. Is this not a point on which charismatics and non-charismatics alike ought to agree?

3. Finally, out of much else that remains to be said about our immeasurably rich topic, I underline, with others, the distinctive role, as paradoxical as it might at first seem, of Christian suffering in defining the present eschatological activity of the Spirit.[51] A perennial danger for the church is distorted perceptions of the resurrection quality of the Christian life. False optimism and trivializing 'possibility thinking' are by no means an imaginary danger, as our own times make all too clear. In fact, in a number of places Paul heads off any easy triumphalism and every form of 'prosperity theology'. Most striking are those passages, which though, strictly speaking, autobiographical, surely intend the suffering he experienced as a paradigm or exemplary for all believers.

Philippians 3:10 is a particularly compelling instance. As part of his aspiration to 'gain Christ and be found in him' (vv. 8–9), Paul expresses the desire 'to know Christ and the power of his resurrection and the fellowship of his suffering, being conformed to his death'. In this declaration, I take it, the two occurrences of *kai* (and) are not coordinating but explanatory. Paul is not saying that knowing Christ, the power of his resurrection, and the fellowship of his suffering are sequential or alternating in the believer's experience, as if memorable and exhilarating times of resurrection power are offset by down days of suffering. Rather, he is intent on articulating the *single*, much more than merely cognitive, experience of knowing Christ – what he has just called in verse 8, 'the surpassing greatness of knowing Christ Jesus my Lord' (v. 8). To know Christ, then, is to know his resurrection power *as* a sharing in his sufferings, an experience, all told, that is glossed as 'being conformed to his death'. The imprint left in our lives by Christ's resurrection power is, in a word, the cross. This cross conformity, as much as any, is the signature of inaugurated eschatology.

Similarly, 2 Corinthians 4:10–11 speaks of 'always carrying around in the body the dying of Jesus, so that the life of Jesus may be manifested in our body', and, again, of 'always being given up to death for Jesus' sake, so that the life of Jesus may be manifested in our mortal flesh'. Here, closely akin to Philippians 3:10–11, the two counterposed notions of the active dying of Jesus and of his

---

51. Among others, the treatment of Dunn, *Jesus and the Spirit*, pp. 326–338, remains particularly instructive.

resurrection life do not describe somehow separate sectors of experience. Rather, the life of Jesus, Paul is saying, is revealed in our mortal flesh (cf. 'the outer self', v. 16), and nowhere else. The (mortal) body is the locus of the life of the exalted Jesus. Christian suffering, described as 'the dying of Jesus', moulds the manifestation of his resurrection life in believers.

So, elsewhere, in 2 Corinthians 12, the apostle, who is able to boast about 'visions and revelations from the Lord' (v. 1), would rather boast about and delight in his weaknesses, and the hardships and persecutions endured for Christ (vv. 9–10). For there, pre-eminently, he has come to understand, the power of the exalted Christ is displayed. Just there, in that suffering, '[Christ's] power is perfected in weakness', and the proven truth is that 'when I am weak, then I am strong'.

Believers suffer on earth, Paul learned from experience, not merely in spite of, nor even alongside, their presently sharing in Christ's resurrection, but just because they are raised and seated with him in heaven (Eph. 2:5–6). The choice Paul places before the church for all time, until Jesus comes, is not for a theology of the cross instead of a theology of resurrection, but for his resurrection theology as theology of the cross.

But what does it mean to suffer with Christ? That question needs careful and probing reflection, especially in those places where the church enjoys relative freedom and affluence and suffering can seem remote and confined to the church elsewhere, but where, with the ebb and flow of current geopolitical developments, we are surely naive not to be preparing for the day when that distance may disappear – perhaps much sooner than we think.

Here I can only point out that in Romans 8:18ff. Paul opens up a much broader understanding of Christian suffering than we usually have. There, probably with an eye to the Genesis 3 narrative and the curse on human sin, he reflects on what he calls, categorically, 'the sufferings of the present time' (v. 18), that is, the time, for now, until the bodily resurrection of the believer (v. 23). From that sweeping angle of vision, suffering is everything about our lives, as they remain subjected, fundamentally and unremittingly, to the enervating 'futility' (v. 20) and 'bondage to decay' (v. 21) that, until Jesus comes, permeate the entire creation. *Christian* suffering, then, is everything in our lives in this present order, borne for Christ and done in his service. Suffering with Christ includes not only monumental and traumatic crises, martyrdom and overt persecution, but it is to be a daily affair (cf. Luke 9:23: every disciple is to 'take up his cross *daily*') – the mundane frustrations and unspectacular difficulties of our everyday lives, when they are endured for his sake.

I end with what I take to be a perennial word to the church in Philippians 1:29: 'For it has been granted to you on behalf of Christ not only to believe in him, but also to suffer for him.' Here the apostle speaks of the 'giveness' of Christian suffering for the church as church. Probably we are not overtranslating here to speak of the gracious giveness of suffering, that suffering is given to the church as a gift.[52] At any rate, Paul is clear, the Christian life is a 'not only . . . but also . . .' proposition – not only a matter of believing but also of suffering. Suffering is not simply for some believers but for all. We may be sure of this, then, as the church embraces this indissoluble correlativity of faith and suffering discipleship, it will more and more comprehend the present eschatological depths of its union with Christ, the life-giving Spirit.

© Richard B. Gaffin, Jr., 2007

---

52. So M. Silva, *Philippians* (Grand Rapids: Baker, 2005), including his paraphrase (p. 81), 'since your suffering no less than your faith is God's gracious gift to you on behalf of Christ'.

6. WORTHY IS THE LAMB: THE DIVINE IDENTITY OF JESUS CHRIST IN THE BOOK OF REVELATION

G. K. Beale

Preface

The conference organizers asked me to write a paper on the Christology of the Apocalypse, set forth as follows:

> The book of Revelation is both the fitting and the perfect climax to God's revelation of Himself in holy Scripture. The Lamb is in the midst of the throne and is reigning *now*, even though the church has to face persecution and conflict, and bear witness in a hostile world. Christ's present reign guarantees his final triumph and that of his people over the world, the devil, and all the forces of darkness. This fact is presented in Revelation as a great incentive for the church to maintain its distinctiveness from the world, its faithfulness to Christ, and its function as light-bearing witness.
>
> Yet Revelation presents Jesus in a way that is unique in the New Testament. Apocalyptic images and vivid, pictorial language are used to convey the message that the Lamb is triumphant and is worthy of all praise. This chapter explores these themes and considers the *distinctive* contribution Revelation makes to the biblical portrait of Christ. The

practical relevance of this is dealt with by demonstrating that we are summoned to render worship to the Lamb in our daily lives, rather than to the alluring idols of this world, which are presented in Revelation in their true form as blasphemous and grotesque beasts.

Due to space constraints, this chapter focuses on only a few passages in Revelation that relate to this theme.

Introduction

Here we look at a few passages in John's Revelation that are not typically viewed to express the divine identity of Jesus Christ, but that nevertheless, I shall argue, convey that very notion. We shall then reflect upon the rhetorical implications of these texts.

Let us look first at Revelation 3:14:[1] 'To the angel of the church in Laodicea write: The Amen, the faithful and true Witness, the beginning of the creation of God, says this.'[2]

Christ is the divine, genuine and true witness of his resurrection as the new creation

Christ describes Himself as the 'Amen, the faithful and true Witness' (Rev. 3:14), which is an expanded explanation of Revelation 1:5, where Christ is described as a faithful witness.

---

1. For more in-depth analysis of Rev. 3:14 (i.e. elaboration of the thesis proposed, as well as alternative explanations) and its following context than can be given here, see G. K. Beale, 'The Old Testament Background of Revelation 3.14', *New Testament Studies* 42 (1996), pp. 133–152, as well as idem, *The Book of Revelation*, New International Greek Testament Commentary (Grand Rapids: Eerdmans, 1999), pp. 297–310.

2. All quotations in this chapter are from the New American Standard Bible. Copyright © 1960, 1962, 1963, 1968, 1971, 1972, 1973, 1975, 1977 by the Lockman Foundation.

Revelation 1:5	Revelation 3:14
'the faithful witness, the firstborn from the dead'	'the Amen, the faithful and true Witness, the beginning of the creation of God'.

The three words 'amen', 'faithful' and 'true' are probably synonymous, but may still have slightly different shades of meaning: *amen* means trustworthy, *faithful* means dependable, and *true* means genuine. Therefore, Christ is a genuine, trustworthy and faithful witness. But to what is Christ a witness?

Christ was a witness to God during his ministry and is now a witness to God's work of new creation in raising him from the dead (note again Rev. 1:5 and 3:14).

In Revelation 3:14 when Christ says he is the beginning of the creation of God, he is not referring to the first creation in Genesis 1 but to the new creation begun when he arose from the dead. But how do we know that Christ's resurrection as a new creation is in mind?

This is clear from the first parallel in Revelation 1:5: Christ as a faithful witness is directly followed by his being firstborn from the dead, just as in 3:14 Christ as a faithful witness is directly followed by being 'the beginning of the creation of God'. Hence, this parallel shows that the beginning of the (new) creation of God is begun in Jesus' resurrection (see the table above). This parallel is demonstrated further by recalling that every one of Christ's self-introductions in each of the other letters in Revelation 2 – 3 is either a restatement or development of something in chapter 1. It is unlikely that the phrase 'the beginning of the creation of God' is the only part of Christ's seven self-introductions that is not derived from chapter 1. It is probable that this phrase 'the beginning of the creation of God' is not alluding to the first creation in the book of Genesis but is an interpretative paraphrase of Jesus as the firstborn of the dead in 1:5.

The same idea that Christ's resurrection was the beginning of the new creation is also found in 2 Corinthians 5:14–17 and Galatians 6:14–15.

Jesus' statement that he is the 'amen, the faithful and true witness' is not only an expansion of 'faithful witness' from Revelation 1:5, but is an expansion of God's name of 'amen' in

Isaiah 65:16, which is repeated twice there; or, put another way,
3:14 expands on 1:5 through interpreting it by Isaiah 65:16, which
itself is amplified. Note the actual wording of the Isaiah text (my
emphasis):

> Because he who is blessed in the earth
> Will be blessed by the God of *amen*;
> And he who swears in the earth
> Will swear by the God of *amen*;
> Because the former troubles are forgotten,
> And because they are hidden from My sight!

Isaiah 65:16	Revelation 3:14
'the God of truth . . . the God of truth'.	'[Christ is] the Amen, the faithful and true Witness'.
(Early Greek Bibles have at this point 'the God of amen'; others have instead 'the true God', and still others 'the faithful God'.)	
Together with Rev. 1:5 (and the allusion there to Ps. 89:37), the textual tradition of Isa. 65:16 and its context represent a sufficient quarry of terms and ideas probably extant in the first century from which the titles of 3:14 could have derived. First, the Hebrew text refers twice to God as 'the God of truth' (*'āmēn*), which is translated in the following ways by different versions of the Septuagint (LXX): *ton theon ton alēthinon* (the true God); *en tō theō pepistōmenōs* ('by God faithfully': Aquila; Jerome, ms. 86 also reads *pepistōmenōs*); *en tō theō amēn* ('by the God of Amen': Symmachus; Theodotian	

Isaiah 65:16	Revelation 3:14
reads *amēn* for the second 'Amen' of Isa. 65:16. Cf. 3 Maccabees 2.11, where God is referred to as *pistos . . . kai alēthinos* [faithful . . . and true]).	*amēn, ho martys ho pistos kai ho alēthinos*

Ho amēn (the amen) is a Semitic equivalent to the Greek 'faithful' (*pistos*) as well as true (*alēthinos*), which is evident from the Septuagint's typical translation of verbal and nominal forms of the Hebrew root *'mn* (to be faithful) mainly by *pistos* (faithful), but also sometimes by *alēthinos* (true).[3] Therefore, the threefold name could be an independent, expanded translation of Isaiah's 'amen'. If multiple versions of the Septuagint translated God's name in Isaiah 65:16 thus (see the table above), so could Christ have (or John, in partially interpreting Christ's words).

Alternatively, since the Greek translations of the Hebrew Old Testament, made before the writing of Revelation,[4] also expand God's name of 'amen' into the threefold name of the God of *amen, faithful,* and *true,* Christ (or John) could be reflecting this interpretative tradition, much as someone today might paraphrase one verse by combining three translations of it from modern English versions (e.g. from the Revised Standard Version, Authorized Version, New International Version).

---

3. See E. Hatch and H. A. Redpath, *Concordance to the Septuagint*, 2nd ed. (Grand Rapids: Baker Academic, 1998), pp. 54, 1138–1139.

4. What enhances the notion that the three readings existed in some form prior to the second century AD is that the vowels of the Hebrew *'mn* could be pointed in three possible ways, which correspond at least to two and possibly three of the Greek Old Testament versional readings and to Rev. 3:14. For a description of these LXX revisions by Aquila, Theodotion and Symmachus and their reflection of readings prior to the end of the first century AD, see Beale, 'Old Testament Background', pp. 139–140.

Whichever is the case, it is probable that Revelation 3:14 is an allusion to Isaiah 65:16 and represents an interpretation of the name of God in that Isaianic text.[5] The word 'amen' is usually a response by people to a word from God or to a prayer in both Old and New Testaments, and sometimes refers to Jesus' trustworthy statements. However, an observation underscoring a link between Isaiah 65:16 and Revelation 3:14 is that these are the only two passages in the entire Bible where 'amen' is a name. That this section of Isaiah would be in mind is also likely since John has been meditating on 62:2 and 65:15 in Revelation 2:17 and 3:12, in addition to focusing on other related texts of Isaiah in Revelation 3:7, 9.

The blessing of the God of truth [or 'amen', or 'faithfulness'], which is only generally referred to in Isaiah 65:16, is precisely understood in the following verse to be the promised blessing of the new creation that he will bring about: 'For behold, I create new heavens and a new earth' (Isa. 65:17; note also the identity of Isa. 65:16 with 65:17 in the repeated phrase of the second line of each verse, 'the former troubles [things] are forgotten [shall not be remembered])'. This name of God is his guarantee that he will surely bring about a new creation, which he promises to do in Isaiah 65:17. Therefore, God promises in Isaiah 65:16–17 to create a new earth, and he gives assurance in verse 16 that he will fulfil this promise because he is completely trustworthy, dependable and true.

And in Revelation 3:14, when Jesus speaks about being a faithful witness, the beginning of the new creation, he is referring to the new creation promised by the amen, true and faithful God (Isa. 65:16) in Isaiah 65:17, which God launched through Jesus' resurrection, to which Jesus was a witness.

---

5. The articulation of the heavenly Christ's name through an exegesis of Old Testament texts has affinities with the practice in Judaism of formulating personal names for angels on the basis of exegeting Old Testament texts (see S. Olyan, *A Thousand Thousands Served Him*, Texte und Studien zum antiken Judentum 36 [Tübingen: J. C. B. Mohr (Siebeck), 1993]).

Observable in both Isaiah 65:16–17 and Revelation 3:14 is a twofold pattern found only here in all of Scripture (see table below).

Isaiah 65:16–17	Revelation 3:14
'the God of truth . . . the God of truth . . .	'[Christ is] the Amen, the faithful and true Witness,
For behold, I create new heavens and a new earth'.	[Christ is] the beginning of the [new] creation of God'.

This unique twofold pattern points even further to Revelation 3:14 being a development of Isaiah 65:16–17.

An allusion to Isaiah 65:16–17 is also corroborated by Revelation 21:5, where the one on the throne says *Idou, kaina poiō panta* (Behold, I make all things new), a reference to Isaiah 43:19 and 65:17; and then he refers to this declaration as *hoi logoi pistoi kai alēthinoi eisin* (these words are faithful and true). This declaration itself is a development of the earlier allusion to Isaiah 65:17 in Revelation 21:1 ('Then I saw a new heaven and a new earth'). In this light, it is not accidental that in 21:6 God or Jesus is called the beginning (*hē archē*). This may imply that the hoped for new creation of 21:1, 5 has already been inaugurated by Jesus' resurrection. This is further hinted at by observing that of the three times the phrase *pistos kai alēthinos* (faithful and true) occurs elsewhere in the book, one serves as an introductory affirmation of the truth that God will make *all* things new (21:5) and a second (22:6) functions likewise as an emphatic conclusion to the same discussion of the new creation in 21:5 – 22:5 (although in 21:5 and 22:6 the words are in the plural).

Therefore, Jesus now applies to himself in Revelation 3:14 what was true of God in Isaiah 65, so that he identifies himself as God. Now Jesus is a genuine and reliable witness to his resurrection as the Lord God himself. He is as trustworthy as God because he is God. He has not minced his words. This is one of the clearest places in all of the book of Revelation in which Christ's deity is expressed.

Therefore, Christ is the divinely faithful and true witness to his resurrection as the inauguration of the eschatological new creation in fulfilment of the Isaiah 65 prophecy.[6] But there is something additional in Revelation 3:14 that has not yet been addressed, which has the potential to enhance its meaning. The background of the word 'witness' needs to be addressed directly.

Christ also presents himself as true, end-time Israel

There is one word for which I have not yet offered any Old Testament background. And that is the word 'witness'. Some might think that there need be no further exploration for additional background to Revelation 3:14, especially since the word 'witness' does not occur in Isaiah 65:16–17. Furthermore, is it not sufficient that

---

6. See E. Lohmeyer, *Die Offenbarung des Johannes*, Handbuch zum Neuen Testament 16 (Tübingen: J. C. B. Mohr, 1970), p. 38, who is representative of others in arguing that the phrase 'beginning of the creation of God' in 3:14 refers to Christ as Lord of the newly created church community but not of the whole new creation. (Codex Sinaiticus could be an early witness to such an interpretation, since it substitutes 'church' for 'creation'; i.e. Christ is 'the beginning of the church'.) This is because Lohmeyer interprets 3:14 in the light of Col. 1:18, which he understands to pertain only to the creation of the church. However, even if for sake of argument it is granted that Colossians 1 is the only key to interpreting Rev. 3:14, Col. 1:18 should not be limited only to the new church community, since it is linked with the cosmic creation of 1:15–17. The following context of Col. 1:19–20, 23 shows that Paul understands Jesus' position in 1:18 as extending beyond the church to the whole creation. Jesus and the church are the beginning of the new creation but do not exhaust it. Others have proposed that Col. 1:18 and Rev. 3:14 are parallel, that both depend directly on Prov. 8:22 and are employed polemically against Jewish-Gnostic ideas about Jesus as a mediating power but not as a supreme one (e.g. C. J. Hemer, *The Letters to the Seven Churches in Their Local Setting*, Journal for the Study of the New Testament Supplement Series 11 [Sheffield: JSOT Press, 1986], pp. 186–187).

Revelation 3:14 further develops the same word 'witness' from Revelation 1:5? While this may be as far as we need to go in discerning the origin of 'witness' in Revelation 3:14, further new creation texts in Isaiah may provide another backdrop against which to understand 'witness' in both Revelation 1:5 and 3:14.

The word 'witness' also occurs in the segment of Isaiah 43:8–21 (esp. cf. 43:10, 12–13, 18–19), where one of the prominent themes is that of Isaiah prophesying that Israel is to be God's witness to the coming new creation (my emphases):

'You are My *witnesses*', declares the Lord,
  'And My servant whom I have chosen,
  So that you may know and believe Me
  And understand that I am He.
  Before Me there was no God formed,
  And there will be none after Me.
I, even I, am the Lord,
  And there is no saviour besides Me.
It is I who have declared and saved and proclaimed,
  And there was no strange *god* among you;
  So you are My *witnesses*', declares the Lord,
  And I am God.
  Even from eternity I am He,
  And there is none who can deliver out of My hand;
  I act and who can reverse it? . . .
'Do not call to mind the former things,
  Or ponder things of the past.
Behold, I will do something new [LXX has 'new things'],
  Now it will spring forth;
  Will you not be aware of it?
  I will even make a roadway in the wilderness,
  Rivers in the desert.

Israel was to be a witness in the future to the fact that the new creation which God had prophesied had been fulfilled in their midst.

Their witness was to show that the testimony of the worshippers of Babylon's idols were really false witnesses, since their idols were not the true God and, therefore, could not prophesy (Isa. 43:9, 12; 44:8). Indeed, God had created Israel in the first place to be a witness to him before the unbelieving world: when he created the nation he told them in Exodus 19:6 what their purpose was to be: 'You [Israel] shall be to Me a kingdom of priests and a holy nation'. The Israelites were to be priestly mediators between God and the ungodly world by being a missionary light of witness to the world. Israel's lampstand in the temple symbolized this mission of being a light to the world.[7]

But Israel repeatedly refused to do this. So God promised he would raise up someone who would be a faithful witness. Israel as a nation would no longer be called God's servant, but God would raise up a Servant who would be a faithful witness (see Isa. 49:1–6; note especially 49:3, 'you are My Servant, Israel'). The New Testament identifies this Servant as Jesus Christ (e.g. Luke 2:32 calls Jesus a 'light of revelation to the Gentiles', an allusion to Isa. 42:6 and 49:6; the same Old Testament allusion is applied to Jesus in Acts 26:23).

So Isaiah 43 (vv. 10–13, 18–19) says Israel was to be a witness to the coming new creation; but only the true Servant, Israel, would be able to be such a witness, which is what Revelation 3:14 affirms of Jesus. The Septuagint interprets Isaiah 43:10 and 12 by adding that God would also be a witness (and the Targum to Isaiah interprets the description of Israel as a witness to be the Messiah). Could it be possible that both the Isaiah 43 ideas of *Israel* and *God* being faithful witnesses are combined in the one *Jesus Christ* in Revelation 3:14? At least, even if only the Hebrew text's notion of Israel being the faithful witness is in mind, we have seen in Isaiah 65:16–17 that this is combined with God being a faithful promiser of the coming new creation. The idea in Isaiah 43 of being a witness to the new creation fits admirably with the allusion to the same concept in Isaiah 65, and explains why Jesus would have combined these two texts into one allusion.

----

7. For an in-depth explanation of this witness, as symbolized by the temple and its lampstand, see G. K. Beale, *The Temple and the Church's Mission*, New Studies in Biblical Theology (Leicester: Apollos, 2004).

The role of witness that Israel should have carried out has been carried out by Jesus, who is really the true Israel because he is the only fully faithful witness through his resurrection to the new creation.

If we are going to be God's people, true Israel, then we must believe in Jesus in order to be identified with him, who summed up true Israel in himself and carried out Israel's role of being a faithful witness to God's new creation in his resurrection. Likewise, the only way we can carry out our primary role of witness as true Israel is to keep in close relationship with Jesus, the faithful Israelite witness. As Christians our main purpose in relation to the world is to witness.

Excursus on the Septuagintal background of Isaiah 43

Commentators are right in seeing Psalm 88(89):27, 37 as the basis for the statement in Revelation 1:5 that Christ is the 'faithful witness', 'firstborn' and 'ruler of the kings of the earth', since all three phrases occur in those verses of the psalm. However, the significance of the allusion is usually not discussed. The immediate context of the psalm speaks of David as an anointed king, who will reign over all his enemies and whose seed will be established on his throne for ever (Ps. 88[89]:19–32, LXX; Judaism understood Ps. 89:28 messianically [*Midrash Rabbah* Exod. 19:7; perhaps *Pesiqta Rabbati* 34.2]). John views Jesus as the ideal Davidic king on an escalated eschatological level, whose death and resurrection have resulted in his eternal kingship and in the kingship of his beloved children (cf. v. 5b), which is developed in verse 6. The faithful witness in Revelation 1:5 is probably also an echo of Isaiah 43:10–13.

Though the Psalm 89 background behind 'faithful witness' is probably carried over from Revelation 1:5 into Revelation 3:14, I have argued above that Isaiah 43 is highlighted there more than in Psalm 89:37. As noted briefly just above, the LXX of Isaiah 43:10 says, 'you [Israel] be my witnesses, and I am a witness, says the Lord God, and My servant whom I have chosen'. Likewise 43:12–13 (LXX) is parallel with 43:10 and has 'you [Israel] are My witnesses, *and I am a witness, says the Lord God, even from the beginning*' (*kagō martys, legei kyrios ho theos, eti ap' hē archē*; my emphasis).

Though some LXX manuscripts in 43:12 omit *martys*, the phrase *martys legei* still could be implied or assumed.

What is striking is that *Israel*, *God* and the *Servant* are all called 'witnesses'. Indeed, the Targum interprets 'My servant' as 'My servant *the Messiah*'. To what are Israel, God and the Servant or Messiah to witness? In context, it is evident that they are primarily witnesses to God's past act of redemption at the Exodus (43:12–13, 16–19) and, above all, to God's coming act of restoration from exile, which is to be modelled on the former redemption from Egypt. Isaiah 43:18–19 refers to the coming restoration as none other than a new creation:

> Do not call to mind the former things,
>   Or ponder things of the past.
> Behold, I will do something new.

Therefore, Israel, God and the Messiah are to be witnesses of the future restoration and new creation. Isaiah 44:6–8 also says Israel is a witness both to God's past act of creation and his coming deliverance of the nation from exile. Both Isaiah 43:10–13 and 44:6–8 also underscore the notion that the witness is against the idols who cannot compare with the true God and his sovereign acts.

Especially noteworthy for the word 'beginning' (*archē*) in Revelation 3:14b is the observation that the witness by Israel, God and the Servant (Messiah) in Isaiah 43:10–13 is to events from the beginning (*ap' hē archē*; likewise, Isa. 44:8), which are linked with the yet future new creation, to which they are likewise to bear witness. This phrase 'from the beginning', and like formulations of *archē* in various contexts of Isaiah (LXX), refer to the beginning at the first creation (40:21; 42:9; 44:8; 45:21; 48:16) or the beginning when God created Israel as a nation at the exodus (41:4; 43:9, 13; 48:8, 16; 51:9; 63:16, 19). But the point of saying that God is a witness . . . still [yet, even] from the beginning in the LXX of Isaiah 43:12–13 (*kagō martys . . . eti ap' hē archē*) is to emphasize the witness to God's past acts of redemption as new creations as the basis for his future act of redemption as an escalated new creation. God has been a witness to his past acts of creating the cosmos and of creating Israel as a nation at the exodus, and he will be a witness *yet* again to another coming creation.

Therefore, the emphasis lies on Israel, God and the Servant being 'witnesses' to the coming new creation as another beginning in the nation's history and in cosmic history. The witness of Isaiah 43:10, 12 is to be understood as a *true witness* because of the directly preceding contrast with Isaiah 43:9, where the 'witnesses' (*martyras*) of the nations (false idols or prophets) are commanded by Isaiah to hear the *truth* (*alēthēs*) and to speak the *truth* (*alēthēs*). The repetition of *alēthēs* highlights the exhortation that the witnesses be *true*. It is not by happenstance that Judaism viewed the witness of Isaiah 43:12 as a *true witness*, since it is explicitly contrasted in the midrashim with those who bear false witness (*Midrash Rabbah* Lev. 6:1 and 21:5).

Therefore, Jesus as the principle, origin or source of the original creation is not in mind, but Jesus as the inaugurator of the new creation is. The phrase *tēs ktiseōs* (of the creation) is best taken as a partitive genitive, although implicit in the idea of *hē archē* may be three ideas: (1) inauguration, (2) supremacy over and (3) temporal priority.[8] The latter two ideas are apparent from the parallel of Col. 1:18 and especially from Revelation 1:5, where 'firstborn from the dead' is directly explained by 'ruler of the kings of the earth'. The first and third notions overlap, since both have to do with the temporal.

Some commentators who assume that *tēs ktiseōs tou theou* (of the creation of God) refers to the original creation do not like the translation of 'beginning' for *archē*, because they think this would necessitate viewing Jesus as a created being along with the rest of creation.[9] However, seeing the phrase as a reference to the new creation results in the different understanding for which I have argued. No doubt, the message about the new creation (21:5) and

---

8. For 'beginning' as connoting temporal priority in Jewish and Greek literature, see T. Holtz, *Die Christologie der Apokalypse des Johannes*, Texte und Untersuchungen 85 (Berlin: Akademie-Verlag, 1971), pp. 145–146.

9. G. E. Ladd, *Commentary on the Revelation of John* (Grand Rapids: Eerdmans, 1972), p. 65.

of the book in general (22:6) is referred to as 'faithful and true' because it is from Jesus who is faithful and true (19:9, 11; 3:14; 1:5).

Using Isaiah in the letter to Laodicea: rhetorical purpose 1

Jesus' purpose in introducing himself as the true and faithful Israelite witness to his resurrection as the new creation is twofold: (1) to convict the Laodiceans about their own ineffective witness and (2) to spur them on and persuade them to be effective witnesses by identifying with him as a witness.

But the word 'witness' is not used in verses 15–21. So where in these verses does it say that the Laodiceans are not faithful witnesses? Verses 15–16 give us a strong hint: 'I know your deeds, that you are neither cold nor hot; I wish that you were cold or hot. So because you are lukewarm, and neither hot nor cold, I will spit you out of My mouth.'

This refers to Christ rejecting their ineffective witness. They either do not witness at all or their witness is constantly made ineffective by their compromising involvement in facets of the local society that are idolatrous, a similar problem seen in some of the other churches in Revelation 2 – 3. But what is the evidence that they are ineffective in their *witness*?

First, in verse 14 Christ introduces himself as 'the faithful and true witness'. Since his titles always relate to a key problem in the churches, this title presumably is a contrast to Laodicea's unfaithful witness. They are unlike him, but need to change by identifying with him and following his example.

In almost all of the Asia Minor cities in which the seven churches were located there were trade guilds or trade unions for various businesses. We know from archaeology alone that there were such guilds in Laodicea for the woolen trade and probably the banking trade. Once a year all the members of a trade would be expected to pay their trade guild dues by attending a trade union meeting at a temple of the patron god who supposedly was responsible for prospering the trade. At this meeting people were usually asked to eat a dinner in honour of the patron god and in honour of the Roman emperor as a god, since he was responsible for the prosperity of all trades.

If people refused to go to these meetings, they would be cut off from their trade, and lose their livelihood. And, if one did not honour Caesar as a god, one was considered to be unpatriotic. Some Christians rationalized and felt that they could still be Christians and attend these meetings. For example, they might have thought that if they were insincere in their heart while worshipping the patron deity during the festivities, they could maintain a good conscience before Christ. But, however they rationalized their attendance, the result was that they did not stand out as Christians, because they identified in some way with the idols of the various trade unions and seemed to be paying sincere homage to the statue of the Roman emperor, which always held a prominent position in temples of various local patron deities. The Laodiceans have apparently become so much like their sinful culture that their culture apparently does not notice that they are Christians and do not know what they really stand for.

That their problem is an ineffective witness is also evident from the fact that all of the sinful problems of the other churches in Revelation 2 – 3 are concerned with witnessing in some way.[10]

Their ineffectiveness as witnesses for Christ is underscored by the picture of lukewarm water in verses 15–16. This lukewarmness has traditionally been interpreted to refer to their lack of spiritual fervour and half-hearted, middle-of-the-road commitment to Christ.

But this is problematic because then Christ is not only recommending that they be spiritually hot but also spiritually 'cold'. In other words, this view has Christ saying it is better to be spiritually cold than merely spiritually 'lukewarm'. It is doubtful on theological grounds that Christ is saying this. The lukewarmness does not refer to their lack of spiritual fervor and half-hearted commitment to Christ. Rather, the lukewarmness refers to ineffectiveness – here the ineffectiveness of their faith and witness.

Hot, cold and lukewarm water were a unique feature of Laodicea and the surrounding region in the first century. The hot

---

10. On which see Beale, *Revelation*, pp. 223–310.

waters of nearby Hierapolis had a medicinal effect and the cold waters of nearby Colosse were pure, drinkable and had a life-giving effect. However, there is evidence that Laodicea had access only to warm water, which was not very palatable and caused nausea. Indeed, Laodicea had grown as a town because its position was conducive for commerce, but it was far from good water. When the city tried to pipe water in, it could manage only to obtain warm, medicinal-tasting water.

The effect of the Laodicean church's witness on their culture is like the unhealthy effect of the water. Perhaps another way to say this is that the effect on Christ of their conduct is like the effect of their own water – Christ wants to 'spew' them out of his mouth. This is because their witness is ineffective and they therefore make him sick to his stomach.[11]

How can we further discern that their witness is ineffective? Verses 17–18 shed more light on this:

> Because you say, 'I am rich, and have become wealthy, and have need of nothing,' and you do not know that you are wretched and miserable and poor and blind and naked,
>
>   I advise you to buy from Me gold refined by fire so that you may become rich, and white garments so that you may clothe yourself, and that the shame of your nakedness will not be revealed; and eye salve to anoint your eyes so that you may see.

Their witness has become ineffective because they have become conformed to the idolatrous world. But how so?

They are trusting in and identifying with the world's security and wealth, instead of trusting in and identifying with Christ. Instead, they need to know that all true, eternal riches are found only in a living relationship with Christ (v. 18).

---

11. So Hemer, *Letters to the Seven Churches*, p. 191 (who cites other secondary sources in support of his view), whose discussion on pp. 186–191 is the basis of my analysis above; cf. more recently S. E. Porter, 'Why the Laodiceans Received Lukewarm Water', *Tyndale Bulletin* 38 (1987), pp. 143–149, also in support of Hemer.

In verses 19–20 Christ encourages the Laodiceans to renew their relationship and witness with him:

> Those whom I love, I reprove and discipline; therefore be zealous and repent. Behold, I stand at the door and knock; if anyone hears My voice and opens the door, I will come in to him and will dine with him, and he with Me.

Though the word 'witness' is not mentioned in verses 19–20, that idea appears still to be in mind from the preceding verses. They are told to renew their relationship with the risen Christ, the fulfilment of Isaiah's prophesied true Israel, who will be a faithful witness to the new creation, which has begun in the resurrection. As the Laodicean Christians re-identify with Christ, they will become like him and be renewed witnesses to his resurrection as the beginning of the eschatological new creation. However, they will not only be like the witness of the human Messiah, as true Israel, but will be reflecting the image of Jesus as the God of Isaiah who is a witness to his own resurrection as the beginning of the end-time new creation, which the faithful Yahweh promised and witnessed to prophetically in Isaiah 65. If they are truly his people, they will reflect his divine image.

Using Isaiah in the letter to Laodicea: rhetorical purpose 2

I have argued that the Laodiceans' witness has become ineffective because they have become conformed to the idolatrous world. But can we say in more depth how they have become conformed to their idolatrous surroundings?

Laodicea is as compromising in their witness as Israel was in the Old Testament. Verse 17 says, 'Because you say, "I am rich, and have become wealthy, and have need of nothing," and you do not know that you are wretched and miserable and poor and blind and naked'. This alludes to Hosea 12:8, which says:

> And Ephraim said, 'Surely I have become rich.
> I have found wealth for myself;

In all my labours they will find in me
No iniquity, which would be sin.'

Indeed, Hosea 12:7 refers to Israel as a merchant, and elsewhere Hosea pictures them as a merchant attributing their material welfare to the benevolence of idols (Hos. 2:5, 8; note the close connection between Hos. 12:7 and the idolatry texts of 12:11 and 13:1–3). But God through Hosea accuses them of being worthless (Hos. 12:11).

The Laodicean Christians believe they are in a healthy spiritual condition because they are economically well off. And, like Israel in the Old Testament, they think that some forms of idol worship are consistent with their belief in God and Christ. Their sinful likeness to Israel is astounding. According to Isaiah 43 – 44 Israel was to be a witness to God as the true God in order to show that the idols of the nations were false gods (note, in this respect, esp. Isa. 43:9–12 and 44:9–20, discussed above!). But Israel failed at this by thinking they could be faithful to God and still worship idols, which could enhance their economic well-being.

The Laodiceans are now in the same boat as Israel. This lukewarm church in Asia Minor claimed to be true Israel, the true people of God. As such they are to witness to Christ as the only true God, the God who prophesied in Isaiah 65, and they are to witness against the idols of the trade unions as false gods. But, tragically, the Laodiceans do not carry out their role faithfully, and so they are doing well economically because of willing cooperation with the idolatrous trade guilds and economic institutions of their culture.

This idolatrous involvement is suggested further by recalling that when John uses the word 'rich' elsewhere, it refers to unbelievers who have prospered because of their voluntary intercourse with the ungodly world system that is based on idol worship (Rev. 6:15; 13:16; 18:3, 15, 19). The Laodiceans' witness became ineffective when they paid allegiance to other pagan gods. How would anyone believe them when they said Christ was the only way and that Christ could provide for you even if you lost your job? Their compromise to keep their jobs, which purportedly prospered due to the oversight of pagan deities, showed they did not believe that Christ could provide in difficult times.

Their healthy assessment of their own condition could not have been more wrong: Christ says, 'but you are wretched and miserable and poor and blind and naked'. They were spiritually the opposite of what they thought. Indeed, verses 18–22 tell us that this need for renewing our relationship with Christ is crucial if we are going to be faithful witnesses; thus the remedy for the readers' ineffective witness is to renew their new creational relationship with Christ and identify with him as a witness to this in-breaking new creation in Christ (vv. 18–22).

They are to renew their relationship with the resurrected Christ by beginning to identify with him as part of the new creation and as faithful witnesses by not being conformed to the world. Note again what verse 18 says: 'I advise you to buy from me gold refined by fire so that you may become rich, and white garments so that you may clothe yourself, and *that* the shame of your nakedness will not be revealed; and eye salve to anoint your eyes so that you may see'.

Each of the three images of verse 18 involve an encouragement for the Laodiceans to separate from identification with the idolatrous world: (1) Purchasing gold refined by fire refers to purifying their lives by removing the stains of idol worship and compromise and undergoing the refining fire of persecution. (2) To buy white garments to clothe themselves refers to having garments not soiled with compromise with ungodly culture, as some Christians in Sardis had done (see Rev. 3:4–5; 19:8). Indeed, 'uncovering the shame of nakedness' is a phrase God uses in the Old Testament when he accuses Israel and other nations of idol worship (Ezek. 16:36; 23:29; Nah. 3:5; Isa. 20:4). (3) To buy eye salve to anoint the eyes in order to see emphasizes their lack of spiritual discernment, especially their ignorance about the lethal danger their association with idol worship poses for their faith (see John 9:39–41).

The command in verse 22 'He who has an ear, let him hear what the Spirit says to the churches,' also found at the end of all the letters, has particular relevance for the church at Laodicea. They above all others have become anaesthetized and insensitive to their spiritual condition and danger. It is not coincidental that the expression 'He who has an ear, let him hear' has its roots in Isaiah 6:10, which is part of a description of and polemic against Israel's idolatry.[12] Just as the idols have 'eyes but cannot see and ears but cannot hear', so Israel is described the same way, since they have become as spiritually inanimate as the idols they had worshipped. The Laodiceans likewise are becoming as spiritually numb as the idols they are partly trusting in.

Therefore, the Laodiceans have become complacent in their ignorant bliss, as a result of the anaesthetized condition brought about by their idolatry. Consequently, the purpose of the command 'He who has an ear, let him hear' is to shock the Laodiceans out of their spiritual insensitivity so they can discern the satanic realities behind the idolatrous institutions in which they are participating. Remember that one of the main purposes of the whole book of Revelation is to shock believers out of their complacent compromise with the world into becoming faithful witnesses to Christ. This is an essential part of what it means for them to worship God on earth.

The threefold exhortation that they buy gold, clean garments and eye salve corresponds to their problems in verse 17 of being poor, naked and blind.

In fact, it cannot be coincidence that history tells us that the city of Laodicea became prosperous for three primary reasons: their *banking institutions* (gold), their *textile trade* (garments) and their well-known *medical school of opthalmology* together with the city's *reputed eye salve medicine*.

These are the institutions in which many of the Christians are participating, which are connected with idol worship. The city's self-sufficient wealth emphasizes that the church has imbibed the independent attitude of the surrounding society. This is how they have become 'conformed to the world'. Instead they have to take a stand for the resurrected Christ and thus risk their livelihoods. They cannot identify with the resources of ungodly society to

---

12. On which see G. K. Beale, 'Isaiah 6:9–13: A Retributive Taunt Against Idolatry', *Vetus Testamentum* 41 (1991), pp. 257–278; and idem, 'The Hearing Formula and the Visions of John in Revelation', in M. Bockmuehl and M. B. Thompson (eds.), *A Vision for the Church: Studies in Early Christian Ecclesiology in Honour of J. P. M. Sweet* (Edinburgh: T. & T. Clark, 1997), pp. 167–180.

solve their spiritual problem. Only the resurrected divine Christ's inexhaustible spiritual resources can help the Laodicean Christians. All the resources we need are in the divine Christ and not in society.

So, the point is that the Laodiceans are to renew their new creational relationship with the risen Christ by beginning to identify with him as Isaiah's prophesied Israelite servant and faithful witness, and not by identifying with the world and being conformed to it. They are to become conformed to Christ's divine image as the faithful witness and not to the images of the world's false deities. Such a renewal may bring persecution, tribulation, suffering and material poverty (cf. Rev. 2:9), which will cause them to realize how much they need to trust him after all.

The three spiritual products they are supposed to buy from Christ are his own attributes – it is he, in his resurrected new creational existence, who will sustain them. Only in the resurrected divine Christ are inexhaustible true riches, clothing and insight.

Indeed, Jesus himself established the fount of all true wealth through his own faithful witness in the midst of suffering during his life, climaxed at the cross (Rev. 1:5). And it is not a chance selection of words that are used to describe Christ's exhortation to the readers to buy these three things from him, since in the initial vision of the resurrected Christ he has already presented himself to all the communities as possessing *gold*, having a *white* appearance and *eyes with piercing vision*. That the portrayal from 1:13b–15 (cf. 2:18) is linked with 3:18 is also suggested by the use of fire (*pyr*) and the perfect participle of the Greek verbal form of the same word (*pyroō*, 'to burn'), both of which occur in these Revelation 1 and 3 texts, the former as part of the description of the resurrected Christ.

In addition the gold may be associated with the vision of the new creation in Revelation 21, where the entire city of the new Jerusalem is said to be composed of pure gold (21:18; as was the street of the city in 21:21). This is a figurative portrayal of the people of God being identified with gold at the consummation of time because they have identified with the golden-clothed Christ during the church age and are reflectors of his glory. That is, they are to renew their relationship by re-identifying themselves with

Christ as the faithful witness to his resurrection as the new creation, so that they also can become faithful witnesses to his
resurrection and be conscious participants in the reality of the
new creation in Christ. The riches found in Jesus are the only kind
of wealth these readers need to buy,[13] since such wealth is unfad-
ing and eternal. In this regard, they should be willing to take a high
profile in the midst of their worldly culture, fearlessly testifying to
Christ in word and character.

Verses 19–20 show encouragements for the Laodiceans to
renew their relationship and witness with the risen Jesus:

> Those whom I love, I reprove and discipline; therefore be zealous and
> repent. Behold, I stand at the door and knock; if anyone hears My voice
> and opens the door, I will come in to him and will dine with him, and he
> with Me.

Verse 21 gives the reward for faithfully obeying Christ's exhortations in this letter and for overcoming the pressures of the ungodly
culture to suppress their witness or to induce compromise: 'He who
overcomes, I will grant to him to sit down with Me on My throne, as
I also overcame and sat down with My Father on His throne.' Christ
overcame as a faithful witness (1:5) and overcame death through
resurrection and was raised up to sit with God on his throne. The
very next time the word 'overcome' (*nikaō*) occurs is in Revelation
5:5, where Christ is portrayed as overcoming through his death and
resurrection (see 5:6–7). Jesus' ongoing resurrection existence there
is described as being so close to God's throne (5:7, 13) that he is to
be considered as sitting on it (as likewise in Rev. 7:17).

This then is a promise to believers that if they overcome like
Christ as faithful witnesses, then they will be raised up as was
Christ and sit with Christ on his throne. That is, if they identify
now with the resurrected Christ as the beginning of the new creation, then they can be become a full partaker of the new creation
at the eschaton through resurrection of their bodies, following the
pattern of Christ's 'overcoming', resurrection and enthronement.

---

13. P. S. Minear, *I Saw a New Earth* (Washington: Corpus, 1969), p. 57.

Conclusion

The main idea of Revelation 3:14–22 in the light of the Isaiah background is the following: if we are faithful witnesses to Jesus as the faithful God of Isaiah and to him as the beginning of the new creation, then we will be resurrected as part of the consummated new cosmos and reign with him. If we are unfaithful witnesses against the idols of our culture, we are false witnesses, and will be judged.

The Laodiceans should view this message as absolutely authoritative and binding upon them, because it is from Christ, whom they are to identify as the faithful and true God of Isaiah, who prophesied the new creation. Accordingly, a crucial part of their witness is testimony to the risen Christ as the true God of the world, which guarantees resistance from the world authorities, since Caesar was touted to be the god of the world.

Appendix: another text in revelation affirming the deity of Christ

Revelation 17:14 says that end-time ungodly world powers 'will wage war against the Lamb, and the Lamb will overcome them, because he is Lord of lords and King of kings, and those who are with him are the called and chosen and faithful.' The basis (*hoti*) for the Lamb's victory over the eschatological beasts in Revelation 17:14 lies in the fact that he is 'Lord of lords and King of kings'. The same title occurs only twice in biblically related material prior to the New Testament: *1 Enoch* 9.4 and Daniel 4:37 (LXX). It is possible that *1 Enoch* is in mind, since its context concerns eschatological judgment (of the fallen Watchers), as does that of Revelation 17.

However, Daniel 4:37 (LXX) is a more likely influence in Revelation 17:14 than *1 Enoch* 9.4 for the following reasons.

1. The wording of Daniel is closer to that of Revelation (note the presence of *hoti* [because] and *estin* [he is], which *Enoch* leaves out):

Daniel 4:37	Revelation 17:14b
'because he himself is God of gods and Lord of lords and King of kings (*hoti autos estin theos tōn theōn kai kyrios tōn kyriōn kai basileus tōn basileōn*)'. Cf. *1 Enoch* 9.4, 'Lord of lords, God of gods, King of kings'.	'because He is Lord of lords and King of kings (*hoti kyrios kyriōn estin kai basileus basileōn*)'.

1 Enoch itself, like Revelation 17:14, may well be alluding to Daniel 4:37.

2. Whereas the Enochian phrase forms part of an address to God, in Daniel and Revelation it is viewed as the basis of the divine power to take away the rule of evil kings.

3. Almost the same title occurs for the Babylonian king in the LXX of Daniel 2:37 ('king of kings'), and 3:2 ('king of kings and of the lords'), and for God in Daniel 2:47 ('God of gods and Lord of kings'), so that these three texts together with Daniel 4:37 (LXX) could be a collective allusion.

4. The observation that the title in 17:14b is followed in verse 15 by the Danielic expression of universality ('peoples and multitudes and nations and tongues') is significant since almost the identical formulas are found repeatedly following the title of Daniel 4:37 (cf. LXX, Dan. 4:37a, 37b, 37c).

5. Finally, that Daniel 4 is the source of the title is supported by earlier observations of Daniel 4 and Daniel 7 allusions in the immediately preceding context of 17:1–14a.[14]

Just as the Babylonian king was addressed by this title (see directly above), so the Roman king of latter-day Babylon (Rome) in John's day was addressed.[15] The title refers to God in Daniel 4 as the one

---

14. See further Beale, *Revelation*, on Rev. 17:1–14a.

15. For the application of the title 'our Lord and God' (*Dominus et deus noster*) and other divine titles to the Roman emperor Domitian, see Suetonius,

who demonstrated his true, divine sovereignty and revealed Nebuchadnezzar as an empty parody of the name by judging the beastly king of 'Babylon the Great'. Now the title is applied typologically to the Lamb. The point is that the revealing angel identifies the Lamb to be the God of Daniel 4. The Lamb demonstrates his deity on the Last Day by judging the beast that carries 'Babylon the Great'. And he exposes as false the divine claims of the emperor and others like him, just as Yahweh did with King Nebuchadnezzar of old.[16]

The called and chosen and faithful are with the divine Lamb and participate in his victory. The reason they participate in the victory is because they have overcome sin, persecution and compromise and have remained faithful, as had the Lamb, and so they have become identified with the Lamb's consummative overcoming of the enemy at the very end of world history. Central to their persevering faith is an unashamed posture of worship of the divine Lamb. These *are* the ones who 'follow the Lamb wherever he goes', and so they also have the same victorious destiny with the Lamb in whom they have trusted as their divine warrior-representative. This is very close to the same conclusion reached above in Revelation 3 (see e.g. Rev. 3:21).

The rhetorical point is to encourage saints and persuade them to persevere through tribulation now, as did Jesus, in order that they might experience the same final victory that Jesus will accomplish over their persecutors.

© G. K. Beale, 2007

Footnote 15 (cont.)

> *Domitianus* 13; Martial, *Epigrams* 5.8; Dio Cassius, *Roman History*, Epitome of Book 67.13.4; Pliny the Younger, *Panegyricus* 33; Philostratus, *Life of Apollonius* 8.4. On the divine titles for Domitian, see Beale, *Revelation*, pp. 5–12, where there is also a summary and evaluation of commentators who try to qualify this evidence.

16. See G. K. Beale, 'The Origin of the Title "King of Kings and Lord of Lords" in Rev. XVII.14', *New Testament Studies* 31 (1985), pp. 618–620, where also other possibly relevant phraseology from the Old Testament and ancient Near East is noted.